THE BRITISH ACADEMY

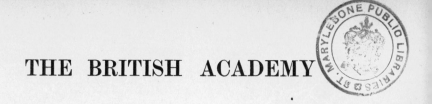

The Samaritans

Their History, Doctrines

and Literature

With six Appendices and nineteen Illustrations

By

Moses Gaster, Ph.D.

The Schweich Lectures

1923

London

Published for the British Academy

By Humphrey Milford, Oxford University Press

Amen House, E.C.

1925

21262

Printed in England
At the Oxford University Press
By John Johnson
Printer to the University

The beginnings of the Samaritans are thus represented by Jews and Samaritans from two diametrically opposed standpoints. According to the Jews, although nowhere clearly stated in the Biblical records, their beginnings are somehow connected with the settlement of foreign nations in the Northern Kingdom by the Assyrian kings. But in all these allusions there is no actual clue to the real beginnings of a schism which was not so much political as it was religious. Herein lies the importance of the problem, which has been recognized as such by the Samaritans and is emphasized over and over again throughout their literature. They feel that the difference between them and the Jews is purely a religious one, and as will be seen presently, their condemnation of the idolatrous kings of Israel is as stern as that uttered by the Jews, but it also includes the prophets who arose in Israel, especially Elijah, who ventured to offer sacrifices to God on a place other than the hallowed Mount.

It is obvious that any sect which separates itself on fundamental principles and claims to itself the possession of the unadulterated truth will endeavour to start its beginnings from the very origins; otherwise it could not justify its claim. It is therefore natural that the Samaritans place their beginnings with the earliest start of Israel's history. There is no necessity of accepting their claim as resting upon an historical basis, but from a psychological point of view it cannot be entirely disregarded, especially when it governs the whole historical development and explains many an incident mentioned in the Bible to which hitherto insufficient attention has been paid. There is always a nucleus of fact, even for the most fictitious developments hereafter, and in our case we have a genealogy of High Priests which seems to justify the claim of historical continuity in the traditions of the Samaritans; later on it will be seen that it represents a parallel tradition to that found in the Books of Ezra and Nehemiah and in the Books of Chronicles; it must, however, be remembered that each one would claim that list of High Priests as its own.

Another factor to be considered in this connexion is the rejection of the whole of the Prophetic literature of the Bible. This fact had a very considerable influence upon the spirit and development of the Samaritans, and also to a large extent contributed to the loosening of the bonds between the various parts. They not only rejected a literature deeply impregnated with a high spiritual conception, with great vision and with a wide

Bible as Shomronim (2 Kings xvii. 29). It must be noted, however, that this word in the form Shomronim occurs only once in the Hebrew Bible; moreover, a careful examination of the passage in 2 Kings reveals the fact that the Shomronim mentioned there can in no way be identified with those who were afterwards designated by that name. There unquestionably it is used for a people dwelling in the land of Shomron who are of purely heathen origin; it describes a population worshipping idols in the same way as the other foreign nations mentioned in that connexion but evidently differing from the Israelites referred to at the beginning of that chapter, and also differing from the exiled priest for whom these nations clamoured, that the plague of lions should be stayed. This priest was, of course, considered to be one of the Israelitish priests who had been carried away into captivity. The application of the name Shomronim to a dissenting sect is perfectly explicable if thereby they wished to denote the heathen origin or admixture with which they charged the Samaritans. In all the other subsequent passages, especially in Ezra and Nehemiah, the people referred to were not called by any specific name, but merely as the indwellers of the towns of Samaria, Shomrayin in the Aramaic—by the way a peculiar formation—which explains the Greek form Samaria and afterwards Samaritans. The Samaritans for their part hotly dispute this interpretation, and they decline to call themselves by the name Shomronim; they call themselves Shamerim, meaning thereby 'those who keep or observe the Law', and they add al-haemet—'in truth', i.e. the faithful observers of the Law. Here we have the prototype of the Greek term 'orthodox', he who keeps the law according to the standard of truth, or the right standard, a word which I believe does not occur before Hierocles or Eusebius.

In the Prophetic Writings reference is constantly made to Ephraim as the head of the Israelitish separatist movement, and in the condemnation uttered against the worshippers of idols and of abominations Ephraim is mentioned. The reason for that condemnation, however, is not to be found merely in the idol worship of the kings, but according to Samaritan tradition it is directed against those who had a temple of their own on Mount Garizim, who claimed to be the true representatives of the old faith, and who for their part condemned the usurpation of Jerusalem of the claim which ought to have been reserved only and solely for the Holy Mount of Garizim.

over by their adversaries. Take one single example : with the exception of four passages, Mount Garizim is not mentioned in the whole of the Biblical writings. Garizim is mentioned only twice in the Pentateuch (Deut. xi. 29 ; xxvii. 12), once in Joshua (viii. 33)—these three referring to the same commandment—and once in Judges (ix. 7), not once in the Prophets and Hagiographa, never in the Apocrypha, and in the New Testament when Jesus meets the woman of Samaria, reference is only made to 'this mountain' (John iv. 20, 21). It is obvious, therefore, that the omission of the name is no accident. The writers in Judaea would of course avoid the mention of a mountain which claimed rival sanctity with Mount Moriah. In a similar manner no one can expect to find in the records of the Jews much that can be in favour of the Samaritans, and vice versa, nothing in favour of the Jews will be found in Samaritan writings. And yet, the Biblical period is certainly the most important. I will therefore endeavour to concentrate my attention upon those incidents which bear directly upon events recorded in the Bible, and carry this sketch down to the period of Baba Rabba, with whom the real history of the Samaritans comes to an end. Herein I will follow the lead of the Samaritans and present their version of their history without thereby assuming that full credence should be given to their statements. They also are partisan records and must be treated as such, but they are the only ones that have come to light in connexion with the Biblical history. I am not concerned here with the theological aspect of the problem, which lies outside the scope of these lectures. They are of a purely archaeological character, and to this I shall endeavour to adhere. Nor is any statement contrary to the Biblical record to be regarded as impugning the truthfulness of the Scriptures ; on the contrary, I believe that the light which these Samaritan records will shed will help to solve many a problem, especially those of the period of the Return from the Exile and hereafter. I am limiting this investigation to the period which comes to an end with the epoch of Baba Rabba at the third or fourth century c. e. to eliminate all chance of Christian or Islamic influence.

If we start with the name of the Samaritans there is already sharp controversy as to its true origin, not to speak of the beginnings of the Samaritans themselves. It is generally assumed that the name Samaritan should be deduced either from an eponymous 'Shemer' or from the locality 'Shomron'. This etymology is favoured by the form in which the word occurs in the Hebrew

lights up some obscure passage of Holy Writ, must be welcomed. The literary activity of the Samaritans cannot be disputed, at any rate in ancient times, as long as they were an independent nation playing a political role and able to defend themselves with weapons in their hands. When their autonomy was broken, when their political existence was destroyed, and when they felt themselves surrounded by a wall of hostile creeds and persecuting rulers, then decay began to set in. From that moment their intellectual activity became stagnant, more especially from the time of Hadrian and a little later, when most of the ancient literature of the Samaritans had been irretrievably destroyed. Still, a few fragments have remained, some of a religious character and some containing records of their national life. Hitherto, as remarked before, that history could only be pieced together from stray adverse allusions, and a picture of the Samaritans was thus drawn which differed strangely from the facts in many essential points. It is only since the time of Scaliger, the first to open communication with the Samaritans in Palestine and Egypt, that more direct information has become accessible. It was gleaned from replies sent by the Samaritans to Scaliger in 1584 and to other scholars like Huntington who had visited them in the year 1671, and later on to Marshall (c. 1675), Ludolf (c. 1685), and de Sacy at the beginning of the last century. In between other letters must have been sent to Europe, a copy of one of these being now in the British Museum. But these letters dealt more with religious practices and beliefs, and very little could be learned from them concerning Samaritan history. It is only since about the middle of the last century that historical records of the Samaritans have become known, such as the Chain of the High Priests, the Tolidah, the Arabic paraphrase of the Book of Joshua, above all the Arabic chronicle of Abul Fath, compiled in the fourteenth century, and other chronicles still in manuscript to which reference will be made later when discussing the Samaritan literature. The scholars who have hitherto written on the history of the Samaritans have drawn most of their information from the Biblical records and have almost entirely ignored what could be gathered from the Samaritans themselves, and the few details which have been taken from the Samaritans have been treated more as legendary matter than as real history. No one as far as I am aware has attempted to dig a little deeper down into the foundations and lay bare some of those facts which had been so carefully covered

and mighty nation which the Samaritans originally were, they have now been reduced to something like 170 souls living under the shadow of the great mountain which to them is the Gate of Heaven. It is, therefore, not an easy task to piece together the real history of the Samaritans from the few references found in the other literatures.

The persecution of the Samaritans was so effective that for close upon a thousand years their very existence was entirely forgotten, and they lived only in the memory of the ancient writers. And yet they must have had their own historical records. The Samaritans, or at least their spiritual leaders, were not illiterate: on the contrary, the priests, who were their real rulers, occupied that position only on the strength of the sacred Scripture. Moreover, they must have possessed a profound knowledge of it in order to justify their claim of being the true keepers of the Law, and they had traditions running parallel to the records of the Bible which they must have preserved. Herein lies the importance of the Samaritans, inasmuch as they would put upon events which happened among them a complexion independent of, and generally different from that portrayed by the Jews, and vice versa, they would treat events happening to Judah which were faithfully recorded in our own Scriptures in a manner wholly compatible with their own interpretation. Thus as far as reliance can be placed upon it the Samaritans have preserved a tradition which differs and is often diametrically opposed to that of the Jews, the latter having become the common property of the civilized world. It is the only one which has hitherto obtained currency and belief, which has practically never been questioned, and which has passed undisputed to our own days as the only record of years gone by. The Samaritans, however, have their own view of all that has happened, and some of this view has still been preserved. But how far can one rely upon the veracity of this tradition?

The partisan spirit must of course have influenced their descriptions; what was sacred to the one was abomination to the other, and the success claimed by one party was hotly disputed and denied by the other. But out of these contending records some facts must emerge to which importance cannot be denied. The parallel narratives among Jews and Samaritans, if divested of this partisan character, disclose certain facts which, if once established, are a distinct gain to ancient history; and every gleam of light, from whichever quarter it may come, which

FIRST LECTURE

THE SAMARITANS: THEIR HISTORY

The Samaritans claim our attention as being the oldest dissenting sect. The importance of a dissenting sect lies in the fact that it intends a critical examination, a searching of the heart among contending factions, of the value of the truth which they possess. Constant strife stimulates spiritual activity and the forces at work prevent the pool of religious life from becoming stagnant. There is constant animation and very often much raising of dust. In the heat of the combat, however, many side issues are introduced and importance is attached to details of secondary value, but after a time one sect or another wins the victory. During this conflict each party has done its very best to annihilate its adversary, often with so much success, that very few traces have been left of the literature of the ancient heresies as they were called. The most important among those who were not utterly destroyed were the Samaritans; they were able to survive the storm that swept over them from every side, and are still living on the very spot where their ancestors worshipped some thousands of years ago. They have retained their faith unchanged, together with the knowledge of their ancient languages, the Hebrew of the Scriptures and the Samaritan or Aramaic of their prayers. The importance of the Samaritans lies in the dissenting position which they adopted towards Judaism and later on towards Christianity, thus representing some of those forces which have contributed so greatly to the history of our modern civilization. Their very antagonism to Judaism has been a powerful factor in moulding the character of the sacred Scriptures, the religious laws and the practices, which through the Bible have dominated the world. But in spite of this the Samaritans have, to a large extent, shared the fate of the other sects. Their history has been written at the hands of their adversaries and consists mainly of stray allusions in the Biblical, Rabbinic and Patristic literature, coloured as they naturally would be by the bias of the writers. Their literature has been destroyed with the exception of a few remnants, and from a great

B

LIST OF ILLUSTRATIONS

the Sabbath, slaughter of animals, clean and unclean animals, marriage laws, divorce, burial, mourning, &c. Calendar like Sadducees'. Mystical and cabbalistic beliefs and practices. Belief in angels. Sectarian movements. Eschatology. Taheb (Shaheb). Immortality. Punishment. Reward. Resurrection. Antiquity of Samaritan tradition.   Pages 40–95

THIRD LECTURE

LITERATURE

General characteristics. Apologetic and polemical. Languages. No development since the fourth century. Only fragments, mostly preserved in later literature. Pentateuch. Palaeographic reasons for its antiquity. Midrashic interpolations. So-called 'barbarous' Hebrew. Zadokite fragment. Scroll of Abisha. Rediscovery of the Pentateuch. Its relation to the M. T. and LXX; fierce controversy. All studies and investigations rest upon corrupt texts. The Greek translation, the Samariticon. Palestinian origin of the LXX. Origin of the number '70'. Samaritan Hellenistic literature. Ezekiel and Markah. Book of Joshua. Its genuineness and antiquity. Decisive importance of the Paseḳ. The prophet Ezekiel and the Book of Joshua. Other biblical fragments. Biblical legends. Targum and its two recensions. Biblical commentaries. Prayer Book; antiquity; composition. Kenosh or Defter. Ancient poetry. Markah. Various treatises on legal practices. Polemical writings. Various chronicles. Their character and value. Mystical and eschatological literature. Calendar and chronology. Literary revival in the fourteenth century. Mostly old material. Samaritan influence on Judaism and primitive Christianity.   Pages 96–158

CONTENTS

FIRST LECTURE

THE SAMARITANS: THEIR HISTORY

SECOND LECTURE

DOCTRINES AND RELIGIOUS PRACTICES

FOREWORD

'AND thou, son of man, take thee one stick, and write upon it, For Judah, and for the children of Israel his companions : then take another stick, and write upon it, For Joseph, the stick of Ephraim, and for all the house of Israel his companions : and join them for thee one to another into one stick, that they may become one in thy hand' (Ezek. xxxvii. 16, 17). Some twenty-five years ago I gripped the stick of Joseph which is in the hand of Ephraim ; and, little thinking what may be the outcome, I have endeavoured during all these years to read the legend written upon it. Without fear and without favour, without historical prejudice or religious bias, I have tried to obtain a sympathetic understanding of the inner life and religious practices of the solitary remnant of the Ancient House of Israel. I did not formulate a theory, nor did I try to fit conclusions to preconceived notions. I did not allow myself to be swayed by the opinion of others, or my judgement warped by misplaced partiality. I went boldly on my quest. I travelled along untrodden paths. I have wandered through many an arid place, my only guide the meagre writings still preserved by the Samaritans. I have scanned them with keen interest, undeterred by their monotony and wearisomeness. As I arrived at the end of my journey, I became aware of the stick of Judah, which had meanwhile been pressed into my hands. And thus in my hands they became joined at last. In these three Lectures I have formulated my conclusions. Let those who will follow me take the same road, and judge me with the same fairness and sympathy as that which I have brought to bear on my theme. Should I have erred, I shall be grateful for correction. I must rest satisfied, however, with the conviction that I have spared no efforts to seek the truth and pursue it.

My thanks are due to the British Academy for the honour conferred upon me in inviting me to deliver this course of Schweich Lectures on 'The Samaritans', and for the permission granted slightly to expand the matter compressed within the space of the three Lectures ; and to Sir Israel Gollancz for his ready and kind assistance.

M. GASTER.

LONDON,
    18 *September*, 1925.

Plate 2

(a) Unknown letter of Abraham son of Jacob to the Samaritans abroad

(*See* Appendix I, pp. 165 ff.)

outlook on the future of mankind, preparing Judaism to become the universal religion of a world united in that grand idea of universal brotherhood, but they also rejected the poetic literature of the Bible, those outpourings of the spirit found in the Psalms and in the lyrics of the Book of Songs as well as the Wisdom literature. In fact they rejected everything that made the Bible the grand monument and great inspiring force throughout the ages. Thus their hopes were narrowed, their outlook reduced, and they concentrated upon the only thing which they possessed of the whole Jewish literature, the Law. They had some fragments of the historical books to which reference will be made later on, but these had no influence on the moulding and shaping of their principles of faith or on their practical application. These the Samaritans continue to possess. This is a fact worthy of note upon which emphasis will have to be laid in elucidating the problem of the antiquity of the Samaritan Pentateuch, for if they accepted the Pentateuch at the late date at which they are assumed to have done, there is no reason why they should have refused to incorporate into their literary property such other books found in the Bible to which no dogmatic objection could be raised. The inevitable conclusion is that at the time when they accepted the Pentateuch the Prophetic and Hagiographic literature was not yet in existence, and that when they became conscious of the differences which separated the North from the South with the building of the Temple in Jerusalem as a rival to that on Mount Garizim, they objected to everything found in the rival kingdom and produced by men of the rival faith. According to the Samaritans, then, their history practically begins with the settlement of the Tribes in the Holy Land. They claim to be the descendants of Ephraim and Manasseh as far as the lay population is concerned, together with a number of adherents from among the other tribes, whilst the priests claim to be the true descendants in an unbroken line from Pineḥas the son of Eleazar, the son of Aaron. Continuing, Samaritan tradition insists that the altar of stones mentioned in Deuteronomy was erected by Joshua himself on Mount Garizim, ' the Mount of Inheritance ', 'Beth-el'. On that altar were written the Words, i.e. the Ten Commandments, being all the words of the Law which, according to Scripture, had to be written on the stones after they had been plastered over with plaster (Deut. xxvii. 2 ff.). The Samaritans furthermore translate the words 'ba'er heteb ', not as is usually done, ' very plainly ', but as ' a perfect copy ', i.e. from the original scroll.[1] Thus according to the Samaritans the establishment of the Tabernacle or Sanctuary took place in the time of Joshua, assisted by the High Priest Eleazar, and was carried out on Mount Garizim, not on Mount Ebal as our Massoretic text has it. This is the chief difference between Jews and Samaritans, of which more will be mentioned later on. A careful examination of the Massoretic text of the Bible will reveal the undeniable fact that a sanctuary of the Lord must have been established on Mount Garizim in the time of Joshua, for he distinctly refers to it in his last oration before the assembled people. ' And Joshua wrote these words in the book of the law of God, and took a great stone, and set it up there under an oak, that was by the sanctuary of the Lord ' (Joshua xxiv. 26).[2] The rule established was, to a large extent, the priestly rule, the Samaritans taking very little notice of the civil government ; for the nation was to be a priestly nation, guided and directed by the Divine Law, of which they alone were the guardians and interpreters.

After a time, a schism arose within the priestly families ; rivalry was latent between the descendants of Eleazar and those of Ithamar, the two sons of Aaron, whilst the memory of the rebellion of Korah was still a living factor. According to Samaritan tradition, the feud between these two lines broke out fiercely when Eli, believing himself to have been offended, separated from the priests of the Sanctuary on Mount Garizim

---

[1] In the same way the Samaritans translate the very same word at the beginning of Deuteronomy i. 5, not as we do ' to declare this law ', but ' he started on the first day of the eleventh month *copying out* this law ', which he finished at the end of the month and gave the copy from the Divine original into the keeping of the priests (Deut. xxxi. 26). It is unnecessary to dwell here upon the dogmatic importance of this interpretation, which ascribes to God His very writing of the Law, so that Moses had only to copy it. The Divine origin, not merely of every word but of every letter of the Law, is not only implied here, but positively asserted ; the midrashic or agadic interpretation thus finds here its full justification.

[2] I must ignore here the view which Higher Criticism chooses to take of the genuineness and antiquity of this chapter. I am dealing with the facts as we find them in Joshua, and they cannot be discussed away, especially as they prove to be of real high antiquity in the light of Samaritan tradition. The LXX changes the whole character of the passage by substituting ' Selo ' for ' Sichem ' and leaving out the words ' the sanctuary of ' (Joshua xxiv. 25, 26) ; it is obvious that we have here an anti-Samaritan alteration which is not without significance for the character of the LXX and for the relation between the LXX and the Samaritan Pentateuch.

Plate 3

(*b*)   Unknown letter of Abraham son of Jacob to the Samaritans abroad

(*See* Appendix I, pp. 165 ff.)

Plate 4

Picture of Vessels of the Temple drawn by Samaritans, with
description in Samaritan

and established a rival one in Shiloh, thus being the first to introduce the schismatic movement, which culminated in the building of the Temple in Jerusalem and came to a final break in the time of Ezra. Eli represented the Ithamar branch, and, as will be seen, the rivalry between the two lines can be followed up, though only dimly indicated, in the records of the events which took place from his time until the final building of the Temple by Solomon and the elimination from the High Priesthood of the descendants of Ithamar in favour of those of Eleazar. It is in any case very remarkable that ever since the establishment of the Tabernacle in Shiloh, where Eli acted as High Priest, a new name for the Divinity was introduced ; the God Ṣebaot appears for the first time in Jewish literature. Whether any special value can be attached to it is a problem that cannot yet be easily solved, but the significance of the appearance of this new distinctive name of God cannot be gainsaid.

Then Eli is joined in his schismatic work by a descendant of Ḳoraḥ, Samuel (*v.* 1 Chron. vi. 18–24, A.V. 33–8), the revolt of the ancestor against Moses and Aaron being the background for this new rebellion.

At that time when Uzzi was the High Priest, according to Samaritan chronology 260 years after the entry of the Children of Israel into the Holy Land, the Tabernacle containing the Ark with the Holy of Holies suddenly disappeared. Legend tells us that it was taken by Uzzi and placed in a cave in Mount Garizim, after which the cave suddenly closed. This was declared to be the sign of God's displeasure at the rebellious action of Eli, with the consequent turning away from Him by the people. God had turned away from them in accordance with the word of Scripture and had hidden His face (Deut. xxxi. 18). This was the decisive moment in the spiritual history of the Samaritans, and considered by them as the turning-point in the spiritual history of the world ; it was the beginning of the period of God's Disfavour, ' Fanuta ', which will last until the world, purged from sin by repentance, will be brought back to the period of God's Favour, ' Rahuta ', but since that time the world has lived under God's Displeasure. This conception has deeply influenced the whole spiritual outlook of the Samaritans and is expressed most emphatically in their liturgy.[1]

---

[1] It may be of interest to point to the parallel legend in Jewish history

In order to give some authority to his sanctuary Eli had taken with him one of the copies of the Law made by Moses which had come into the possession of Ithamar. This was identical with the copy now in the hands of the Samaritans, and was later on placed in the foundations of the Temple built by Solomon in Jerusalem.[1] In the light of this assertion of the Samaritans, some points in the history of Saul and David and of their dealings with the various priestly families may become much clearer than has hitherto been the case ; one gains a different impression of the killing of Aḥimelekh and the priests of Nob by Saul, and of David's friendship with Abiathar on the one side and Aḥimaaṣ on the other ; in the former case Aḥimelekh represented the rival family of Ithamar, which was in friendly relations with David and was therefore suspected by Saul of conspiring against his kingdom ; in the latter, one belonged to the Ithamar and the other to the Eleazar family. David's actions, therefore, may have rested upon certain political considerations and attempts at conciliating one line of priests with the other. Finally Solomon granted supremacy to Abiathar, thus relegating the descendants of Ithamar to the second place. Such are the results one can glean from the appearance of these names in the contemporary history, and it has evidently been read in this light by the Samaritans, who, however, claim for their High Priests that they are the true descendants of Eleazar and Pineḥas, to whom the everlasting Covenant had been promised after the events in Moab (Num. xxv. 12, 13). It must not be forgotten that though practically obliterated, Sichem was still considered the holy city, where the kings of Judah and Israel

which is preserved in 2 Macc. ii. 4, according to which, at the destruction of the Temple, Jeremiah carried the Ark and the holy vessels to a cave in the mountain where Moses had died and deposited them there. The cave was closed by Jeremiah, and no one was able to discover it. Nor will it be found until the time 'when God will gather the people together again, and mercy come' (2 Macc. ii. 7). It is precisely the same tale as that of the Samaritans, only in this case the Ark and vessels are from the Temple of Jerusalem, whilst with the Samaritans the Ark and vessels were taken from the Temple on Mount Garizim.

[1] Though merely a legend, yet in a strange way this to some extent corroborates the very ingenious theory of Professor Naville, who, without knowing the Samaritan tradition, suggested that the Scroll of the Law found by Ḥilkiah in the foundations of the Temple at the time of repair might have been a very old copy buried in the foundations in accordance with ancient practices.

Plate 5

Chased metal case of the Scroll of the Law with Samaritan Inscriptions

had to be crowned down to the time of Rehoboam and Jeroboam (1 Kings xii. 1).[1]

This is not the place to discuss the reasons which prompted David to select Jerusalem as the religious as well as the political centre. The Samaritans say he conceived the idea of transferring, as it were, the holiness of Mount Garizim to the Sanctuary on Mount Moriah. But whatever his motive may have been, it was deeply resented by the Samaritans, who saw in it a definite break and a defiance of all God's ordinances. An examination of their polemical literature will reveal the fact that all the arguments in their disputations against the Jews turn on this capital sin, nor have they words of opprobrium strong enough with which to designate the Sanctuary; instead of Bet Mikdash, they call it with a slight change of letters, Bet Maktash, 'the House of Shame'. They point a finger of scorn at the origin of the House of David and at the birth of Solomon from Bathsheba. Nor is better treatment meted out to the prophets who arose later, and of whom a good few seem to have been known to them. Curiously enough, as far as I am aware, no mention is made of the prophet Ezekiel. There may be a reason for this, but it is highly problematical and I should only like to advance it tentatively. It is that I believe the prophet Ezekiel to have been in greater sympathy with the Northern Tribes than with the Tribe of Judah, but of this more later on.

We now pass on to that crucial period in the history of the Samaritans upon which the Jews have fastened for the purpose of reducing the Samaritans not merely to a dissenting sect but to a sect of pagan origin and doubtful proselyte character, being converted through the fear of lions. The story of the final destruction of the Israelitish kingdom is told in 2 Kings xvii, and mention is made there of numerous heathen colonies which were settled in the land of Samaria by the kings of Assyria, one of them being the Kutim. This is the name which was afterwards applied to the Samaritans, although its use in Rabbinic literature is anything but fixed; sometimes Min and occasionally Shomroni are used instead. Be that as it may, Samaritans and Kutim are treated as identical terms, and the opprobrium attach-

---

[1] With but one or two exceptions Sichem is not mentioned in the whole of the Biblical writings after this period; not one single prophet refers to it, any more than to Mount Garizim. It is not difficult to draw conclusions from this fact; it was the desire of obliterating every reference to the seat of the hated Northern Sanctuary.

ing to the latter has been connected with the origin and religious practices of the Samaritans.

In following up the traces of Ephraim and the period when for the first time the name Kutim or Shomronim is used, it is of importance to study very carefully the writings of the prophets from the time of Isaiah down to those who returned from the Exile. These will show us the attitude which they adopted, and we shall be able to gather from their utterances the position which Ephraim or Israel, i.e. the tribes of the Northern Kingdom, held in their eyes during the centuries which elapsed from the First Captivity or the time of Tiglat Pileser, *c.* 736, king of Assyria, down to the time of the return of the Jews from the Babylonian Exile. Nowhere is any reference to be found to foreign inhabitants in the Northern Kingdom of Israel. Whilst Isaiah predicts the doom (vii. 8, 9), he still holds out the hope of God's love for the tribe of Ephraim and his associates (xi. 11–13).

Close upon a hundred years later Jeremiah speaks most emphatically of Ephraim still enjoying God's love and mercy (ch. 31), and foretells the complete restoration jointly with Judah, with a slight attempt at reconciliation, under the rule of ' King David ' (Jer. xxiii. 5, 6), which as will be seen is more fully elaborated later on by the prophet Ezekiel. The latter takes up, as it were, the thread of Jeremiah's prophecy. But never by a single word does Jeremiah allude to the fact that the country has been absolutely denuded, or that Ephraim has been supplanted by a mass of proselytes whom afterwards the Jews refused to recognize as being of the old race. No suspicion is raised here against the purity of Ephraim or of the Tribes of Israel ; they share the fate of the Southern Kingdom, both being sent into captivity and both being brought back from captivity. It is evident from these prophets that no notice was taken of those peoples who are mentioned in 2 Kings, and who are also found under different names in the petition sent to the Persian king in Ezra iv. 7.

If we now turn to the prophet Ezekiel who is in exile and a younger contemporary of Jeremiah, we see the same longing of uniting the two branches of the tree, and find him working passionately towards the unity of North and South. He apostrophizes Ephraim and his associates in the same terms as those in which he speaks of Judah and his associates, and urges them by the command of God that they should henceforth be as one in His hands. By word and symbol he works for unity. In vain would one search through all these writings for the remotest allusion to a strange population having occupied the Northern Kingdom or peoples brought from distant parts of Assyria or Babylonia supplanting, even in the smallest degree, the old Israelites in faith or race.

Between these two prophets I now place the prophet to whom no doubt belongs chapter nine to the end of Zechariah. I believe this to be the work of that priest and prophet Zechariah whom Jewish tradition declares to have been killéd by the people in the courtyard of the Temple because of his fierce denunciations of their evil deeds. A legend has been created around his seething blood, according to which it would not cease boiling over in spite of Nebuzaradan having slain the leaders of the people over it in expiation of the sin, until he threatened to slaughter the babes as well. I believe that these prophecies uttered by a Zechariah who was contemporary with Jeremiah, and who lived at the time of the Babylonian Conquest, have been joined to those of another Zechariah who lived close upon a century afterwards. They were not marked off but kept together at the end of the other prophecies, and the editors who put them there were therefore fully justified in placing them where they now are. But to whichever period or date these chapters may be assigned their importance cannot be ignored, inasmuch as they played a decisive role in the development of the Messianic idea and the Battles of the Nations ;[1] but here again, on the threshold of the destruction, and in spite of the reference to Javan, we still hear the prophetic voice speaking of Joseph and Judah in one breath (ix. 13), both being considered as existing in full strength (x. 6 ff.), both the object of God's denunciation and of God's love.

Totally different, however, is the attitude of the post-Exilic prophets, as will be seen later on. The word Ephraim as well as any reference to the Northern Tribes have disappeared altogether; Haggai, Zechariah, or Malachi do not mention them, and the few allusions to Ephraim found in Chronicles refer to historical events of centuries long before. They have dropped entirely out of the ken of these prophets and writers. But even then, centuries elapse before we find the inhabitants of the North called by such a derogatory name as Kutim, with its insinuation

[1] Charles, R. H., *Eschatology, Hebrew, Jewish and Christian*, London, 1899, p. 120 f.

that they were no longer of pure Israelitish descent, but foreign proselytes who under fear of the lions were converted to a special kind of Judaism.

Unless I am greatly mistaken, Josephus, who unreservedly expresses his antipathy to Samaritans, is the first to use the word Kutim, explaining that they are the Samaritans.[1] The Scroll of Fasting, Megillat Taanit, of the Maccabaean period, no doubt contains references to violent collisions between the two sections, and a number of days are declared festive days, on which no fasts were allowed because they marked the time and date of reported victories over their enemies. Yet the name Kutim does not occur in the whole of the old text; even in chapter ix, where Mount Garizim is mentioned, the word Kutim is not found, only appearing in the gloss which belongs to a much later period, many centuries afterwards, where the story is told of the Samaritans approaching Alexander with the desire of destroying the Temple of Jerusalem. As far as can be traced, the word Kutim does not occur at all in Jewish literature before the first century C. E.

In the later literature, owing to various reasons and also because of complete forgetfulness of the real meaning of the word used, the words Kuthean, Saduki, and Min, i. e. apostate, are often used for one another and make it almost impossible to determine which of the three is meant.

If we turn once more to the prophet Ezekiel no trace can be found of any heathen nations having been substituted for the ancient tribes in the Northern Kingdom. He does not refer to a single one; on the contrary, Ephraim is still for him the leader of a number of tribes and associates and treated as of equal value and importance as Judah and his associates. The whole aim of the prophet is to bring about a reconciliation between the two. Ephraim is still the dominating factor, and in his vision of the future he divides the land into twelve portions. In xxxvii. 16 f., by the order of God, he is told to take two rods and write on the one the names of Ephraim and all the tribes of Israel, his associates, and on the other the House of Judah. He is then told to join these two sticks together, and he again repeats the statement that the rod of Joseph was in the hands of Ephraim. Thus in c. 580, less than fifty years before the return from the Exile, the prophet Ezekiel still knew of the existence and power of

---

[1] *Antiq.* ix. 14. 3 (§ 288).

Ephraim, with whom the other tribes of Israel had joined. There is no trace of any doubt of purity of descent or that they were not the genuine tribes inhabiting the northern part of Palestine. Again, his geographical allocation of the various tribes is of extreme importance. It differs to a large extent from the division found in actual history, and he takes as his eastern and western borders the Jordan and the sea (xlvii. 14 ff.). He also declares the family of Ṣadoḳ to be the only one among the priests to whom the future guardianship of the Temple should be entrusted (xlviii. 11). This injunction is of great significance because it establishes anew, by the authority of the prophet, the unquestioned supremacy of the Ṣadoḳite family which claims to be the descendant in a direct line from Eleazar and Pineḥas. On the other hand, he suggests that the secular ruler should be 'David', i.e. a descendant of the House of David. David has thus become a symbolical name for the House of David. The Temple is to be established in the centre of Palestine, but the political supremacy is to remain with the Tribe of Judah.

Any one who studies his description of the Temple to be and the place in which it is to be erected in the future, will find that he rejects Jerusalem and selects a central spot in Palestine, which could be nothing else but Sichem or Mount Garizim. Whether that name actually occurred originally and was afterwards left out, or whether it is a mere allusion to be interpreted later on, must be left an open question. So also is the curious definition of the geographical boundaries which agree with those found in the Samaritan Hebrew Book of Joshua, of which more later on when discussing Samaritan literature. In his geographical distribution every one of the older tribes reappears, and the names of Ephraim and the Northern Tribes also occur. To the prophet Ezekiel no change had evidently taken place, and those who might then have been inhabiting Samaria were of no consequence whatsoever. This of course could only be the case if the nations mentioned in Kings and Ezra were garrisons taken from various parts of the Assyrian and Persian empires and transferred from time to time from one place to another. Altogether a careful examination of the writings of Ezekiel, and especially of the legal code with which he was acquainted and which has been subjected to special investigation to be published at another time, may point to a different conception of the home and origin of Ezekiel than has hitherto been tacitly assumed; it looks as if he were of one of the Northern Tribes.

Now the Book of Kings is recognized as being merely a summary of events which happened in Judah and Israel; for further information the reader is always referred to the Books of the Chronicles of the Kings of Judah and Israel. In the same way chapter xvii of 2 Kings must also be considered as containing a summary of the events which happened in the Northern Kingdom during some length of time. Assyrian monuments mention Sargon in lieu of Shalmanasar as the king who exiled the Israelites, but though these monuments emanate from Sargon himself, the details concerning the plantations of the new peoples are nowhere clearly defined. At the same time, it must be remembered that the whole population was not carried away into captivity, a comparatively small fraction, consisting of high officials and dignitaries, together with the official representative of the priesthood, being all that went into exile. Not only did a large population remain behind, but, unless the statement in the Second Book of Chronicles xxx. 1 ff. is to be doubted, the tribal divisions were maintained in the time of Hezekiah and the Temple on Mount Garizim must have remained in existence down to the time of Josiah, since nothing is said anywhere of the destruction of this Temple, thus leaving it an open question whether it was that dedicated to Baal or whether, according to the statement of the Samaritans, it was the old Temple dedicated to the worship of the God of Israel, which Josiah destroyed.[1]

On looking through the lists of the peoples who had been established in the small province of Samaria or the habitat of the tribes of Ephraim and Manasseh in addition to the indigenous Israelitish population which had remained there, it must appear rather remarkable how space could have been found to settle so many nations. The lists found in 2 Kings xvii. 24 ff., and in the letter which was sent in protest to the Persian king remonstrating against Zerubbabel's attempt to rebuild the Temple in Jerusalem (Ezra iv. 7), show that not one of the names of the nations mentioned in Kings appears in the later list; even the name of the Assyrian king is entirely different, being Asenapper instead of Shalmanasar or Sargon.[2] Moreover, five nationalities are mentioned in Kings, whilst nine are given in Ezra, in addition to others who are simply referred to anonymously as, 'the rest

[1] 2 Kings xxiii. 19–20.
[2] Asenapper seems to be the popular pronunciation for the literary Ashurbanipal, 'She' being pronounced 'Se' like the Ephraimites : v. Judges xii. 6.

of the nations whom the great and noble Asenapper brought over and set in the cities of Samaria' (Ezra iv. 10). How can these differences be reconciled, and how could still larger numbers have been settled in the few towns of Samaria, always remembering that the indigenous population was still there, and how could such a change have taken place in less than 150 years? It is the second point which has first to be established before we consider the alleged plantation of the new peoples.

In the year B.C.E. 726, Hezekiah, then king of Judah, invited the Northern Tribes, now that their political existence had almost come to an end and shortly before their chief priests were carried away into exile, to join with him in celebrating the Passover in Jerusalem.[1] By this means he tried to reunite all the tribes, not so much under his political sway as under the religious rule of the central Temple of Jerusalem. To this invitation some of the tribes responded favourably, among them being Manasseh, Zebulun, and Asher (v. 11), as well as some of Ephraim and Issachar (v. 18). Nearly 100 years later, in the year 630, during his great War of Reformation, Josiah still met the tribes of Manasseh and Ephraim, Simeon and Naphtali, in Northern Israel.[2] Neither Hezekiah nor Josiah mention any heathen nations; they do not even refer to their existence, still less to their having supplanted the original Israelitish inhabitants ; nor do they say that the land had become a desert. Now these nations which are mentioned under different names at different times must therefore represent, not, as has hitherto been considered, new settlements of colonists, but simply garrisons drawn from these various nations. It was a known practice of the ancient kings to settle garrisons in conquered territories, a policy followed by Egypt and Assyria, later by the Persian kings, then by Alexander, and finally by the Romans. Everywhere soldiers were drawn from distant countries and settled in various fortified camps, which were often changed when the attitude of the nations from which they had been drawn and their loyalty to their overlord had undergone serious political changes. If a province rebelled the king could not rely upon the loyalty of his troops in distant parts which were drawn from the rebellious provinces ; hence the change of the garrisons and the names of the nations in the second list as far as can be ascertained. The Persian kings themselves placed Jewish and Samaritan garrisons in

---

[1] 2 Chron. xxx. 1 ff.   [2] 2 Chron. xxxiv. 6, 7.

C

Assuan, whilst Alexander settled Jews and Samaritans in Egypt as well as in the northern countries of Bactria; similarly the Seleucids, especially Antiochus the Great, settled Jewish garrisons in the northern provinces, as testified by Josephus.[1] This being the case, the whole situation assumes a different aspect.

The Samaritans became a political sect of Palestine, heavily garrisoned by Assyrian, and later by Persian, troops. During the period with which we are now dealing the country was for the time being under Persia, Cyrus, Darius, and Artaxerxes being the kings mentioned.[2]   Moreover, Samaritan tradition says that these various nationalities were slowly drafted back into Assyria and Babylon after the re-settlement of the Israelites or that portion of them which had returned from the so-called First Exile under the leadership of the High Priest Serayah, the occasion for their return being described in the Book of Kings.

The reason for the conversion of these various heathen garrisons was, according to 2 Kings xvii. 25 ff., the plague of lions which infested the country.   The colonists ascribed this calamity simply to their ignorance of the worship of the god of the land, but, considering that the best part of the population were still living there, the allegation is curious; nor does it explain how the return of the priest from Babylon could banish the lions. Surely more than one priest must have been left behind who could teach them the worship of the god of the land and thus save its inhabitants from the plague.   The facts as recorded in the Book of Kings are evidently greatly reduced; they are a mere summary of the events, from which the writer never expected the consequences to flow which have subsequently been derived therefrom.   In the Samaritan tradition the matter assumes a totally different aspect, and all the difficulties which this obscure passage presents are easily cleared away.   They state that by having carried into exile the High Priest and the priests who ministered in the Sanctuary at Beth-el, i. e. Garizim, the service of God had come to a standstill.   No more sacrifices were

---

[1] *Antiq.* xii. 3. 3, 4 (§ 147).

[2] This will explain the very curious fact that the garrison of Assuan appealed to both the High Priest of Jerusalem and to the Governor of Samaria, Sanballat, to come to its assistance when the town was taken and the temple destroyed by the Egyptians. Sanballat, however, was not the spiritual head; he was probably invested with the same power of governor as that afterwards conferred upon Nehemiah.

brought and none of the ordinances kept, with the result that the curse which had been threatened in Leviticus and Deuteronomy came to pass. With the cessation of worship, drought set in, famine followed, and wild beasts overran the land. 'And if ye walk contrary unto me, and will not hearken unto me; I will bring seven times more plagues upon you according to your sins. I will also send wild beasts among you, which shall rob you of your children, and destroy your cattle, and make you few in number; and your high ways shall be desolate.'[1] This punishment had overtaken them for their sins; it was this which had brought exile upon their priests, and in this calamity were involved not only the inhabitants of the land who had strayed from the true worship of God, but the new-comers as well. It is, therefore, in the name of the whole community that the governor and garrison for the time being sent the request to the king to have the High Priest returned and the worship re-established.

The Samaritans then go on to say that the king graciously hearkened to their request, called the High Priest Serayah, and gave him permission to send out a proclamation throughout the land that all who wished to accompany him and return to their ancient homes might do so. Special note must be taken of the name of the High Priest, who is not Dositheus or Dustai, two names which occur in Jewish tradition.[2] Now this Serayah asked the Jews, and among them their leader Zerubbabel, to join with him in the return and the re-establishment of the Sanctuary on Mount Garizim. In this instance the invitation is just the reverse of what we read in Ezra iv. 1 ff. There the situation is that the adversaries, evidently the Samaritans, approach Zerubbabel and Joshua, the High Priest and the elders, and ask permission to join in the rebuilding of the Temple at Jerusalem.

According to Samaritan tradition the Jews refused to join with them and so caused some delay, but this was removed by the explanation of Serayah and by the disputation which followed.

In the light of history and by reason of the position which the Samaritans occupied at the Persian court and in Babylon because of their numbers, it is not unlikely that a discussion such as that fully described by them may have taken place before the Persian king, called by them Surdi. This disputation follows

---

[1] Lev. xxvi. 21-2.   [2] See my Book of Joshua.

the same lines as those found in all the later ones between Jews
and Samaritans, namely, that the Samaritans tried to prove from
the words of the Law that Mount Garizim was the chosen spot,
and that those who built a Temple in Jerusalem and worshipped
there had deliberately broken the Law; this time they went
farther and said that a copy of the Samaritan Pentateuch as well
as one of that in the hands of Zerubbabel were subjected to the
ordeal by fire. Zerubbabel's copy, of course, was burned to ashes,
whilst that thrown into the fire by Serayah leaped out three
times unhurt. King Surdi then decided in favour of the
Samaritans and sent them back with gifts.

Here there is a curious anachronism. The Samaritan chronicler,
who worked on fragments and confused reminiscences, places
Serayah as a contemporary of Zerubbabel, although the latter is
very much later. He was the priest who returned in the time of
the Assyrian kings in order to avert the plague of lions. The
Samaritan chronicler wrongly introduces here the dispute which
arose later on in the time of Zerubbabel and Joshua, and makes
Serayah the protagonist instead of another High Priest, or rather
probably Sanballat. Some confusion, however, may have arisen
in olden times between those who, according to the Samaritan
records, returned at an earlier period, called by them the
First Return, and those of the Second Return at the time of
Zerubbabel. Serayah, however, represents the First Return from
the Exile and the rebuilding of the Temple after or about the
same time as Josiah, while the disputation alleged to have been
held with Zerubbabel must be relegated to a later period. This,
however, does not affect the possibility of such disputations
having taken place between Jews and Samaritans or between
Zerubbabel and Sanballat.[1]

That the Samaritans wielded great power at the court is
obvious from the fact that on their mere representations all work
on the rebuilding of the Temple at Jerusalem was stopped for
many years. It is also to be noticed that the Samaritans are
never mentioned by name; they are called neither Kutim nor
Shomronim, but merely Adversaries, and no reason is given in the
Biblical record for the refusal of Zerubbabel and his companions
to acquiesce in the wish expressed by those 'Adversaries' to join
with them in the worship of the God of Israel in Jerusalem. It is,

[1] Much confusion would be avoided if more than one Sanballat could be
assumed to have been leader or political ruler of Samaria.

however, perfectly clear and easy to understand the refusal of the Jews to accept the invitation of the Samaritans to worship with them on Mount Garizim, but if the Samaritans came and offered to worship in Jerusalem, why should they have been refused?

None of the nations that had slowly filtered in from the neighbouring countries and settled in the partly desolated Judaea could have been meant by the title 'Adversary'. These had fraternized with the Jews until the great reform of Ezra and Nehemiah. The only adversaries to be so treated, and not so much from a political as a religious point of view, were those who held similar religious convictions and who could not easily be distinguished from the rest of the Jews except by the fundamental difference of the place of the Sanctuary. In all other respects they were justified in saying that they worshipped the same God of Israel, for they held the same laws and observed the same practices. This point will be developed much more fully later on when the religion of the Samaritans will come under review. Even if it were admitted that they were proselytes brought into the Jewish faith through fear of the lions and then converted through the teaching of the old priest, they could still have been considered as worshipping the God of Israel, and could only have been styled 'Adversaries' if for one reason or another they looked with jealous eye upon the rebuilding of the Temple in Jerusalem. Now these 'Adversaries' played a very decisive role at the time, but it is only if we grant that the Samaritans or northern Israelites had returned in large numbers and settled in the land of their fathers, that we can understand that the feud between the North and South was rekindled and fanned to a flame on a purely religious basis. The influence of the Samaritans among the Jews at that time must have been very extensive; not only did they wield sufficient power to prevent the rebuilding of the Temple in Jerusalem, while they enjoyed the privilege of having rebuilt one on Mount Garizim a long while before, but the difference of their religious observances was so slight as to render them almost indistinguishable. This was a grave danger to the new community, which had come back from Babylon chastened in heart and wholly changed in its religious outlook. Every trace of ancient idolatry had been shed, and pure monotheism was now the outstanding form of their worship and belief. It was probably this hatred of idols and freedom from pagan worship which had appealed so strongly to the Persian kings in contradistinction to the other

nations, and which may have influenced their decision in favour
of the Samaritans and Jews, assisting them in the rebuilding of
their temples dedicated to the worship of the one God. Be that
as it may, the spiritual leaders of the new community, the prophets, realized the danger which threatened the Jews lest they
be absorbed by the Samaritans. For many centuries the Temple
had stood on Mount Moriah.[1] If now all the utterances of the
prophets were to be blotted out, all remembrance of the glorious
times of Hezekiah and Josiah, Solomon and David, to be forgotten,
all the worship to which they had clung to be declared heretical,
what future lay before the people ? Why strive to build a new
Temple ? Why establish it once again on the old, and at the
same time upon a new basis ? If these thoughts gained credence
all enthusiasm and activity would be killed and all the high
hopes which had animated them on their return from the Exile
would only be an ugly dream. The leaders had, therefore, to
concentrate their efforts upon combating an insidious propaganda which threatened to lure away the people from their
allegiance to their old literature and old convictions ; they could
not turn their backs upon the history of centuries, and so they
engaged in a strenuous fight, which started with the return of
Zerubbabel and Joshua and was continued by the prophets
Haggai, Zechariah, and Malachi. A new light is thus thrown
upon the activity and tendency of these prophets, and one understands much better the words and actions of Zechariah in his
relations to Zerubbabel and Joshua.

Zechariah's desire, like that of the people, was to re-establish
the Temple on its old foundations in Jerusalem. The relations
between the Samaritans and the returned Jews must have been
of a friendly character at the beginning; after all, they were
conscious of being parts of one nation, they practically spoke the
same language, worshipped the same God, followed the same
injunctions, and had the same laws. The Jews could, therefore,
easily have intermarried with the Samaritans, for it is not to be
assumed from the records of the time of Ezra and Nehemiah,
that the Jews had so far forgotten themselves as to intermarry
with the heathen inhabitants. If they did so at all, it could

---

[1] I may state here that the text of the Pentateuch in the hands of the
prophets must have already had the reading which is found in the Massoretic Text, in which Mount Ebal is mentioned instead of Mount Gerazim
as the place where the altar should be established, evidently only temporarily,
and built of the twelve stones with the inscriptions thereon.

only have been with their own kinsfolk who had returned long before they had, who occupied a commanding position, and the leader of whom had been entrusted with the military governorship of the land. It was therefore the object of the prophet Zechariah and those who worked with him to weaken the influence of the Samaritans and at the same time to give to the Jews, despondent and dispirited as they were, new courage and new confidence. The old rivalry between the secular and the priestly power was revived just then by the rival claims of Zerubbabel and Joshua the High Priest. The prophet had to make his choice, and the choice fell upon Joshua: the reasons seem obvious.

The Samaritans, together with the other hostile colonists and peoples, had denounced the Jews to the kings of Persia as preparing for revolt, giving the rebuilding of the Temple and the rebuilding of the walls of Jerusalem as the outward signal of such preparations. If, then, the scion of the royal house of David had been appointed ruler of the Jews, this would have proved the truth of the denunciation and would have strengthened the belief that such a ruler would try and revive the ancient glory of his ancestors, and with the aid of wealth and armed power realize his ambition. The prophet had, therefore, to advise the elimination of such a dangerous element, and though, as he puts it, ' however large the mountain may be ', meaning the power of the Samaritans in their Mount Garizim, ' it would be as nought before Zerubbabel ', yet Joshua was to be the chosen one of the Lord. He had chosen Jerusalem and rebuked the adversary. A priest would be inoffensive; moreover, he was indispensable, since no temple worship could be contemplated which was not under the direct administration of the priests. The prophet then adds : ' I will bring forth my servant the Branch ' (Zech. iii. 8). The reference here is to Joshua, the priest who is designated as the real branch of the house of Eleazar, and not, as has hitherto been thought, in any way connected with the House of David or any foretelling of the Messianic period, for which there is not the slightest justification. The whole object of Zechariah is to prove that Joshua was the only man qualified for the position, contrary to the claim of the Samaritans, who bespattered him and denied his right to it. In chapters iii and iv the ' Adversary ' appears, Satan, the evil Adversary, who evidently tries to convince Joshua, the High Priest, that Garizim or Sichem was the place chosen by God. He is rebuked by the prophet, who says : ' May the

Lord rebuke thee, who has chosen Jerusalem.' The very word
which occurs over and over again in Deuteronomy in connexion
with the choice of the sacred place which will be made by God,
' yibḥar', is used on this occasion, 'haboher'. Although the
Adversary has bespattered the High Priest, who is described as
being dressed in filthy garments, meaning thereby that his claim
to the high priesthood was not justified, the Prophet insists that
these garments should be taken away and that he should be
clothed in glorious garments befitting the High Priest.

The Samaritans maintain that their High Priests are the only
ones in the line of true descent from Aaron and Eleazar, and that
those of Jerusalem are either from Ithamar or from some
secondary line. This the prophet tries to nullify, and states
emphatically that no one else is the rightful man who is to serve
in God's courtyards. Not only was Joshua the rightful priest,
but those who were with him were also ' anshe mofet', meaning
singled out for being a Divine proof. Any idea of reading into
this chapter any Messianic portents is quite impossible ; the
Messianic idea as an active or conscious force never arose in
Judaism before the Maccabaean period, and the theory which has
been advanced, especially by modern scholars, that Zerubbabel
went back to Jerusalem with the idea of establishing the Messianic Kingdom has no foundation whatsoever. Zerubbabel merely
went back as a political leader and Joshua as the spiritual one,
just as we find it later on in Ezra and Nehemiah, but in a somewhat different order, and as we find it among the Samaritans in
the persons of Serayah and Sanballat, if we may assume the
existence of a Sanballat at the time of Serayah, and if there be no
anachronistic mixing up of dates and persons. In order to allay
the fears of the people completely the prophet adds that seven
fountains would be opened from the stone upon which Joshua
had stood, the seal broken, and the sins of the land, referring to
the others, washed away, whilst the people of Judah would henceforth be able to live peaceably, ' each under the vine and the fig
tree '.

But the prophet did not give up the hope of reuniting these
two families ; in the vision which the angel explains he sees two
olive trees, i.e. two branches of one olive tree feeding the bowl
of the golden candlestick, and again he refers to these two olive
trees as being the two sons of Iṣhar (iv. 14). Here the prophet
plays upon the word ; it may mean oil, but it is also the name of
the brother of Amram, thus perhaps alluding to the two priestly

families. These two will be reunited in the future, though neither through strength nor through might, but through the Spirit of the Lord. To them belongs the future, although Zerubbabel may take a hand in the temporary rebuilding of the Temple.

This vision, however, was not to be realized. Zerubbabel failed in his mission because he could not hold out against the Samaritans; he had come with the hope of rebuilding the Temple and town, and he was frustrated in both his aims. His political mission came to an end, and with it his political authority waned and he disappeared from the scene. The people became disheartened, and friendly relations were re-established between Jews and Samaritans to such an extent that intermarriage took place. The political renaissance, however, did not affect the Jews very much, nor did their aims lie in that direction. From being a political nation they had returned a religious people, and this became their absorbing interest, upon which they centred all their activity. Hence the importance attached to the function of High Priest and the efforts which were made by the prophets to retain him in office and to encourage the people in their hopes of ultimate success. Because of the obstacles raised by the Samaritans, which threatened the very peace of the inhabitants, the prophets strained every nerve to encourage them, and held out a vision of a future of life in peace and comfort. Zechariah continued his work, preaching and encouraging and laying emphatic stress on the fact that Zion was the Holy Mount and Jerusalem the Holy City (viii. 3), where God would dwell in the place which he had chosen for his Sanctuary.

Again, in Haggai, chapter ii, 11 f., the prophet asks the very pointed question about the touch of the impure which defiles the flesh that the priest is carrying; unquestionably, the people alluded to here must be the Samaritans. From the priestly point of view they were declared impure and their contact carried with it Levitical contamination. The heathen nations could hardly have been meant, since it was not likely that any Jew, and especially a priest, would be brought into such close contact as to expose himself to defilement, nor would it be necessary for the prophet to explain that the touch of such a person was defilement. It could only refer to the Samaritans, whom the people would not consider impure unless so described by the prophet.

If we now turn to Malachi, we find in chapters i and ii the expression of the despondency which settled upon the Jewish community after the failure of Zerubbabel to rebuild the Temple. Their high hopes had been dashed, their expectations far from realized, while those who feared the Lord could only meet in secret and whisper to one another words of comfort or of doubt. To these the prophet speaks words of encouragement, and finishes his exhortation with a reference to the prophet Elijah, who will come again and decide, as at the sacrifice on Mount Carmel, between the followers of strange and objectionable worship and those who proclaim the true worship of God.

I must state here again with all strength that any attempts to read into these chapters prophecies of Messianic anticipations which should have been fulfilled at the time of the Return are entirely unjustifiable. The Messianic idea did not assume such a concrete form at that period in the history of the Jews ; it only developed slowly through the course of the centuries after the Exile, when the prophecies had unfortunately not been fulfilled literally and the time of peace and happiness fore-shadowed by them had become a mere hope for the future instead of a reality of the present. The peace and prosperity alluded to by the prophets referred to the very time in which they lived and to the circumstances in which they developed their common-wealth. There is no trace of political aspiration ; it is a con-centration upon the spiritual life and the immediate Divine protection which occupied the mind and hearts of the people. As a result of the rebuilding of the Temple, they expected a visible sign of that Divine protection, and with the frustration of the rebuilding their hopes drooped. The prophets then arose and encouraged them anew, and gave them the assurance of final realization. Later on this finality was connected with the Messiah, and at a still later period was brought into close relation with the final Day of Judgement.

The decisive turn came, however, in the time of Ezra, when, by means more efficacious than the mere rebuke of political or religious collaboration, the severance or break was made irrevo-cable. The history of Ezra as told in the Bible is very involved and obscure ; his position is never defined, his authority does not seem to have been great, nor is his activity clearly described, although later tradition, both Jewish and Samaritan, has ascribed to him a very important action in connexion with the Pentateuch, which has assumed extraordinary proportions with the higher critics and which is not justifiable by any state-ment anywhere. The only ground for all this superstructure,

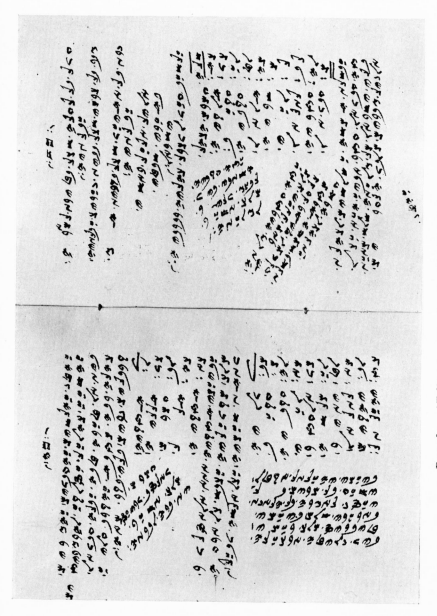

Plate 6

Page from 'Tolidah' written by the late High Priest Jacob

which credits Ezra with the extraordinary activity of compiling the Pentateuch as we have it, rests upon two points: upon the title by which he is mentioned, 'Sofer Mahir', and upon the fact that on one occasion he caused the Law to be publicly read to the people, not only the text, but also 'meforash vesom sekhel' (Neh. viii. 8). This is not the place to enter into a minute examination of the title or the meaning of the words here quoted in the original. Rabbinic tradition explains the latter by saying that Ezra not only had the text read in Hebrew but also interpreted it in the Targum or Aramaic language, so that it could be fully understood by the people, thus making the origin of the Targum contemporary with him; but no word is found in Jewish literature of any other activity of Ezra as far as the text of the Pentateuch is concerned.

As for his title, it is noteworthy that his genealogy is given, though many links are missing, and that he is described as the Sofer Mahir. The word Sofer, which occurs frequently in the history of David and in the latter part of Kings, as well as in Jeremiah, means more than a mere scribe.[1] In all these passages the Sofer is a very high functionary, either equal to the High Priest or commander of the army. Ezra's position could, therefore, not have been that of a mere scribe, but that of a man who held a special post of commanding rank. It is also curious to note that no High Priest is mentioned through all the period of Ezra and Nehemiah, nor on the other hand is Ezra designated as the ministering High Priest of the time. If we turn to his genealogy the problem becomes more complicated still; he is described there as the descendant of Aaron the High Priest, in direct succession through Eleazar and Pineḥas down to Serayah (Ezra vii. 1–5). The same line of succession, a little more amplified, occurs in Chronicles (1 Chron. vi. 4–15). This is carried down to Jehozadak the son of Serayah, who was carried into exile. Many generations must have passed away between the time when Jehozadak went into exile and Ezra's appearance on the scene, a period of close upon 150 years. It therefore seems evident that Ezra was the rightful successor to the High Priesthood and the descendant of the Joshua who had come back with Zerubbabel. The object of this genealogy was obviously to enforce Ezra's claim of speaking with the authority of a High Priest. Only under such

---

[1] 2 Sam. viii. 17, xx. 25; 2 Kings xii. 12 (A.V. xii. 10), xix. 2, xxii. 3; Jer. lii. 25.

a supposition can the extraordinary fact be explained that Ezra and Nehemiah acted as though no High Priest existed.

If we compare this genealogical chain with that given by the Samaritans we shall find a remarkable similarity between them ; of the fifteen names given by Ezra, no less than eleven are also found in the list of the Samaritans: one is doubtful and three differ, whilst in one place the same gloss is added. In the Samaritan chain Jonothan, in the Bible the High Priest Joḥanan, is mentioned as being priest at the time of the building of the Temple by Solomon.

Now Ezra had obtained permission from King Artaxerxes to rebuild the Temple and the walls of Jerusalem, and evidently came to the decision to break finally with the Samaritans. This was the dominant motive in the activity which he displayed, and it is only from this point of view that it can be understood. It will also explain the virulent hostility displayed by the Samaritans whenever they mention the name of Ezra. According to the unanimous tradition of both, Ezra transcribed the Hebrew text from the old characters still found among the Samaritans into the Aramaic script. There could only have been one reason for such a drastic step, namely, to break completely and to eliminate the Samaritan text from circulation among the Jews, to relegate it to a place of inferiority or declare it spurious as well as incorrect and unreliable, as was often declared in the Rabbinic writings, and to wean the people from any contact or any knowledge of the old script. The new alphabet formed the impassable barrier between the two.

The Samaritans, however, go farther, and allege that Ezra not only changed the character of the alphabet but also falsified the text. They state that he eliminated the tenth commandment according to their recension, and in Deut. xxvii. 4 altered the word Garizim into Ebal, as the mountain upon which the altar should be erected of the twelve stones and with the words of the Law written upon them. This they assert was done to destroy the claim of the Samaritans, which rests upon their tenth commandment and that passage in Deuteronomy, and thus to repudiate once and for all their claim of possessing the true text of the Law and the true place of the Sanctuary. It is now easier to understand why the Levites read the Law to the people under the command of Ezra and with the assistance of Nehemiah. This was Ezra's final step to bring about the complete separation of Jews from Samaritans, a step which he could only have undertaken with the full support of the new Governor of Judea, who was a man occupying a high position at the court of the King.

More than ten years had elapsed since Ezra had first come back to find the very curious situation which had developed during the seventy years since the time of Zerubbabel and the prophets Haggai and Zechariah. The Jews, weak and cowed by the hostility of the Samaritans and of the other nations who worked with the latter, must have entered into friendly relations with those who claimed to be of the same kinship and who worshipped the same God. There was no personal hostility between the two sections apart from religious differences, and, as is clear from the Bible, intermarriage had taken place between Jews and Samaritans down to the time of Ezra and Nehemiah, not only among the lower classes but also among the highest in the land and the leaders of the Jews. At the time of Ezra and Nehemiah there were men of both sections who kept up friendly relations with one another, and who were opposed to Ezra and Nehemiah. As both these latter avoid mentioning the Samaritans by name, one must assume that they are referred to as the Ashdodim, who were able to impose their language upon the new-born children. It would be difficult to state with certainty what language was spoken in that small town of Philistia, or how great the population could have been, but it must have been extraordinarily great if their women were able to marry a large number of Jews, so large indeed as to affect the speech of the younger generation. If, on the other hand, we assume the Ashdodim to be a euphemistic expression for Samaritans, there is no difficulty in understanding that they spoke the Samaritan dialect of Aramaic, and that the children had therefore to be weaned from it and brought back to a knowledge of Hebrew. That Aramaic had become the popular language is now an undisputed fact, though the Aramaic of the Jews differed dialectically from that of the Samaritans; the origin of the Targum is the best proof of the widespread knowledge of this language among the Jews of Palestine.

In order, therefore, to carry out his decision, Ezra had first to break the family relations: hence the stern decree of divorce. It was not merely a question of keeping the stock pure, for large numbers of the other nations had become assimilated, and intermarriage with strange proselytes was not as strongly forbidden then as became the case later on. It was the danger to the religious life which was involved; not the fear of idolatry, because all trace of idolatry had been expunged, but the more serious risk of losing their religious identity and of turning their backs on Zion and Jerusalem.   How great this danger was, is best proved by the fact already referred to, that intermarriage had taken place between the highest in the land; Nehemiah himself (xiii. 28) mentions the son of the High Priest Joiada, who had taken to wife the daughter of Sanballat, his contemporary in Samaria, and not to be confused with the Sanballat of the time of Zerubbabel.   Sanballat is called the Horonite, the name being probably used here as a title of opprobrium for ' stranger ', ' Aher '.[1]

This will explain the failure of Ezra's activity until his work was taken in hand by Nehemiah and carried through owing to the authority wielded by the latter.   The High Priest and his family, the princes of Judah, and all those who lived in amity with the Samaritans unquestionably offered great opposition and resistance to Ezra's reformative work and were able to thwart it during the years that Ezra was alone.   They objected to his drastic methods and made his mission abortive.

Josephus (*Antiq.* xi. 7. 2 (§§ 302 f.)), tells a parallel story of the marriage between the son of the Jewish High Priest and the daughter of Sanballat. He calls the man Manasseh and connects with this episode the building of the temple on Mount Garizim by Sanballat, whom he makes a contemporary of Alexander the Great.[2]

Modern criticism connects with this Manasseh the alleged adoption by the Samaritans of the Pentateuch which the former is supposed to have brought with him.   No trace of such a fact can be found in the Samaritan chronicles, nor is the intermarriage mentioned between the house of the High Priest of Jerusalem and any of their governors or rulers; in one chronicle, however, Sanballat is mentioned as ' Cohen Levi ', ' the Priest

---

[1] Sanballat was already in 536 leader of the Samaritans. In 456, during the time of Ezra, the name of the son of the High Priest who married the daughter of Sanballat is not given; he is only mentioned in Nehemiah in 445, so the marriage must have taken place whilst Ezra was still there, and nearly a hundred years after the first Sanballat had appeared on the scene. This latter could therefore not be identical with the Sanballat mentioned by Nehemiah, but may have been his father or grandfather, which would explain Josephus's mistake (*Antiq.* ibid.).

[2] He has evidently been misled by the fact that at least two Sanballats must have existed.

the Levite', and in another as 'Levite' only, but he is never identified in any way with the High Priest. On the contrary, according to the Samaritan chronicles, a large number of exiles came back and settled in the land under the High Priest Abdael, no less than 37,000 being mentioned as having returned. Josephus for his part has no hesitation in giving the number of those who returned under Zerubbabel and Ezra as forty myriads, exclusive of priest, Levites, and assistants. Thus we have one exaggeration against the other, for a careful examination of the work of Josephus will reveal the unsuspected fact that he seems to have been fully acquainted with Samaritan history and Samaritan traditions; much, of course, he controverts, and whenever possible turns it in favour of the Jews. Take, for example, the incident to which Nehemiah alludes in one sentence, when he says that the Samaritans had correspondence with the leaders of the Jews; Josephus turns this into a whole story of a denunciation on the part of the Jews against the Samaritans who had been sent to the court of the Persian king Artaxerxes.[1] This same story, however, greatly embellished and given in much greater detail, occurs in the Samaritan chronicle, as well as that of the final break started by Ezra and completed by Nehemiah which reappears in Samaritan history in a manner much more clearly defined than the form in which it has been preserved to us in the Books of Ezra and Nehemiah.

It is in the light of these facts that one can understand much more easily the origin and tendency of the Books of Chronicles.

If we examine them carefully, we shall find that they are devoted almost exclusively, not so much to the extolling of the priesthood as to the proof that the worship in Jerusalem was the only legitimate one, and that all the priests and Levites connected therewith were the only ones who could prove pure descent, since those who could not produce their genealogical lists had been eliminated; moreover, they continued to carry the genealogical lists down to the latest possible period that can be determined. This was a proper sequel to the work of Ezra and Nehemiah, namely, that only those should be allowed to serve and minister whose genealogies were above suspicion.[2] Under

---

[1] *Antiq.* xi. 4. 9 (§§ 114 ff.).

[2] Much stress was laid on such lists, and this explains the drawing up of the list of the birth of Jesus in Matt. i and Luke iii. They seem to have been indispensable, and in the midrashic literature of Jews and Samaritans we shall again come across such genealogical lists also applied to wicked people, in

these priests, one must, of course, understand those who may
have joined from the Samaritans or other parts of the Northern
Kingdom, being attracted by the newly established power of
Judea under Nehemiah and by the slowly growing strength of
the dwellers of Jerusalem. Like the Samaritan genealogical
lists, the Books of Chronicles starts with Adam, who is considered
by the former as the first High Priest; then the line is carried
down to Moses, and is followed by an elaborate description of the
Levites and priests whose organization has been carried out by
David in connexion with the new Temple. The books are at the
same time a kind of apotheosis of the House of David, and a eulogy
of all the good kings who ruled in Jerusalem and kept faithful
to the Law of God.

The author of the Books of Chronicles, however, takes care to
point out that at the time of the split under Jeroboam (2 Chron.
xi. 13 ff.) all the true priests left Northern Israel and went and
settled in Judah. The tendency is obvious: it all serves one
and the same purpose, to deny the claim of the Samaritans that
their priests were the true descendants of Eleazar and Pineḥas
and that they had kept the old tradition unchanged.

Thus far the Bible record and the chronicles of the Samaritans
run parallel.

Naturally the question is: Is it not possible for the Samaritans
to have copied or borrowed their material from the Bible?
Any one, however, who is slightly acquainted with the virulent
hatred which animated these two sections of the Jewish people
would not for a moment maintain such an improbable hypothesis.
Nor do they agree in their descriptions. Each one gives his own
view of the events as they happened, but both seem to go back
to a common source. In a way they supplement one another and
complete the picture of the time, of which information is very
scarce, while the documents preserved are in a very fragmentary
state. Ezra finishes abruptly, Nehemiah finishes abruptly, and
Chronicles likewise. Even if we assume that the first chapter
of Ezra be a continuation of the Books of Chronicles, the second
book, i.e. Nehemiah, still remains unfinished. There follows a
profound gap until the story starts again with the advent of
Alexander.

As already remarked, the Samaritans know nothing of Manasseh

order to prove that Haman or Bileam or Pharaoh were links in a long chain of
similar bad progenitors.

nor of any building of the Temple, either by him after having been driven out of Jerusalem, or else, as stated by Josephus, by Sanballat after he had obtained permission as a favour from Alexander, though their history is carried swiftly to that period ; but if Josephus's statement be correct, that Sanballat obtained the favour of being allowed to build a temple on Mount Garizim, then the Samaritan contention is justified that they were well treated by Alexander ; according to the Jews it was the latter who received preferential treatment at the hands of Alexander, inasmuch as he gave them the right to destroy the temple of the Samaritans which existed on Mount Garizim. Jewish and Samaritan literature contain precisely the same legend down to the minutest detail concerning the meeting between Alexander and the High Priest ; Jewish tradition is doubtful whether the name of the priest was Jaddua or Simeon the Pious, whilst the Samaritan tradition has no hesitation in giving the name of the High Priest as Ḥiskiah. Alexander is received by both in the same pompous manner ; he comes with the intention of destroying the town for alleged enmity, but instead of destroying it he prostrates himself before the High Priest, and explains the reason for his sudden change of attitude by telling his generals of a vision which he had had before the decisive battle with Darius, in which he had seen the image of such a man as the High Priest promising him victory. In answer to his request to have statues erected in the Temple, the High Priest promises to erect him lasting ones, and when he returns from his victorious expedition in Egypt and inquires after the statues, he is presented with a number of boys all born since his last visit and all called Alexander. In the Samaritan version the High Priest afterwards continues in a long philosophic and moral discussion, which is given in full in the Samaritan chronicle. One fact is certain : when he built Alexandria he carried away with him a large number of Jews and Samaritans and settled them in Egypt, and thus carried the strife which was rampant between them from Palestine to Egypt, an act which afterwards had very important consequences.

The Samaritans then continue and tell of a King Simon of the Jews who persecuted them to the extreme, preventing them from keeping their feasts and even from reading the Law according to their own tradition. Unless a confusion has been made here with John Hyrcanus, who destroyed their temple and persecuted the Samaritans in 127 B.C.E., this could only have been the aforementioned Simeon the High Priest. Ben Sira wrote a special ode in honour of Simeon, praising him far above other men. Whether he obtained that attribute from Jewish tradition through some act of vindication of Jewish claims against the Samaritans can only be a matter of conjecture, even if Samaritan tradition should prove correct. But be that as it may, after Simeon's death the Samaritans recovered their freedom of action and freedom of worship. According to the same tradition, a large number of Samaritans emigrated to various parts, owing to the persecution, some of them settling round the so-called river of Kutah. They eventually returned from thence, and that is how the Samaritans explain the name Kutim being given to them by the Jews: it refers to this section of the Samaritans, for they repudiate entirely any connexion with any heathen nations.

After the death of Alexander, Palestine became the battle-field of the Ptolemies and the Seleucids ; the country was ravaged by the armies of both sides, and Ptolemy carried away many Jews and Samaritans as captives to Egypt, thus greatly increasing the number of the two factions already in that country.[1] The difficulties which existed between these two sections grew in consequence of the increased numbers, and fights between them are mentioned by Josephus.[2] These all had a religious origin: the disputes which arose chiefly concerned the place whither the offerings should be sent, whether to the Temple of Jerusalem or that of Mount Garizim. The real object of the fights, however, was not merely the direction whither each of these sects should send their offerings, but probably referred to the royal gifts which the kings used to send to the recognized religious centre. Outwardly there was no difference between the Jews and Samaritans : they followed the same Law, observed the same practices, and the minor differences which existed between them could not have been distinguished by any one who did not belong to either of the two sects. The matter was, therefore, brought before the king for decision.

With this is intimately connected the history of the so-called LXX, i.e. the Greek translation of the Pentateuch, but discussion of this point must be reserved for a later stage, when the literature will come under review. One thing is certain: from a careful examination of all the data available in Josephus and the

---

[1] Josephus, *Antiq.* xii. 1. 1 (§ 7).   [2] *Antiq.* xii. 1. 1 (§ 10).

Rabbinic tradition, as well as in the Samaritan chronicles, we come to the conclusion that the story of the translation having been made on that occasion has no real basis. It is the legendary embroidery round an historical kernel which had already become obscure and confused at the time when the so-called Letter of Aristeas was compiled. It suffices to state here that the question under consideration was not to obtain a translation of the Pentateuch for the royal library, but a discussion between the two contending sections as to the authority and genuineness of the sacred book upon which they both based their claim. According to Josephus the Jews won, and according to the Samaritan tradition the Samaritans were the victors. But leaving this aside for the moment, the discussion throws important light upon the history of the Greek translation, while at the same time the controversy contributed to intensify still more the hatred of one section for the other, which showed itself later on at the time of the Maccabaean revolt.

When Antiochus Epiphanes endeavoured to unify all the nations under his sway in the worship of the Greek gods, he was helped to a large extent by the apparent sympathy with Greek culture and Greek ways shown by the chief families of Jerusalem : the High Priest himself had not disdained to accept the heathen form of worship and to view with approval the establishment of a statue of Zeus in the very Temple. The same treatment was, no doubt, also meted out to the Samaritans, and Josephus does not lose an opportunity of asserting that the Samaritans offered less resistance than the Jews, and allowed their temple on Mount Garizim to be dedicated to the heathen god. The charge was just as much justified in this case as was the countercharge made by the Samaritans that the Jews had not hesitated to erect a statue of Zeus at Jerusalem. It is, however, true that certain circles of both nations accepted the order of King Antiochus and submitted to a temporary alienation from their ancient faith. How far the Samaritans acquiesced in order to shake off the rule of Antiochus, and to free themselves from heathen religion, can only be gathered from their further history, which shows that they continued to worship according to their ancient forms in the Temple on Mount Garizim ; indications in their chronicles point to the same fact, but only through slight allusions. There was no hero among the Samaritans, who, like the Maccabees, took up the fight, and they, therefore, had very little to record from the personal point of view. There was no outstanding figure upon whom to concentrate their attention and to whom they could point as the one who had freed them from the hated yoke. They, no doubt, benefited by the victory of the Macca- bees, although it is very difficult to say how far they may have assisted the latter, for to them the re-establishment of the Temple in Jerusalem and the worship of God there was not a result to be desired. On the contrary, whenever trouble beset the Jews and their Temple, the Samaritans did not hesitate to take a share in it and to rejoice in the evil which had befallen. There was no love lost between the two parties, and no sooner did John Hyrcanus obtain practical autonomy for Judea than he attacked the Samaritans, destroyed their Temple, and annexed those portions of their territory which abutted on the northern frontier of Judea. Ever since the Return the Samaritans had been slowly losing the political supremacy which they had enjoyed, and this gradually passed into the hands of the Jews. They remained, however, more formidable foes than the Romans, although from a religious rather than from a political point of view, and the allusions to the enemies of the faith, apostates and those who were doing their best to lead the people astray, found in the pseudepigraphic literature must henceforth be brought into connexion with the relations between Jews and Samaritans. Hitherto the antagonism which is reflected in the pseudepi- graphic literature has been explained as the antagonism of rival sections within Judea, and many factions have been more or less invented or their position exaggerated in order to account for the strong admonitions often found there. As will be seen later on, the rivalry between two Jewish sections never reached so great a height as to justify such outbursts of vituperation as those found in the Book of Enoch, the Testament of the Twelve Patriarchs, &c., unless they were directed against a downright hostile sect like the Samaritans. The latter still wielded a great influence over the popular mind, and proved a serious danger to the development of Judaism on specific lines. Many an his- torical allusion will be found embedded in this literature if studied from that point of view, just as has been found on a careful examination of the writings of the last prophets and of the Books of Ezra, Nehemiah, and Chronicles for the preceding period.

The Rabbinic as well as the Samaritan tradition recalls many events in which this antagonism often led to bitter fights and bloodshed. The Samaritans endeavoured to mislead the Jews in the Diaspora, and lighted beacons on the hill-tops on wrong dates, to indicate the new moon as calculated in Jerusalem, for this was the sign agreed upon by the Jews. By so doing they confused the calendar, and made it impossible for the Jews outside Palestine to keep the festivals on the appointed days, and thus contributed to the appointment of messengers or apostles who carried messages from Jerusalem to different parts; these were the precursors of, or rather paved the way for, the activity of the Apostles of the Christian faith. As a result the Jews declared the country of the Samaritans contaminated, and were taught to avoid passing through it, and everything possible was done to prevent contact with them.

They, for their part, and they themselves own it, introduced and strewed dead men's bones in the court of the Temple of Jerusalem in order to pollute it, besides substituting mice for doves in the boxes which the men were carrying to Jerusalem, and which were consequently let loose in the Temple. They even went so far as to insinuate that the Jews kept an image of a small man hidden in the Holy of Holies, which they worshipped, and which the Samaritans alleged had been seen by one of the heathen kings. He had asked permission to enter the Holy of Holies, and had been refused by the High Priest, being told there was nothing to be seen. He, however, insisted and entered, whereupon he saw that idol, and in his wrath he slew a large number of Jews including the High Priest. Here we have the precursor of the much more infamous allegation made by Apion. The Jews retorted by asserting that the Samaritans worshipped a bird, an idol called ' Ashema '.[1]

Although the Samaritans rejoiced at the downfall of Jerusalem in 70 c.e., they also suffered very heavily. The Roman government failed to distinguish between Jew and Samaritan in the same way as the Greek or Egyptian governments before it, and we, therefore, henceforth find Jews and Samaritans treated alike by Roman legislation, the oppression which fell upon the Jew being also extended to the Samaritan. The tragedy of the one section was shared by the other; and the laws affecting the observance of the faith, circumcision, and other ceremonies were applied to both Jew and Samaritan. The Samaritan chronicles

---

[1] This is nothing else but the Samaritan way of reading the Tetragrammaton, which, like the Jews, they avoid pronouncing, reading it Shema to this very day, while the Jews read Adonai. This fact is not devoid of importance, as will be seen later on.

mention a good many of the Roman emperors who passed severe laws against them, but one of the worst fates which befell them was the destruction, under Hadrian in 130, not only of their place of worship, but of practically the whole of their literature which had been collected in Sichem. This was a very severe blow, from which the Samaritans never entirely recovered ; it also explains the fragmentary character of the literature which has been preserved. The Jews maintained their internal organization and religious power for centuries, and were thus able to unify their spiritual life, to a certain extent, and to carry on unbroken the literary and spiritual development. Not so the Samaritans. With the downfall of their political autonomy, the various tribes which made up its entity fell to pieces, and started an independent religious life, which has hitherto not yet been even surmised. They proved a ready soil for the growth of many of the dissenting movements and sectarian developments, to which attention will be directed when discussing the doctrines and faith of the Samaritans. This also explains the slow decay which overtook them.

Like the Jews, they also basked in the favour of some of the emperors, and the legends again appear in both literatures concerning the history of the Emperor Antoninus Pius and his relation to each of them. Both tell us of his friendly intercourse with the leading man ; among the Jews it was the Patriarch Judah, among the Samaritans it was the High Priest. According to the latter, that intercourse was of so intimate a character that he eventually became a proselyte of the Samaritan faith and showed his favour to all its followers. But evil times again overtook both Samaritans and Jews under the Greek emperors of Byzantium, and at their hands they suffered very greatly until the Byzantine emperors embraced Christianity and it became the officially recognized church. Then began a period of such intolerable oppression that the advent of Islam and the freedom which they enjoyed under Mohammedan rule was the beginning of a new life.

The connexion between Samaria and the Far East is also shown by their sympathy for the Parthians and Sassanians in their wars against the Byzantine emperors. Many of the followers in the armies of those kings were probably Samaritans, if we take the word in its widest sense as covering the Northern Tribes who had not returned from the Exile.

In the fourth century the Samaritans were allowed to breathe freely for a while under the leadership of Baba Rabba, who carried on guerrilla warfare against the local garrisons of Samaria until at length he freed the country from the hostile armies. According to their chronicles he re-established the worship as of old, reorganized the people, and divided the land thus re-conquered amongst various houses, appointing officials to regulate the internal administration of the community on a solid basis. The period of Baba Rabba was also the period of the recovery of the ancient documents and the first attempt at preserving them. It succeeded in so far that many of the old fragments have come down to us, and as some of the greatest poets and religious writers flourished in his time, their writings have also been preserved.

In any case, those monuments which existed at that period have been preserved by the Samaritans with unfailing care and fidelity. The student, therefore, is fully justified in using the material thus preserved as reliable documents for the elucidation of contemporary events, and for drawing from them all the information possible for the explanation of the problems contained in the history of the Jews, and enunciated by the latter in accordance with their own principles.

We can now see that these two traditions run parallel to one another, that many a point which is obscure in the one is illuminated by the other, and that the background which has been wanting for Biblical history, for incidents of the time of the Maccabees, for a proper understanding of some of the pseudepigraphic writings, and for many of the movements in Egypt and Palestine in which Jews and Samaritans were concerned, can be found in the Samaritan traditions. One is incomplete without the other, and both must be taken together if the historical truth is to be established on a firm and sure foundation.

SECOND LECTURE

DOCTRINES AND RELIGIOUS PRACTICES

THE difficulty of piecing together the chequered history of the Samaritans and of establishing its relation to Jewish history, both Biblical and post-Biblical, has to a certain extent been overcome by the discovery of some of their chronicles. Late though their compilation may be they none the less contain very ancient material, and, as I have endeavoured to show, material of a very reliable character. If studied with caution and compared with the records found in Jewish and non-Jewish history, they will yield much that is of importance for a proper understanding of the past.

But difficult as the study of their history is, it is still more difficult to arrive at a proper appreciation or even to give an adequate description of the doctrines and practices of the Samaritans. Here, until almost quite recently, all sources failed us. True the Pentateuch was there, but nothing was known of the way in which they applied the laws contained therein except from stray allusions, sometimes favourable and sometimes unfavourable, which are found in the Rabbinic writings, and later on from those few letters exchanged with Europe from the sixteenth century onwards. Gradually further material came to light from which something of practical value could be gleaned, as for example the Liturgy, although this mostly contains hymns of various ages which merely allude to the claims of the Samaritans and to the underlying principles which inspired the poets to their composition. Happily, however, information is now at hand which embraces all the problems of human life. These have been carefully examined with the object of trying to find traces of pagan practices or beliefs, or any syncretism with the practices and ceremonies of the nations surrounding them. If the theory be true that the Samaritans were the descendants of the ancient proselytes, the fallacy of which has been shown in the previous lecture, some such traces must inevitably be found in their doctrines and ceremonies. Even the Jews themselves at their bitterest only allude to one fact which was proved to be of a legendary character and due to a misunderstanding. As is well known, Palestine under the Greek government was the hotbed of religious movements, and since the Greek conquest various mystic sects established themselves. Moreover, the Ancient Mysteries were not unknown in Palestine, for it was the very centre of that syncretistic movement which swayed the ancient world prior to the rise of Christianity, and which was further developed in the course of the next centuries. These movements, however, had no influence upon the faith and doctrines of the Samaritans, nor did they in any way help to shape and mould the spiritual outlook of the worshippers on Mount Garizim. The most minute investigation has failed to indicate a single trace ; on the contrary, the result has been to fortify still farther, and confirm more strongly, the conviction that the Samaritans are none other than a purely Jewish sect. It is Jewish not only in its origin, but it is also Jewish in the wider sense of its development, and the reason for this is not far to seek. Both Jews and Samaritans draw their inspiration from and rest their faith and doctrines on one and the same source, the Pentateuch. Anticipating for a while the conclusions to be derived from a study of the Samaritan Pentateuch, its antiquity and genuineness, which is reserved for the third lecture, it must be accepted here as the starting-point of the investigation. The laws and prescriptions found in both recensions are the fundamental basis of the ceremonial life of Jews and Samaritans. This was already clear from the letters received from the Samaritans : they were asked to give an outline of their faith and practices, and in reply they affirmed unhesitatingly throughout the centuries during which the correspondence was carried on their strict adherence to the Law of Moses, who to them is the highest and only prophet, and to the fulfilment of all the laws and prescriptions in his books which are of Divine origin. In that respect they differ in nothing from the Jews, and this statement is fully corroborated by the tradition of the Rabbis; some of the latter who were less influenced by political considerations even went so far as to say that all the laws observed by the Samaritans were if possible observed with greater strictness by them than by the Jews, and that a Jew could unhesitatingly make use of anything prepared or done by the Samaritans if said by the latter to have been prepared in

accordance with the law of Moses.[1]   It is, therefore, evident that
to both Jews and Samaritans the highest authority was invested
in one and the same book, i. e. the Pentateuch.

To assume that the Samaritans borrowed the Pentateuch from
the Jews at the time modern Higher Criticism alleges, would
run contrary to the historical development of religious life.   A
book must be recognized as of supernatural origin if it is to be
an infallible guide and if obedience to it can be claimed by the
people.   The hypothesis that the prophets, as it were, proclaimed
the principles of morality and ethics and also laid the foundation for the practical application of those abstract theories, means
reversing the only process by which these doctrines can be
explained.   Again, if the origin of those principles of morality
and of all the ceremonial laws which flowed from them were in
reality the work of the prophets, the Samaritans would under no
consideration have accepted a book which to them was of such
contaminated origin.   They rejected the prophets and everything in any way connected with Jerusalem, while as far as
the Law in the main was concerned they agreed with the Jews
on almost every point.   In addition, however, they introduced,
or claimed to preserve from still higher antiquity, a section of the
Pentateuch by which they justified the fundamental difference
between them and the Jews.

The text of the Samaritan Pentateuch contains an additional
tenth commandment, the Jewish ten being reckoned as nine;
this tenth refers to the selection of Mount Garizim as the Holy
Mount and the place where the altar should be established.[2]
The verses in question are repeated afterwards in Deut. xxvii, &c.
With this exception there is no essential difference between
the Samaritan and Jewish text of the Pentateuch.   The Pentateuch, therefore, could not be the result of the work of the
prophets before the Exile, for they were all described as
sorcerers, wizards, and heretics by the Samaritans, and still less
could it be the work of Ezra, the man who, as has been seen
before, was the chief author of the final schism between the two
sections.   There is also internal evidence to be gleaned from the
evolution of their spiritual life and religious development, which

---

[1] v. Strack, H. L., and Billerbeck, P., *Kommentar z. Neuen Testament aus
Talmud u. Midrasch*, vol. i, *Matthäus*, München, 1922, pp. 538-60, where there
is an exhaustive treatment of the relations of Samaritans and Jews in post-
Biblical times.

[2] v. Appendix.

enables us to recognize an old common origin of these principles found among Jews and Samaritans.

It must be borne in mind that the admonitions and remonstrances of the prophets were always directed against the kings and the leaders, and not against the masses. The latter must have had very little in common with the court form of worship, as it could otherwise not have been changed from one form to another as easily and as often as we find it in various acts related by the prophets. A people does not change its faith and religious practices at a moment's notice or at the bidding of a king, especially when there is no adequate power behind the command to force them to do so, for the people are always very conservative in all matters of religious ceremonies. Their whole life depends upon an exact and accurate carrying out of beliefs and religious practices, and they will not be swayed from one extreme to another at the command of any one, whoever he may be. If the Samaritans were of heathen origin, and the Pentateuch which they accepted had been of recent compilation, it would have been impossible for the whole nation to have changed its faith without a strong protest, at the mere bidding of a priest who for some reason undisclosed adopted all the laws contained in the Book of Moses, or without at least retaining many, if not most, of their ancient customs. The revolt of many of the priests and Levites, including the son of the High Priest, against Nehemiah's decree, which apparently could not touch the family life without touching the religious principles, shows how quickly the people resented violent changes.

Already from very early times the Jews had felt the necessity of adapting the ever-changing forms of life to the letter of the Law. Many ceremonies and laws contained in the Pentateuch could not be applied literally without the greatest confusion and the greatest hardship. Some, in fact, were absolutely impossible of being carried out at all, unless an interpretation were added which made these laws practical. How was the Sabbath to be kept, how the commandments concerning the fasts and the feasts, how the festival of the Passover or that of the Tabernacles? How were questions of matrimony and divorce to be settled, when the latter is not even mentioned in the Pentateuch? Then there was the slaughter of animals, the formulation of prayers, the time and place, not to speak of innumerable questions connected with Levitical purity and impurity, forbidden food, and how to distinguish those birds which were allowed to be eaten

from those which were not allowed to be eaten, questions which
arose out of daily life and to which the text of the Pentateuch
gave no definite answer. At every turn of life they knocked
against a closed door, and therefore some means had to be found
to answer these questions and to satisfy these demands. In order
to find a way to apply the laws, and at the same time to satisfy
the letter and spirit of the text, the sages of old had recourse to
a peculiar system of interpretation, on the one hand to indicate
the method of application, and on the other to justify the practice
which had grown out of this peculiar exegesis. How old it
might be can already be inferred from the action of Ezra, who
had to interpret the Law and justify his action from the words of
the text. The science of this exegesis is called Midrash, a word
already found in the Books of Chronicles; [1] and the principle
which underlay it is as follows : the text was scanned very carefully, and if a redundant expression were found anywhere, however
it may have crept in, that redundancy was seized upon as having a
definite meaning; for nothing, not even a single letter, was considered superfluous in a book written by God : if, therefore, it were
found in the text, it had intentionally been put there to allow of the
specific interpretation which was placed upon it. The new law
thus evolved was called the Oral Law in contradistinction to the
Written Law. The form was believed to have been handed down
from the time of Moses, the assumption being that the germs of
that interpretation were to be found in the text itself, and that
this interpretation should be applied and developed in the course
of time as circumstances dictated. Thus every practical ceremony, nay every doctrine, had to find its source and justification
in the text of the Pentateuch. Such an interpretation and
application, however, could only be understood if the text itself
had already been consolidated and fixed for a very long time
down to the minutest form, so that it had become a standard
book which had come down from hoary antiquity, and which
was surrounded by a halo of holiness which commanded obedience
and awe. Unless the Pentateuch had been considered of so ancient
and sacred a character, there would have been no possibility for
having recourse to this artificial exegesis; if Ezra and the sages
could have compiled a Law themselves, they could have enlarged
upon it and introduced into it such alterations and modifications
as would have suited the requirements of the moment. It will

---

[1] 2 Chron. xiii. 22 ; xxiv. 27.

be seen later on that, in fact, some slight amplifications were introduced into the Greek and Samaritan versions for popular use, but these are quite infinitesimal and are the result of that exegesis.

Although practically little was known of the Samaritan traditions and the manner of their observance of the Biblical laws, some scholars have noticed some similarities between Samaritans and Jews and even Samaritans and Karaites. Without investigating the matter deeper, and without going to the original source of information, they hastily assumed that the Samaritans were always the borrowers. According to them, whatever is found among the Samaritans resembling Jewish, Christian, Mohammedan, Karaite, or other sectarian practices, it must have been borrowed by the Samaritans. Any one, however, who has studied the history of religious practices and cults, of beliefs and ceremonies which affect the daily life of a nation, will definitely reject the idea of continual borrowing of practices which are invested with a sacred character, and which change the whole current of religious convictions. No nation has easily given up even its own superstitions in favour of others, unless forced to do so by extraneous agencies or through a tyranny which made them embrace another faith altogether. None of these forces acted upon the Samaritans, and if anything, they are the only people who have had neither reason nor occasion to change. As already remarked, their tradition has been riveted to the same place for so long, and has been handed down direct from generation to generation, that the utmost reliance can be placed upon it. There have always been Samaritans living in Sichem and worshipping on Mount Garizim for at least 3,000 years or more, and why at every turn of the wheel they should have changed their mode of life, accepted different laws, altered their prayers and worship and adopted a new conception of the future, no one has yet been able to explain; they must have had some way of living, they must have observed the Sabbath and the biblical laws even if they had been the proselytes of the 'lions' of the sixth century B.C.E. Why should they have changed? It is quite different with the other local sects: it is a natural phenomenon for a younger sect, separating itself from synagogue or church, to turn to an older dissenting sect and lean upon it for support in its endeavour to protest against what it believes to have been innovations. The Karaites, in their opposition to the Rabbis, would have learned only too willingly from a sect which had defied those same

Rabbis; Christianity would easily borrow from a sect which worshipped God independent of Jerusalem, although still venerating the Bible, while Islam would and did borrow indiscriminately. No trace of the dependence of the Samaritans upon Islam has yet been adduced, nor has any real evidence been brought forward which weakens the antiquity of the Samaritan tradition.

One must remember that the Samaritans were always on the defensive, for they had to protect their own claims, which rested upon their Bible and upon their traditions; and although the Rabbis accuse them occasionally of having falsified the text, they none the less bear testimony to the strict observance by the Samaritans of the laws contained therein. The Samaritans dared not give up a minute particle of their tradition, if they did not wish to lay themselves open to the much graver charge that they could not justify their claim of being the keepers of the Truth or observers of the Law according to the Truth. Moreover, there was nothing to be gained from imitating the outward forms and ceremonies of the others, and in their thoughts and in their writings they have never shown any desire of modifying their antagonism or of changing their hatred for everything Jewish.

Now the need for this oral interpretation of the Pentateuch was felt by both Samaritans and Jews, and both proceeded in a parallel manner. Both evolved fundamental principles of interpretation, but whilst agreeing in these fundamental principles they developed in the course of time in an independent manner. The details which were filled in by Jew and Samaritan vary much, and in some cases the conclusions reached are diametrically opposed to one another. The parallelism on the one hand, and the difference on the other, prove, at any rate, that one has not borrowed from the other except perhaps in such high antiquity as belonged to a remote past. This is also shown by the curious fact that in some points the Samaritan Oral Law agrees with the so-called Sadducean interpretation, whilst in many others it agrees with the so-called Pharisean. All, however, seem to belong to the time of the Second Temple, and no new developments can be traced in the later writings, with the exception of perhaps one or two points which will be mentioned later on.

If we examine Samaritan conditions more carefully, we shall find that their case is identical with that of the Sadokite priests. Like the latter, the priests were the ruling caste; they were the custodians of the Law, its sole interpreters, and the judges and guides in all religious and legal matters affecting the people. There was as little difference in the religious and secular life of the Samaritans as there was in that of the Jews. Everything stood in the service of religion and every ceremony was a religious act. Like the Jews, the Samaritan priests had to be very jealous of the prerogatives which they possessed to justify their claim of being the true keepers of the Law according to the Truth; the most trivial deviation from that norm would have been very serious, whilst the slightest leaning towards the practices of the hated Jews and the rival priesthood would have been fatal to their position. Considering the virulent hatred between the two sections, it is unthinkable that one should consciously have borrowed from the other or introduced into its practical application of the Law methods applied by the other party, the more so since both relied upon the same source for their inspiration and guidance. Moreover, the Samaritans were still more handicapped, inasmuch as they possessed the Pentateuch only, and could not rely upon the writings and teachings of the prophets.

Their whole code of law had to emerge from the words of the Pentateuch if it were to cover every shade and form of religious life. They would, therefore, have every reason for preserving intact whatever they believed to be their own religious faith and practice.

In one point, however, the case is quite different as far as the Samaritans are concerned, for the power and prerogative of the priests has never been challenged. Throughout the ages they have been the sole rulers and guides. They have kept their Chain of High Priests from Adam down to our own days, and although it is doubtful in some places, there cannot be any question that the priesthood has continued to wield the power vested in them by the Law. They have never been removed from Mount Garizim, and so have been able to preserve practically unchanged whatever form of tradition they may have possessed. There was no reason why they should not persevere in the same practices, while the permanency of abode round the Sanctuary and the personal guidance of the priest forbade any contemplation of change. Once fixed, the Oral Law remained binding upon the Samaritans as it has remained binding upon the Jews. This does not mean that changes were not introduced during the course of time, but merely that the old tradition has remained; whatever new additions were made—if and when will have to be determined, and the dates thereof are still wanting—they must have followed the same principles of Biblical exegesis as those by which the Oral Law was evolved out of the text, for a whole system was evolved which covered the religious life of the Samaritans, and which has remained rigidly the same throughout the ages. To this very day the Cohanim, i.e. the descendants of Aaron, or from the middle of the eighteenth century, the Levites, still enjoy the same privileges as those described in the Pentateuch. They receive tithes from the people as well as a portion of the slaughtered animal, and they take a personal part in every form of life, thereby approximating their position to that which the priests assumed in the Christian church, who probably followed the example of the Samaritans. They are present at circumcision, they sanction and attend betrothals, they draw up the bill of divorce, they are present at the last hour of the dying, and take part in the funeral, although they keep at a safe distance in order to preserve their Levitical purity. Down to the seventeenth century they still used for purification ashes of a red heifer, which had been provided by a generous Samaritan from Damascus in the fourteenth century.[1] They also perform the service in the Kinsha, and on every occasion their authority is invoked.

If, then, under these circumstances it is found that the Samaritans follow practices which resemble those of the Jews, they must be of such high antiquity as to be traced back to an ancient common source, old enough indeed to have been the common property of both sections before the definite break occurred. It would be just as absurd to assume that the Jews borrowed those practices and ceremonies from the Samaritans as it would be ludicrous to believe that the reverse had taken place, and sufficient has been shown to make such an hypothesis impossible. The only explanation, therefore, is the one which has just been stated, namely, that both go back to an ancient common source, an explanation which is quite natural considering that both rest their Oral Law upon one and the same written text.

It is obvious that such a text must have been in the hands of Jews and Samaritans for a very long time before it could have assumed the character of a sacred book of Divine origin, in which every word and letter was of importance, and where the peculiar forms occurring in it were intended to convey to its followers

---

[1] Fully described in the additions to the Tolidah, found in another MS.

more than was found in the written text. If, therefore, such
deductions have been made, it is obvious that the text must have
been a very old one and in evidence long before any period
when modern scholars allege it to have been accepted by the
Samaritans. Centuries must elapse from the moment that the
text was rigidly fixed until it could be used as a basis for such
an interpretation, centuries even before the LXX, so that the
stream of tradition must run much higher up to touch its
ultimate source, the definite text of the Pentateuch.

Now these peculiarities of the text were the pegs on which to
hang, by special hermeneutics, those interpretations of the Law
which led to the growth of what is now called the Oral Law.
That Oral Law was not a new invention, but was considered by
Jews and Samaritans alike as a very ancient tradition, as old as
the time of Moses, who is himself credited with having commenced such an interpretation when handing over the written
Law. Not a few such traditions are called by the Jews 'Halakhah of Moses from Sinai', although this statement is not to be
taken literally, for many laws so designated in the later writings
are of a much later origin. It must, however, be assumed that
some of those which had found willing acceptance, and which
corresponded to the practices followed by the people consciously
or unconsciously, with or without reference to the sacred text,
were codified as Sinaitic traditions at a later period. This alone
shows that a number of laws existed among the people which
were credited with a very high antiquity.

Now it is one of the cardinal beliefs of the Samaritans that
the Pentateuch as it stands now was actually written by the
Hand of God, and this is a point upon which they insist over and
over again; the only thing that Moses did was to transcribe it
(*bĕ'ēr*, Deut. i. 5), and hand it over to the priests and elders to
be kept by the side of the Ark of the Covenant and to be read
periodically to the people. There is, therefore, not a single word
that is superfluous, not a letter that can be missed, although
there is often a redundancy of style and apparent unnecessary
repetition of the same command ; e. g. the seething of a kid in
its mother's milk is forbidden three times in almost identical
words. I have taken this example in order to show later on how
Jews and Samaritans have interpreted the same verse and the
conclusions derived therefrom for the Oral Law and for daily
practice. Again, this attempt to interpret the Law, to smooth
out difficulties, to insert occasionally the explanatory word which

E

finds its justification in the Oral Law, is already found in the Greek translation, which in these peculiarities agrees in many points with the Samaritan text as now preserved. If then we find them in the Greek text we are carried back to the third century B.C.E. for the existence of such a developed system of exegesis, for it must have been old enough to have found its place already in the very text from which the Greek translation was made; it cannot be assumed that the Greek translators were responsible for these insertions, modifications, and changes. They were faithful translators of an old original, and they would not have dared to make such alterations or additions of their own, however strong the desire may have been of smoothing and explaining the translation before them, had they not already found them in the text from which they made the translation. Finally this exegesis is not limited to the legal compilations of the text; words and allusions in the Hebrew text were often the starting-points for whole series of legendary matter, which in the beginning were only briefly alluded to, but which afterwards were fully developed in independent writings which drew their inspiration from the words and allusions of the Hebrew text. A section of the old Hellenistic literature, a part of the Sibylline Oracles, and later the number of pseudepigraphic writings find their ultimate source in this curious exegesis of the text of the Bible. More was to be read into it if the deeper problems of human life were also to be solved by reference to the text of the Pentateuch.

This high antiquity also explains the similarity between the old so-called Sadducean 'Halakhah' and the Samaritan tradition. The word 'Halakhah' among the Jews has assumed the exclusive meaning of traditional interpretation of the written law, i.e. the practice of the Oral Law. This, however, was not the original meaning, but is a later development in which the original meaning seems to have been forgotten. But the author of the Arukh has still preserved the true meaning of the word, which he derives from the Biblical 'halakh', to walk', i.e. to take the proper road, to walk before God, to walk on the road which leads to the fulfilment of the command. This is the word which is generally used in the Pentateuch to denote the practical carrying out of the Law, and occurs as far back as the story of Enoch in Gen. v. 24; while the very same term is used of Noah that he walked with God' (Gen. vi. 9), i.e. he went in the true way which led to God, he led a pious life. The exegesis by which the 'way' was indicated to the pious was called Midrash Halakhah, and the word must have long been in use in that connotation for it afterwards to have become identified with the practice of the Oral Law. Originally it referred to the practice of the written Law and the best manner in which it could be carried out, so that a man might choose the good way and not the evil way.

The Samaritans have also preserved the use of that word in the form 'hillukh', which is none other than 'the Way',[1] and which with them is the guide to the performance of the Divine Law. In the Samaritan the word also has the meaning of ' Code of Laws', both written and oral. By following up the line of development among the Samaritans, we have found the existence of a parallelism upon which stress has been laid. Both applied the same method to the same principles, but an examination of the method employed by the Samaritans and the results achieved satisfies us that they came to a standstill at a time prior to the rise of the Jewish sects of Sadducees and Pharisees, for the Samaritans have some points in common with the one sect and some with the other. In the light of this result we shall be able better to understand the real meaning of these two sects so described by Josephus, concerning which divergent views have been expressed hitherto. A different interpretation, however, suggests itself to me, which may solve many of the problems connected with the two so-called sects, and which places the development of the Oral Law on a totally different basis in their relation to one another.

Before discussing the Sadducees and the Pharisees as represented by the traditions preserved in Josephus and the later literature, it is necessary to establish one fundamental fact, that in all these traditions we only find the record of points in which one differs from the other, and that nothing is said of all those doctrines which were common to both. Concerning this latter it must not be assumed that there was any fundamental difference between Sadducees and Pharisees in the religious doctrines and principles, as well as in the practices which had grown out of the written law and which constituted the Oral Law, i. e. the law transmitted from mouth to mouth and not written down until a long time after the period which closed with the destruction

---

[1] ' I am the Way ', John xiv. 6, and ' the way of God ', Matt. xxii. 16; Mark xii. 14.

of the Temple. The differences which did exist between them
only arose after the Maccabean revolt ; before that there was
uniformity in the interpretation of the text of the Bible and in
its practical application as a religious norm. We may say that
the period from Ezra to that of the Maccabees was one of absolute
rule on the part of the ' Sadokite ' priests, meaning thereby that
the Law was interpreted and applied by the priest only, beginning with the High Priest in Jerusalem and finishing with
every priest or Levite in the villages and communities ; for,
according to the Law, they were the judges and arbiters, and the
undisputed guides in all matters of faith and practice. It follows from this that the Oral Law or Halakhah must trace its
origin to a very early period, so far back that its beginnings cannot be stated definitely. There are various strata dividing the
old Halakhah from the later and the latest, although it must be
clearly understood that one did not necessarily supersede the other.
With very few exceptions, the old Halakhah has been preserved
in its entirety in the later, where a supplementary development
of some points has taken place in order to cope with ever-growing
necessities. This absolute absorption of the old by the new
makes it very difficult to distinguish one from the other, and it
is only when the two vary in their interpretation, or when some
definite change has been made, that it is possible to discover
which is the old and which is the new. But as, generally speaking, the religious life remained unaltered, there is no reason to
believe that any real change took place through the subsequent
ages in the practical performance of the prescriptions of the
Law and its manifold ceremonies. Only in the method of interpretation could a slight evolution be discerned. As shown by
Geiger,[1] the oldest Halakhah is characterized by the fact that it
draws its conclusions from the literal interpretation of the text
as it stands ; redundancy of expression, apparent superfluous
words or letters, are the basis and justification for this Halakhah.
The system evolved later on is far more elaborate, and it is only
by comparing these various methods of arriving at a definite
Law that one is able to differentiate between the old and the
new.

Scholars who have dealt with the problem of the Sadducees
and Pharisees have had no difficulty in pointing out that Josephus
described their differences in a manner compatible with Greek

---

[1] *Urschrift u. Uebersetzungen der Bibel*, Breslau, 1857, *passim.*

thought. He declared the Sadducees and Pharisees to be different Jewish sects, which were opposed to one another, and characterized them in such a manner as to exaggerate one point or minimize another. To be real sects fundamental differences had to be emphasized, and he therefore magnified small differences to make them fundamental principles. The information gleaned from the Rabbinic literature does not agree with the description given by Josephus, and to this very day many of the points have remained obscure. The few allusions to the Pharisees in the New Testament are misleading, and all the information which can be gathered from the Talmudic literature is of comparatively late origin, when everything had disappeared, and only vague remembrances are attached to the name of Sadducee. This word is used promiscuously for Kuthi, Nokhri, Min, and the views held or supposed to have been held by a ‘Ṣadoḳi’ often turn out to be the views held by quite a different sect, if the word may be used in that connexion. Josephus, as is well known, took his nomenclature from the Greeks, and described as sects parties whose real religious differences were not deep-seated enough to entitle them to such a denomination. If, e.g., the remark in Mishnah Joma (f. 18 b) be correct, that a High Priest suspected of being a Sadducee was approved by the Pharisees and officiated in the Temple on the Day of Atonement, and the reasons for that suspicion are indicated, then surely the differences between the two parties could not have been as profound as, for instance, those between the Jews and Samaritans. Besides, nothing reliable was really known about the tenets of the Sadducees after the destruction of the Temple, and although all the references to them are tinged with partisan colouring, the remarks still do not reveal the same rivalry in dogma and principle between Sadducees and Pharisees as one would expect after reading Josephus. Again, Josephus gives no reasons for the principles held by the one or the other. They could only differ among themselves in the interpretation and application of the Law, for this Law was common to both and neither could deviate from it without forfeiting its character as a Jewish sect. What is stated here about these two sects applies equally to the others mentioned by Josephus and Philo, such as the Essenes, &c., while the Assideans, i.e. Ḥasidim, already existed and formed an important section of the community at the time of the Maccabean revolt. Unfortunately, our information concerning all these sects is reduced to the few references in Josephus, the Rabbinic litera-

ture, and the New Testament writings, and the way was therefore open for all kinds of speculations. The Rabbis never call
themselves Pharisees, and the only possible interpretation seems
to be that Pharisee means 'separatist': those who separated
themselves from that interpretation of the Law which up to then
had been the exclusive pronouncement of the priestly caste. But
this does not mean that there was any religious difference between
them. The views held by the one were shared by the other : the
practices were absolutely the same, the differences being merely
of a theoretical character and rarely applied to practical life.
The Samaritans, however, have their own tradition concerning
them, and in one of their chronicles reference is made to Sadducees, Pharisees, and Assideans. The Samaritans identify themselves with the Ḥasidim, those who are pious and strict observers
of the Law, and say of the Sadducees that they are the people
who strictly applied the letter of the Law and never deviated from
it. Samaritan tradition, however, makes no mention of the fact
that the Sadducees denied the immortality of the soul or reward
and punishment after death, nor is there anything of a dogmatic
character such as is ascribed to them by Josephus. Of the
Pharisees they merely say that they are the men who give
a wider interpretation and application to the Law in ceremonies
and practices.

As far as I am aware, no one has ventured to explain the great
influence which the Sadducees wielded, nor has attempted to
reconcile the facts that they were the real judges down to the
time of the destruction of the Temple, and that after that
calamity they disappeared entirely. No purely religious party
could have been utterly destroyed by the mere fact of the destruction of the Temple. Other tendencies made themselves
manifest among the Jews before the destruction, and a number
of sectarian movements have been recorded as having risen after
the disappearance of the Temple and its service. There must,
therefore, be another and more profound reason for the existence
of the Sadducees before the fall of Jerusalem, for their claim of
supremacy, their demand to act as the judges, and for their assumed
negation of all the eschatological principles which occupied such
a large place in the speculations and beliefs of the centuries just
before and just after the common era.

It cannot be made sufficiently clear that the difference between
the Sadducees and the Pharisees was not one of religious conception, of interpretation of the text of the Bible, or of its strict

application. A most minute examination of all the available sources only reveals secondary points of no vital importance, many of which concern the service in the Temple and the observance of precepts connected with Temple worship, matters which scarcely reached the outer world and only affected a very small circle. A number of these were of a purely theoretical character, and it is impossible to understand how, on the strength of these minute differences, such virulent hatred, such open antagonism, and such terrible fights, which led to the slaughter of thousands, could have been engendered and carried out. The cause of difference between the two sects must lie far deeper. They were not sects in the religious meaning of the word, but two parties divided on political fundamentals; the one, the Sadducean, represented by the priests, wished to retain its political prerogative and power, not only for the present, but also for the future, while the other, the Pharisean, represented by the lay scholars, wished to separate the spiritual from the temporal power, and take the latter out of the hands of the priesthood.

Why should the Sadducees have assumed the position which they held both in the Temple and in the courts of law or Sinhedrion, and why should the High Priests of the time of the Second Temple have endeavoured to trace a direct descent from Aaron and Eleazar or rather from Eleazar and Pinehas? This has been tacitly accepted as a matter of course, although no explanation has been forthcoming why this should have been the case. There is general agreement that the Sadducees more or less existed before the Maccabean revolt, that they traced their lineage from the first High Priest, and that the party to which they belonged was the so-called aristocratic or wealthy section of the community, the Pharisees being of a more democratic character. In a way this distinction is correct, but the reason for the cleavage between the two parties has still to be found, as well as for the attitude taken up by the Sadducees in connexion with the application of the Law and their alleged denial of eschatological beliefs.

The privileged position granted to the Sadducees, or rather to the High Priest who was head of the party, can best be explained in the light of the historical events mentioned in the first lecture. The High Priests of the Jews and Samaritans were invested with the ruling power, which they claimed in virtue of their priestly origin. It must be remembered that according to the Torah, the priest was the judge and guide and the ultimate authority whose

decision was final. He was also the Shofet mentioned in Deut.
xvii. 9. This, according to Samaritan interpretation, was not a
secular judge but the High Priest, and it was therefore in their
interest to retain that supreme authority. In every circumstance
of life they played the decisive role; in secular as well as religious differences the people had to appeal to them alone for
justice, since they interpreted the Law according to the words of
Scripture. They also developed the Oral Law, and thus the basis
of the ancient Halakhah after the Return remained in the sole
possession of the priesthood down to the time of the Maccabees,
and rested exclusively upon an interpretation of the Law which
they applied with extreme rigour. Since every case had to be
brought before them, there was no room for a lay judge. But
in order to occupy that doubly distinguished position, and to
strengthen the loyalty of the people, it was necessary in each case to
prove that these High Priests and the priestly families connected
with them were the direct descendants of Aaron, and especially
of Pineḥas, and invested with that supreme authority which the
Law accorded to them. Hence, in both cases, the scrupulous care in
preserving the genealogical lines to show an unbroken continuity
as High Priests throughout the ages. At the time of the Second
Temple it was of the utmost importance for the High Priests to
prove the purity and directness of their descent from Ṣadok,
a descendant of Pineḥas, and not from Abiathar, the latter being
a descendant of the Ithamar line. The value attached to this
record of unbroken lineage is further shown in that passage of
Josephus (*Antiq.* xiii. 3. 4 (§ 78)) where the Jews substantiated their
claims before Ptolemy as against those of the Samaritans; they
not only brought the Law, i.e. the text which they held and
which differed from the Samaritan recension in that it eliminated the alleged tenth commandment found in the Samaritan
text, but also produced as witness the records of their High
Priests, thus proving that their High Priests were of the real
descent. They thereby established their tradition as the true
and reliable one.

This explains why the people would grant that pre-eminence
to the Sadducees, i.e. the descendants of Ṣadok, since it was in
full accord with the word of Scripture, and at the same time
proved that the latter were the keepers of the Truth and not the
hated Samaritans. The Samaritans, of course, adduced the same
proof, being just as careful and scrupulous as the Jews to preserve
such genealogical tables, showing that their High Priest was the

real descendant in the direct line. As already remarked, this also explains Ezra's insistence upon his descent from the same priestly line, for this would invest him with the power and authority inherent in a man who could claim to be a keeper of the true Law ; it also gave him the authority of placing it before the people in the manner in which it was done, and demanding obedience to it and to those laws which even cut deeply into the family life. Hence, also, the whole tendency and meaning of the Book of Chronicles. Here the genealogy starts with Adam, but the largest part of its contents is to prove the Davidic origin of the establishment of the Temple, with its organization of the priests and Levites, when Solomon placed Ṣadoḳ at the head of the priestly families. But in order to keep that position and pre-eminence the Ṣadoḳites were bound to insist upon the strict observance of the letter of the Law which was their charter, and the priestly families connected with them could only draw their authority from a literal interpretation of the text. They dared not go beyond the four corners of the Pentateuch if they did not wish to risk losing their position. It was only because they kept rigorously to the old traditions that they maintained their position as the secular judges, invested with the full authority of deciding the Law. They were also protected by the ministrations in the Temple, for the whole service lay in their hands, and this, of course, gave them that additional authoritative position in the life of the commonwealth, which could not be disputed by any layman.

The Pharisees' name after all can best be connected with the root פרש ' to separate '. This old interpretation seems to be the only correct one, and throughout the whole of the Talmudic literature the root פרש has only one meaning, that of separation, segregation, secession. It is, therefore, not a question of a sect but of a section of the Jewish population, among them scholars who were not of priestly descent, who separated or seceded from the political rule and mastery of the priesthood. The Pharisees were therefore those who declined to accept the unquestioning rule and the right of interpretation and application of the Law by the priesthood, limited as it was to the words of the Pentateuch only; and inspired by the glorious traditions of their historical past, drew additional lessons—not necessarily of a legal character—from the teachings of the prophets.

The great upheaval brought about by Antiochus Epiphanes, which among other things had swept away the ancient institution of the Great Assembly, had left the field free for the development of new parties, while the victories of the Maccabees had brought again to the mind of the people the memories of ancient glory. The words of the prophets rang in their ears, and they looked forward to the fulfilment of those ancient promises. Moreover, the Prophetic Writings, especially those of Jeremiah and Ezekiel, pointed to a descendant of David who would revive ancient times. For the Pharisees the everlasting covenant with Pinehas was limited to those who ministered in the Temple, whilst another covenant had been made with David which they recognized as just as valid as that made with the priesthood. Centuries had passed, and a new glamour now surrounded the name of David and his descendants. They had, as it were, receded into a past which the people were anxious to renew, for the military prowess of David and his successors seemed the best guarantee for the preservation of their own autonomy and for the realization of some of the promises of the prophets and for the greater glory of the future. In order, therefore, to strengthen their own position and reduce the power of the priests to a minimum, the Pharisees imported from Babylon Hillel, the reputed descendant of the House of David, and placed him at the head of their schools, and so gained through him and his descendants the political leadership of the people. The priesthood, however, held fast to its own prerogative, and as long as its own rights were not affected it looked with indifference on those stirrings of the soul and on questions which become louder and louder, questions concerning the fate of human life here and hereafter. From the priestly point of view, it was quite sufficient for them to declare that whatever kind of beliefs the people might cherish, whatever new hopes might be entering the mind of the nation, these were of no binding character nor invested with any legal authority; they were beliefs which the people might cherish or might ignore without thereby affecting their position as Jews. So long as the Temple stood, atonement for sin and redress for evil were there ready to hand, and they, as priests, made the necessary intercession between man and God. They could thus deny the immortality of the soul and resurrection, not as beliefs which the people might hold, but as not being proven from the text of the Pentateuch. Apparently there was nothing in the text which could give to these beliefs the same dogmatic value and the same legally binding authority as that accorded to the laws then in existence, an infringement of which came under the category of sin and for which a sacrifice of atonement had to be brought, as, for example, murder, cruelty, adultery, idol-worship, breaking of the Sabbath, &c., and similar moral or ceremonial laws. This, however, does not mean that the Sadducees denied the immortality of the soul or the belief in resurrection as maintained by Josephus (*Wars*, ii. 8, § 14) and the New Testament (Acts xxiii. 8), but that they denied there was proof for these beliefs in the Law. If Josephus add that they do not believe in the existence of angels, it may be the result of their own interpretation of the word 'malakh', which has the double meaning of 'messenger' and 'angel', for the few passages in the Pentateuch where the word occurs are open to both interpretations. None of the other books now forming the Bible had any legal value, and neither Sadducees nor Pharisees ever drew any binding legal conclusions either from the words of the prophets or from the writers of the Hagiographa; they may be a great moral asset, but they did not form part of the legal code, and could therefore be safely ignored. They were, however, afterwards used to strengthen the adoption of those beliefs which apparently were new, but which seem to have been adumbrated in the Pentateuch, although open to divergent interpretations.

Gradually the priests realized this deep-set movement and sought to answer these demands of the people in their own way. They therefore looked forward, not to a descendant of the House of David, who had been removed in the person of Zerubbabel by the authority of the prophet Zechariah immediately after the Return, but taking the words of the Bible literally, explained that the future ruler would also be a descendant of the priestly family. He would belong to the tribe of Levi, since he would be a prophet like unto Moses, as foretold by the Lord in Deut. xviii. 15 and 18.

But the priesthood became discredited through the apostasy of some of its leaders during the period of forcible Hellenization. They adopted Greek ways and went so far as to tolerate the introduction of Greek worship in the Temple. Moreover, the line of direct descent from Pinehas was broken by arbitrary appointments on the part of the Seleucids and Ptolemies, and the authority of the priests weakened accordingly. As mentioned above, the people turned their eyes longingly towards Babylon, where the descendants of David were known to live. They wanted a popular ruler, a man like themselves who was accessible to them, and who was not living retired within the four walls of the Temple, keeping away from any contact with the rest of the people, lest his purity be defiled and he deprived of his right to sacerdotal functions.	The opposing side, the Assideans or Ḥasidim, took the field and separated themselves from the priesthood—hence the name Perushim.	By continuing the old traditional practices, they laid the basis for the new authority and transferred it from the priests to the laity, and vested it in the men who claimed to be equally well versed in the words of Scripture, and who were able to interpret it satisfactorily. Further, they brought in a secular head from Babylon in the person of Hillel, and made the cleavage between the two parties fundamental, a gulf too deep to be bridged.	These Perushim, Pharisees, like Ezra 'explained' the text in a manner more compatible with the general tendencies of the time ; they showed greater latitude in their interpretation and by waiving the severity of the literal interpretation, they introduced a broader outlook of the way in which the theory and practice of the Law could be adjusted without doing violence to the text.	Exegetic beginnings which lay far back in antiquity were now fully developed ; rules of interpretation were formulated, and every law, every jot, and every tittle was used for the purpose of sanctioning the new development now carried out by the scribe and scholar in lieu of the priest and Levite.	In consequence of wresting the legal power from the priestly caste, the latter became a political party anxious to retain its privileges and authority, and thus the conflict became an open fight between the temporal and spiritual powers.	This would explain the fierce hatred between the two, since the victory of the one meant wresting the power from the priest, whilst if the Sadducees succeeded all the words and promises of the prophets would apparently be annihilated and the future no better than the present ; for, let it be remembered, the Messianic idea gained impetus and force with the Maccabean successes.	Simon, who was the most successful, when appointed head of the Jews, is distinctly mentioned as leader only until the time of the prophet : 'Simon should be their leader and High Priest for ever, until a faithful prophet arose' (1 Macc. xiv. 41).	Only a priest was contemplated ; the future lay with the prophet and a descendant of priestly lineage.	The Maccabees were of a priestly family and were therefore supported by the priestly party.

As the Messianic idea grew, the breach between the two

parties widened still more, for according to Sadducean teaching the Messiah to whom the people looked with vague aspirations and hopes could only be of the tribe of Levi, i.e. one of their own class. The ideal to which Ezra and Nehemiah looked in the future was also a priest who would arise for the Urim and Thummim (Ezra ii. 63), which by the way seem to have disappeared from the time of the building of the First Temple in Jerusalem. The Pharisees for their part looked to the House of David for their Messiah.

In time the people grew strong enough to object publicly to having a priest and king in one and the same person, and it is well known that they once pelted with citrons the then ruling High Priest Jannai as he exercised his priestly function in the Temple, shouting at the same time : ' Be High Priest but leave the kingdom alone ', an act which resulted in a fearful slaughter of the people. The reason is very clear. The people refused to recognize the right of the priest to the secular power, and looked to the House of David to send them the expected Ruler, not, let it be noted, a Redeemer. The Messiah is in no way connected with moral redemption ; he is only to be the temporal leader and ruler of the people, and will simply be king and nothing else.

When King Janneus lay on his death-bed, his last injunction to his wife Alexandra was that she should now seek the help of the Pharisees. In his lifetime he had leaned towards the party of the Sadducees, but he foresaw that the victory would lie with the popular party, and he therefore recommended his wife not to seek support from the former ; true, she could not represent any Messianic idea, but she could help in forwarding the ideal cherished by the mass of the people. And it really came to pass that the future lay in the hands of the descendants of Hillel.

When Herod came into power he also waged war against the Pharisees, and in them he had his bitterest enemies. Now that the throne was secular, and by tradition and belief belonged to the descendant of the House of David, the Pharisees could never tolerate its usurpation by the descendant of an Idumean. At that time this was the fundamental principle which divided the two parties.

But the Messiahship, however vaguely conceived as yet, was the bone of contention, and the people waited for the time when their expectations and hopes would be fully realized. This explains the history of Jesus, whom the people acclaimed as the descendant of David, and whom the Sadducees condemned for that reason ; not because the people acclaimed him as king, but because the people acclaimed him as the Son of David.

In his way Josephus fights shy of the whole principle of the Messiah ; the priestly tradition was too strong for him, and he therefore avoids any direct allusion.   When he mentions the Samaritan of about the same time as Jesus, who claimed to be the Samaritan Messiah and of whom I shall speak anon, Josephus puts him down as a madman, or as one who wished to deceive the people, thus entirely altering the character of the movement among the Samaritans.   The apocryphal and pseudepigraphic literatures also give ample evidence of these two currents of thought ; thus, while in the Apocalypse of Moses it is just dimly indicated, in the Testament of the Twelve Patriarchs it is from Levi that the future ruler will come.   Again, trace of the Davidic tradition is to be found in some of the others.

The destruction of the Temple destroyed the last hope of the priesthood of being the spiritual and temporal rulers and they therefore disappeared, because they were a political party.   On the other hand, the popular party with the House of David at its head retained its power and prerogative for many centuries ; the Patriarchs as they were called, who were the official rulers of the Jews under the Roman government, were all descendants of Hillel, and their power continued afterwards in Babylon until the ninth century, when it was revived for a while in Bostanai. Differences of interpretation, however, were not limited to Pharisees and Sadducees ; other schools sprang up which obtained a considerable following, in so far as each one drew its lessons from the text, although in accordance with principles differing from those held by the others.   It is this text of the Law which was common to all down to its single letters, which alone can explain the rise of the sectarian movement at so early a period, and is the same reason which produced other sects in the subsequent centuries.   None of them claimed to hold a different Law : it was only a question of interpretation or of finding a justification for new beliefs and practices in the actual words of the text.   A careful examination of this point will help towards the solution of the problem of the text in the hands of these various sectarians, and of the antiquity of the wording found in those texts upon which they based their own interpretation ; for it will presently be seen that this affects the Samaritans.   This is also a reason why the Sadducees disappeared with the destruction of the Temple.   The Law remained intact and quite independent of the men who attempted to interpret it according to their own views and tendencies, and this was all that was required.

The view expounded above of the real character of the Pharisees and Sadducees, of their mutual relation to the text of the Pentateuch, of their interpretation and application of it to practical life, which constituted what is known as the Oral Law, is fully borne out by the attitude adopted in this matter by the sages, the Fathers of the Synagogue. As mentioned above, they ignored the priests altogether, and limited the handing down of the tradition to Joshua, the Elders, the prophets, and the men of the Great Assembly.

When compared with the Samaritans, the relation between the two parties becomes still clearer. The Samaritans clung to the undisputed theocracy, and refused to acknowledge a secular leadership; no king ruled them, the only authority being that of the priesthood, which has remained so to this very day. We find, however, that they possess traditional laws which are parallel to those of the Jews, and which have been evolved from an interpretation similar to that evolved by the Jews. Many go back to very ancient times, and would therefore fall within the period when the descendants of Ṣadoḳ were still ruling in Jerusalem as High Priests; but the Samaritans also have other traditional laws common to the Jews, which are found among the so-called Pharisaic doctrines. It therefore becomes a question whether traditions thus denominated are not of a more ancient origin preceding the rise of the Pharisees, but which continued as general practices among the Jews, even after the extinction of Sadducean rule. As has been pointed out before, there can be no question of Samaritans borrowing direct from the Jews, nor has any borrowing been traced to a definite period after the destruction of the Temple. On the contrary, the Samaritan traditions all point to a time anterior to that event. The relations between Pharisees and Sadducees will therefore have to be reconsidered as far as the evolution of Jewish Oral Law is concerned, and the difference between these two sections reduced to a much smaller compass without thereby affecting the political cleavage between the two.

A few words may still be added here about the so-called 'Zadoḳite fragment.' The critical judgement of scholars seems to have gone astray in accepting this document as a very old one, referring to a specific Zadoḳite sect somewhere in Damascus, for the numerous legal prescriptions have been declared to be identical with, or similar to Sadducean ; it was assumed that the sect lived there before the destruction of the Temple. Now it is a well-known fact that the Sadducean party disappeared altogether with the destruction of the Temple, so according to scholars this document must be anterior to that period. No trace, however, of real Sadducean teaching has been found, and Professor Ginsburg was able to demonstrate just the reverse, namely, that these prescriptions agree much more closely, though in an exaggerated form, with Pharisean teaching.

The line of legal demarcation between these two parties can, however, not be strictly drawn, and, as stated before, much that is believed to be Pharisean is purely Sadducean or rather common to both, and there is nothing in the mass of legal prescriptions found here which could not with equal justice be ascribed to either of them.

But if this document be examined carefully in the light of Samaritan traditions, it will not be difficult to discover many very close affinities. The strict observance of the Sabbath and the peculiar laws about purity of food and body strongly resemble the methods of Samaritan sectarian teaching like Dustan and others. Most striking is the objection taken to the Messiah from the House of David in place of the Restorer from the House of Levi. This is the outstanding doctrine of the Samaritans, and, as has been shown, is the touchstone for Pharisaism and Sadduceeism. It is also the only point in favour of its Ṣadokite kinship, which, however, is impossible in view of the virulent language against David (p. 5, l. 3 ff.). Besides other affinities with Samaritan traditions, there is the remarkable use of the name Belial for Satan, to whom sinners will be handed over for destruction (p. 5, l. 19). This is precisely the name given by the Samaritans to the evil power which, in the form of the serpent, tempted Eve ; it also occurs under the form of Beliar in the Sibylline Oracles and in the Ascensio Jesaiae. The Jews, however, have never used it in that way.

We are dealing here with one of the many offsprings of sectarian teaching which flourished particularly in Galilee and the northern part of Palestine. It is of comparatively late date, somewhere about the middle of the fifth century if not later, as is also shown by the peculiar language, to which attention will be drawn later on.

If we now examine the traditional laws of the Samaritans, we shall find a number of them agreeing with what is known as Sadducean tradition and a number with Pharisean. This fact alone is sufficient to prove that the Samaritan tradition is independent of the Jewish, and belongs at any rate to a period anterior to the victory of the Pharisaic interpretation, for had they been influenced by the latter and accepted their exegesis and legal forms, the Oral Law of the Samaritans would not have been able to show traces of a more archaic Halakhah.

This is not the place to enter upon a detailed description of the manifold ceremonies and practices observed by them. The correspondence to which reference has been made does not contain a hint, although later information is now to hand, which offers ample material for that purpose. This will be more fully discussed in the third lecture in connexion with the literature. It suffices to state here that many of the observances are testified from very ancient times, and, as will be seen later on, the state of the Samaritan text of the Pentateuch points to a very ancient origin of these doctrines and practices. It is impossible to assume that the Samaritans deliberately and systematically evolved a code of laws of an eclectic character, selecting some from the Sadducees and others from the later Pharisees. There was not much intimacy or love between Samaritans and Pharisees, and still less between Samaritans and Sadducees. This must be perfectly clear from the fact that the Sadducees were the High Priests of the Temple of Jerusalem, or the living protagonists of the Temple of Garizim. The Samaritan priesthood would surely not have gone to the Jewish priesthood to derive from them the method of interpretation and the strict application of the letter and spirit of the Law, if they wished to maintain their independence and decry the Jews as heretics and apostates. A few examples will emphasize the real difference between the Samaritan and Jewish traditional law as represented by the two sections of the people.

We begin with the calendar, upon which the whole religious year, the keeping of the festivals and the observance of the fasts, is dependent. The difference here is fundamental, for the one entirely vitiates the character of the festival as held according to the other : either the one or the other is correct. We find that Jewish tradition has ascribed an almost mystical character to the fixing of the calendar and the calculation of the new moon. The secret of declaring the new moon or arranging the intercalary months was one of the great privileges of the San-

hedrin, and was afterwards carried on by the Patriarch with
great jealousy until political circumstances demanded the establishment of a fixed calendar.

According to Samaritan tradition, the secret of the calculation of the new moon was first given by God to Adam, and was
transferred from generation to generation until it came to Moses,
who passed it on to Pineḥas; he was the first to establish the
Samaritan calendar according to the astronomical calculation of
the meridian of Mount Garizim. Since then it has remained in
the hands of the High Priest. The actual calendar of the
Samaritans also differs greatly from that of the Jews; festivals
and fasts do not agree, with one important exception, where it
agrees with the Sadducean calendar, i.e. in the counting of the
Omer. The Sadducees started counting the Omer from the Sunday after the first Sabbath of Passover, so that the Feast of
Pentecost always fell on a Sunday; the Samaritans do likewise.
The reason for this application of the law by the Sadducees is
nowhere given fully, but in one of the Samaritan compilations
dealing with the law all the arguments which the Sadducees
might have brought forward to justify their calculation are set
out in detail.

Out of the darkness of Samaritan tradition there emerges the
peculiar figure of a heresiarch called Dustan. They place him
at a time shortly before Alexander, and there is no reason why
the accuracy of this tradition should be doubted; he is not to be
confused with a Dusis who flourished many centuries afterwards.
Very little of a positive nature is known of him and his teaching,
and later traditions may have been mixed up with the older
ones, even if these have not been entirely forgotten. But from the
few fragments which are extant we can gather that some of the
principles which he preached approximated his teaching to that
of the Sadducees, and that he taught a much more rigorous
interpretation of the text than ever advocated by the most conservative follower of the latter party. He also approximated the
practices of the Essenes in the extreme observance of Levitical
purity, so much so that the shadow of a man falling upon a grave
was sufficient to declare that man impure. He further attempted
to regulate the calendar anew, establishing months of thirty days
each, evidently in order to avoid those difficulties which arose
from the observance of the new moon alone and without definite
co-ordination between the solar and lunar years. The difficulties
arising out of this calendar among the Jews have already been

mentioned in the first lecture, whilst, as remarked before, the priesthood treated the fixing of the new moon as a special privilege which was entrusted to the High Priest. It was only later on that it was wrested from him by the secular Pharisees when they took away the privileges from the priesthood one after the other, and transferred them to the secular head, who claimed to be a descendant of the House of David. This suggestion of a new calendaristic calculation of the months brings to mind the Book of Jubilees, in which traces of a teaching going back to a very ancient period and observed by one of the sects which had much in common with the Samaritans have probably been preserved, as well as some ancient Jewish traditions. Dustan also eliminated the Tetragrammaton from the text of the Penta-teuch as far as possible, and substituted Elohim for it, thus taking us back to a period when even the High Priest, out of special reverence, no longer pronounced the Ineffable Name except on the Day of Atonement.

The Tetragrammaton was one of the pivots round which turned the whole mystical literature, and the fear of pronouncing it, the method of substitution, and the schemes and esoteric speculations used by all the sects are too well known to need more than a brief allusion. This Tetragrammaton appears in every magical document, and the fear of transliterating it was so great among the Jews that they merely copied the Hebrew letters and inserted that form into the Greek text whenever the name occurred. The Greek fragments of Akylas which have since come to light in Genizah palimpsests corroborate the ancient tradition of the Fathers of the Church that the Tetragrammaton was written in Hebrew characters; it is, of course, the ΠΙΠΙ of the Patristic literature. Later on, when discussing the mystical tendencies among the Samaritans, this problem will again be met in con-nexion with the mystical meaning attached to the Tetragram-maton. It was unquestionably in order to avoid its profane use or pronunciation that Dustan endeavoured to eliminate it from the text and substitute another more innocuous name of God. Again, if this be the case—and there is no reason to doubt it—the begin-nings of mystical speculations must be placed at a far higher antiquity than has hitherto been assumed. Moreover, the reason for the assumption of a late date is very simple: there is no literature extant. Practically speaking, we are in the domain of speculation, and we must, therefore, be content to draw such conclusions as are warranted by even the slightest references, especially if they be corroborated by later and more ample evidence.

Too little is known of the other ancient practices of the Samaritans to allow us to see wherein the reform of Dustan consisted as well as the reason for his more ascetic and mystical tendencies. If we compare the traditions of the Samaritans with the Jewish Halakhah we shall be struck by the fact that many of their laws agree with what has been termed the ancient Halakhah, always remembering that it is often not easy to distinguish between what is ancient and what is more recent. The only means of determining this is by examining the system followed by the Samaritans in evolving that Halakhah from the Biblical text, and finding out whether they base their Oral Law on the simple interpretation of the text of the Bible, on its words, letters, &c., in much the same way as the authors of the ancient Halakhah have done, or whether they have evolved the system of a later period of a more abstruse and involved interpretation. Subjected to this test, I can unhesitatingly say that as far as all the ceremonies and practices of the Samaritans are concerned, their code of traditional law, as found in MSS. in my possession, is based exclusively on a simple interpretation of the words of the Law. We are thus sometimes able to trace the reason, not given expressly anywhere else, for differences of interpretation between Sadducees and Pharisees. It is, however, impossible to give many details here: these must be reserved for the publication of the original texts with the necessary commentary. But I will give one or two examples which will suffice for my purpose. I take the law of the slaughter of animals.

No direction for slaughter is given in the Bible with the exception of the word 'shaḥaṭ'; this is evidently a technical term referring to a special kind of cutting to prepare the animal for food, differing from 'zabaḥ', which is used specifically for sacrifice, 'shakhat' being a more general term. The slaughter of animals was a practice which had to be performed daily, and yet no definite instruction can be found in the whole of the Biblical Scripture which directs the way in which it should be performed so that the meat should be fit for food. Slaughter also took place in the Temple, but even then only outer signs of blemish were indicated which caused the animal to be declared unfit for sacrifice; it had to show an obvious defect. Otherwise there was no other direction. Among the Jews, therefore, we have to rely absolutely upon a continuous tradition which was later formulated by the Rabbis under various headings, but which no doubt preserved many ancient practices. The slaughter was invested with a sacrificial import; it had to be performed by a pious man of unblemished character, who was well versed in the Law, and he had to use a knife specially constructed for the purpose. He had to cut the jugular vein and examine both the external and internal aspects of the animal to discover blemishes which would render it unfit for food, a practice which has continued to this very day.

The same principles prevail among the Samaritans, and they state definitely that these are the traditions handed down to them by the Elders and by their forefathers, the 'Pure Ones'. In addition to the prescriptions followed by the Jews, they have one more which must be of extreme antiquity, of which one single indication is given in the Bible in connexion with the sacrifice of birds. A word is used which occurs in two passages only (Lev. i. 15 and v. 8), i.e. 'malak', the meaning of which already seems to have been forgotten in very early times: Onkelos merely transcribes it and the Greek translates, 'to wring the neck of the bird', which is contrary to the words of the text, where it says that the neck should not be severed; a later tradition explains that it should be nipped off by the nail, for which no justification is to be found in the words of the text. The Palestinian Targum uses a word 'ḥazam ('azam)' which occurs only once in the Mishnah, and the real meaning of which is very doubtful.

The Samaritans, however, have taken this word as the basis for an additional law in connexion with slaughter, and in their code of laws have extended it from birds to animals. They give a full description of the way in which it is to be carried out, which if rightly understood means: after cutting the throat with a special knife 'the spinal cord is severed' by the very same knife as that which cut the jugular vein, and thus immediate extinction of life is brought about. Curiously enough this seems to have been the method of the ancient Egyptians as seen in a small model of a butcher's shop exhibited in the British Museum. It is a method which could not have been learned from the Rabbis and which is very archaic in character; even the ancient Halakhah is silent about it, and a later opinion, at a time when the real meaning of 'melikah' had been entirely forgotten, goes so far as to declare that birds need not be slaughtered in accordance with the principles generally established for the slaughter of animals. This, of course, has remained a solitary opinion of no legal value.

Of a similar traditional character is the Samaritan interpretation of the injunction not to seethe a kid in its mother's milk. which occurs three times in the Pentateuch, in Exod. xxiii. 19, xxxiv. 26, and Deut. xiv. 21. This multiplication of the command has given rise to the ancient interpretation among the Jews that it must not be taken literally as it stands, but that it means that meat and milk should not be cooked together and so not eaten together. This interpretation is already fully set out in the Palestinian Targum together with an additional sentence which throws light on some very mysterious words accompanying these verses in the Samaritan Bible, but which cannot be discussed here. Onkelos interprets in a similar manner, and both evidently reflect a practice established from very ancient times, which by then had become law. The Samaritans follow precisely the same law, but they also give a different reason for this application of the commandment. In their case they apply one of the peculiar methods of exegesis, i.e. by counting the letters as numerals.[1] According to the explanation given to me in 1905 by the then High Priest, Jacob the son of Aaron, it is derived from an ancient oral tradition still living among them, and which, I believe, he said he had found in an old commentary. The numerical value of the word ' g^{e}di '=' kid ' is seventeen, and the number of animals assumed to have been included in Deut. xiv and allowed to be eaten is seventeen. These seventeen must therefore not be seethed in milk, and if this has been done they may not be eaten. As this is almost a daily practice of life, the Samaritans would not wait for the Jews to teach them such an interpretation, nor would they later on adopt such a practice when by so doing they create obvious difficulties for themselves.

This interpretation of ' gedi ' is not a solitary example of Gematria as practised by the Samaritans, for there is the famous one of the word בשגם in Gen. vi. 3, which by a numerical calculation, i.e. 345, is equal to the name of Moses, for whose sake, according to the Samaritans, the world was created, and who was to live 120 years, the exact number mentioned in that verse. Other parallels can also be easily adduced, such as those at the end of the allegory on the Taheb, and the whole mysterious

[1] This use of letters in their numerical value already occurs in the Sibylline Oracles, and later in the Apocalypse, and must therefore be very old. v. Dornseiff. *Das Alphabet in Mystik und Magie*, Leipzig, 1922.

calculation therein which rests upon a kind of Gematria connected with the names of God.

There is one more point which might be noticed here with profit. The Bible enumerates a certain number of birds which are forbidden to be eaten, but gives no characteristic sign, as is given for the mammals and fish, by which to distinguish the clean from the unclean. How then could a man distinguish between one such set of fowl and another? The only way was by examining all these laws and finding out the features they had in common or the features which were missing, and then drawing up a list of the peculiar signs by which to distinguish one from the other. The signs by which the clean and unclean are to be distinguished are again practically identical among Jews and Samaritans; such as the fourth toe at the back, the bird which does not hold the food in its claw, the gullet which is considered as a kind of maw for chewing the food, and so on. As this was an urgent necessity an answer to the question had to be found.

This is not the place to multiply examples, since reference can only be made to one or two in order to show how the ancient Halakhah has also been a living practice among the Samaritans, and how they have derived it exclusively from the words of the Pentateuch which was theirs. This can be shown further in many of the other customs and practices followed by the Samaritans. In their strict observance of the Sabbath they go beyond the tradition of the Jews, and refuse to allow a light to be kindled, sitting in darkness. They put a greater restriction upon the distance they are allowed to walk on the Sabbath, and also refuse to accept the principle of the Erub.[1] Further, they forbid the drinking of wine or any intoxicating liquor on the Sabbath and festivals, for they assert that the observance of these days is equivalent to the service in the Temple, and according to Lev. x. 9 no priest was allowed to drink before approaching the altar. This is in contradistinction to the Jews, who do precisely the reverse, and celebrate the Sabbath and festivals by the blessing over a cup of wine. Many other details upon which it is unnecessary to enter here have been discussed by Geiger in his *Urschrift*, where he has shown that more than one ancient Halakhah finds support in the peculiar reading of the Samaritan recension, and is often also supported by the LXX; this is an obvious proof that the

[1] A symbolical legal connexion for the strict observance of the Sabbath.

Samaritan text represents a traditional source common to Samaritans and Jews.

Let us turn for a moment to a few of those laws which affect human life. The marriage ceremonies are extremely archaic and the betrothal makes the damsel the lawfully wedded wife of the husband. On that occasion the priest plays an important role; the dowry is fixed in conformity with the Biblical prescription and is called Maher,[1] special blessings are pronounced by the priest, and a contract is drawn up called the Mikhtab Hadebiḳah —'the writing of joining', the word being taken from the text of the Bible in Gen. ii. 24, where it says 'a man shall cleave'. and where, by the way, the reading of the Samaritan text is of considerable importance as it agrees with the quotation in the New Testament, for it says, 'And they *both* shall become one flesh',[2] a reading which bears specially upon the principle of divorce, a subject, however, which cannot be proceeded with here. The document is signed by witnesses, the formula for the signature agreeing almost entirely with that found in the Papyrus of Assuan. The whole draft is in conformity with the prescriptions of the Bible, according to which the betrothal causes the damsel to be considered as the lawfully married wife, so that any transgression on her part is liable to punishment with death. With the Jews betrothal and marriage are two distinct functions, and the position of the woman under each is entirely different. Moreover, many details given in the Bible are inserted in the Samaritan betrothal bill, such as those referring to vows, obedience, &c., which are not found in the Jewish contract. Thus while running on parallel lines, the contents in Samaritan and Jewish documents differ considerably.

Similarly, in full concurrence with the letter of the Bible, the Samaritans also draw up a bill of divorce which agrees, yet disagrees, with Jewish documents of a similar kind. It remains, however, an open question whether the woman is allowed to sue for divorce and can have the documents drawn up on her behalf by the priest, or whether the authority rests with the husband alone. It seems that a certain authority allows the priest to draw up a bill and to direct the divorce to take place.

All these laws and practices, however, only affect the material aspect of human life; its relation to God is regulated by com-

---

[1] Not 'mohar', as punctuated by the Massoretic Text.
[2] Matt. xix. 5 ; Mark x. 7, 8 ; 1 Cor. vi. 16 ; Eph. v. 31.

mandments and precepts found in the Pentateuch, which are
further elaborated by additional laws. Thus the problem arises
of how to approach God in the more spiritual way of prayer.
No provision for this is made in the Bible. Moses' prayers
often consist of a single sentence, nor is any other prayer recorded
which can be a sufficiently clear guide to the worshipper. Again,
nothing is recorded of the worship in the Temple, either in the
time of Eli or at a later period. The dedicatory prayer of
Solomon is no help, and nowhere can we find any definite
description of the form of prayer. It is the same with the
Apocryphal books, with the exception of the individual prayers of
Judas Maccabaeus, Tobit, and Susanna, which after all are merely
individual outpourings of gratitude, hope, or solicitation. The
Psalms are also nothing else but individual outpourings; later
on they were used as hymns in connexion with the worship, but
they are not real formulas for prayer. A few traces of the ancient
Liturgy, however, can be reconstructed, but as far as can be
ascertained from the meagre records in the Biblical Scriptures, no
definite form of collective prayer seems to have been evolved
during the whole of that period. It would, of course, be rash to
come to any conclusion, but as the fundamental worship consisted of the sacrifice in the Temple of Jerusalem, it is possible
that collective prayers were recited in conjunction with the
sacrifices. The individual form of prayer is mentioned in connexion with the bringing of the first-fruits and is a kind of
confession of faith, or an expression of thanksgiving of an
individual character. As it was incumbent upon every one to
recite it in precisely the same manner, it may have been the
starting-point for a collective confession of faith. On the other
hand, tradition as found in Rabbinic literature knows a peculiar
form of worship, a kind of liturgy consisting of two parts, one
being the recital of the Shema, and the other the recital of the
Amidah; the latter, however, is now universally regarded as not
being older than 100 C.E., long after the destruction of the
Temple, though the former, the recital of the Shema, was the
essential part of the prayer recited by the priests and Levites in
the Temple at the dawn of day. It consists of the two sections
of Deut. vi. 4-9 and xi. 13-21, to which was added at no doubt
a much later period another section, Num. xv. 37-41. The same
tradition has it that the Ten Commandments were recited in
the Temple, and that delegates from the various communities,
representing distant congregations, were present in rotation

at the sacrifice.   They used to recite the first chapter of Genesis, either the whole in one day or the corresponding section for every day of the Creation, while the priest performed the threefold blessing[1] commanded by the Law.   On the Sabbath the Law was read in sections which more or less corresponded to the number of weeks, so that the whole of the Pentateuch was divided into fifty-four sections, exclusive of those which were read on special festival days.   On such occasions a portion of the Law which contained the commandment bearing on the festival in question was read from the scroll, this also being the case on the New Moon.   Some blessings were recited by the High Priest, which were later on embodied in the blessings recited before and after the reading of the lessons from the prophets.   A few blessings are also mentioned, such as grace before and after meals, or on some special occasion.

But except for these few portions, the rest of the Jewish liturgy was in a fluid state for many centuries after the destruction of the Temple ; in fact, it was forbidden to write it down for the very purpose of not giving it a definite fixed character, and it was only after the seventh or eighth centuries that the first notions of an exact order of prayers became known, although psalms and hymns had already been introduced at an early date.   One more feature, however, must be mentioned in connexion with these psalms and hymns, namely, that they originally consisted of a collection of verses selected from various parts of the Bible, thus forming a kind of mosaic ; this already is the character of the hymn found in 1 Chronicles xvi. 8-36. This collection of verses or catena is the connecting link between the psalms as found in the Bible and incorporated as such into the liturgy, and the hymns composed later on by men like Yannai, Kalir, and others.   They may have had older predecessors, but owing to the fact that they were not written down as part of the liturgy they were lost or forgotten in the course of time.

If we now examine the form which the liturgy of the Samaritans has assumed, we shall find that all those elements of the Jewish prayer-book which may be presumed to be very old, and to have existed long before the destruction of the Second Temple, are the essential elements of the Samaritan Prayer-book.   We find here the same portions of Deuteronomy, the Shema', with the slight difference that the two initial words 'Shema' Yisrael',

---

[1] Num. vi. 24-6.

Plate 7

Second half of the Samaritan Ten Commandments with the additional
verses from Modern Scroll. (Exod. xx. 7–xxi. 15)

(*See* Appendix III, pp. 188 ff.)

which are only an appeal to the people to listen, are omitted,
though the specific words which form the proclamation of faith
and belief in one God have been retained ; nay, these are
repeated over and over again in the course of the prayer, and to
them are added the words ' Līt elah ella aad '—' There is no
God but One '. This formula is already found repeated in Markah
at the end of a number of poems and stanzas, as well as in the
far more ancient prayer ascribed to Joshua, and there can therefore be no doubt of its Samaritan origin : it is from them that
Mohammed borrowed his formula, ' Lā ilāha illa llahu '—' There
is no God but Allah ', to which is added ' and Mohammed his
Messenger ', in precisely the same way as the Samaritans speak
of Moses as the Prophet or Messenger of God.

We find further that the Samaritans recite the Ten Commandments daily during their prayers. It must be noted that the
practice of reciting the Ten Commandments was at one time
suppressed at the Temple of Jerusalem, the reason given being
because of the Minim, but the true reason seems to be, however,
in order not to attract special attention to the difference between
the Samaritan and Jewish forms ; [1] as will be seen later on, the
Samaritans have added to the Ten Commandments found in the
Jewish recension another commandment which they count as
the tenth, in which reference is definitely made to Mount Garizim
as the place where the Sanctuary of the future should be
established. [2] This was the cardinal point of difference between
Jews and Samaritans, and it must have been the policy of the
priests of Jerusalem to ignore the Samaritans as much as possible
and not draw attention to the differences between them if it could
in any way be avoided.

A large part of the liturgy also consists of an anthology or
catena of Biblical verses called ' katef ' by the Samaritans,
(i. e. florilegium), and consisting of verses specially selected from
the Pentateuch, which correspond, as it were, to the character of
the Sabbath or festival on which they are recited. On special
occasions additions are made which the Samaritans call Muzaf,
corresponding to the Musaf of the Jews, but meaning something
different. With the Jews ' Musaf ' means an additional service,
with the Samaritans ' additional verses ' ; these are often simply
indicated by some catchword, which is not of an arbitrary
character, but which is intimately connected with the divisions

---

[1] Berakhot, 11 a.   [2] v. Appendix.

or smaller sections of the Samaritan Pentateuch called Ḳiṣṣim. But more of this anon.

Another characteristic fact is that the first chapter of Genesis forms an integral part of the prayers on every occasion, which are finished with the priestly blessing. Mention must be made here of the Jewish tradition known as Taḳanah, i.e. an institution established, the origin of which is ascribed to Moses. Here again the same difficulty exists in separating the older from the later institutions, but when examining Samaritan tradition we see that some are found among them and others are not. This is the case of the Shema ; the form of the Tefillin, in fact the ordinance of the Tefillin, of which no indication is given in Scripture, is traced back to Moses. The Samaritans, however, know nothing of it. They interpret the passage 'These words shall be upon thine heart' as referring to the Ten Commandments ; 'And as a sign upon thine hands', from which the Jews have derived the ordinance of the Tefillin, the Samaritans translate 'They will be a sign upon thine hands', i.e. symbolized by the ten fingers, and therefore apply the last meaning. They interpret 'And thou shall write them upon the door-posts' as referring to the same thing, with the result that most of the Samaritan inscriptions consist of an abbreviated form of the Ten Commandments inscribed in stone on the door-posts. Among the Taḳanah mentioned by the Jews is the reading of the Law on the Sabbaths. These Biblical lessons on the Sabbath and festivals are believed to be an ordinance of Mosaic origin, whilst the ordinance of reading portions on Mondays and Thursdays is traced back to Ezra ; in the same way the time for prayer, evening, morning, and noon, is traced back to the three Patriarchs, Abraham, Isaac, and Jacob. The Biblical tradition in Daniel and Psalms points to prayers being recited three times daily, evening, morning, and noon, which corresponds exactly to the number of times and the hours when the Samaritans are directed to recite their prayers. They have also retained the practice of reading a lesson from the Bible on every Sabbath, but decline to read it on Mondays and Thursdays, this evidently being a later innovation.

The antiquity of the weekly sections of the Law has hitherto been somewhat obscure. It must, however, go back to a very old practice, for curiously enough no one seems to have noticed that Philo's commentary on Genesis, limited as it is to three books, has followed this device : each of the books corresponds to one of the weekly sections for the Sabbath reading from Genesis. The practice must therefore have been established already long before Philo, and it need cause no wonder that the Samaritans also divided the Bible into as many sections as there are Sabbaths in the year. Like the Jews, they took care to arrange the divisions, which in the main agree with those of the former, in such manner that during leap year certain sections are divided again to provide for the four extra Sabbaths, whilst in the ordinary year these are united so as to make up the regular number. The whole problem of the Sabbath lessons and other minor divisions of the Pentateuch into open and closed sections by the Jews and into Ḳiṣṣim or more uniform sections by the Samaritans has been fully discussed by me elsewhere. Here it is sufficient to draw attention to the same parallelism in the development of the use of the Pentateuch in Divine service.

Although the Samaritans have preserved this ancient ordinance, they have rejected a large number of others, which are also given under the same heading of Teḳanah or Mosaic Halakhah among the Jews.

We also find in Daniel (vi. 10) that when he bent his knee and prayed, he turned his face towards Jerusalem. In the same way the Samaritans are enjoined to turn their faces towards Mount Garizim whenever they pray. This principle was evidently accepted by Mohammed in his Ḳibleh, the orientation of which was originally towards Jerusalem, but was afterwards changed towards Mecca. In every case the turning is towards the place where the sanctuary is believed to have been established.

When the sacrifices could no longer be brought, the Samaritans, like the Jews, inserted those sections of the Pentateuch into their prayers which contained the commandments of the observance of the festivals and the prescriptions concerning the sacrifice, their sections being almost identical with those found in the Jewish Prayer-book. In both cases it is explained that the prayer uttered represents the sacrifice. The Samaritans also have hymns, some of which are of extreme antiquity and are ascribed to Moses, Joshua, and the messengers; these, very likely, are the men who were sent to spy out the land, although the word 'malakhim', which is used, might equally well mean that they were hymns recited by angels. Later on a large number of poems were composed by which the Prayer-book has been greatly enriched, and down to the last century some Samaritans were still writing liturgical poems which found their place in it, some being recited in full and some only in portions. The composition of these hymns, their metre, rhyme, acrostics, &c., should form the subject of a special inquiry in connexion with such hymns as the Psalms or Odes of Solomon, or the beginnings of the hymns of the Syriac Church, the hymns of the Apocryphal Acts, especially those of Thomas, and the oldest fragments of the Jewish liturgy. The resemblance between many of them is very striking, but this is not the place to dilate upon them: I must be satisfied with having drawn attention to a problem which may be fruitful of results. Thus far we have been moving in an atmosphere which is akin to that in which the oldest Jewish liturgy was evolved. No traces of a prayer corresponding to the Jewish Amidah is found in the Samaritan liturgy, although the other part of it runs parallel to the older form of worship among the Jews.

Some writers have declared that the Samaritans do not believe in angels; it is, however, difficult to find a source for this assertion, for there is nothing in Jewish writings to confirm this statement. What was probably meant was that the Samaritans did not accept the developed angelology in the shape it assumed later, and which is so fully exemplified in the pseudepigraphic writings, notably the Book of Enoch. The Samaritans did not ascribe to angels any power whatsoever of good or evil. Their belief in them was, no doubt, limited to the few allusions in the Pentateuch, for they do not deny what is expressly stated in it, and therefore believe in angels as messengers of God; they know two or three, and speak of a fourth, whom they call Kebala‘, a word which has hitherto baffled all who have studied Samaritan doctrines, although the origin of this name is perfectly simple. It is a word which occurs in Num. iv. 20, where it says: 'They shall not enter the sanctuary lest they see the "covering up" of the Holy of Holies and die.' כבלע את הקדש ומתו. Now the Samaritans translate את as 'within or with', and therefore translate the verse: 'lest they see Kebala‘ within the sanctuary and die.' The word Kebala‘ is a hapaxlegomenon, and was therefore misunderstood by them; thus a new angel was created.

The whole angelology and demonology among the Samaritans is very primitive. In the Book of the Birth of Moses the angels come and sing hymns in almost the same manner as that described in the New Testament. Markah records the part played by angels at the death of Moses, and in the Asatir we find the elements being represented by angels, the angel of fire, water, wind, &c. The Samaritans could not deny the existence of evil powers of some sort any more than could the Jews. The Pentateuch records the worship of idols, the stars of heaven, images, beasts, birds, &c.; wizards and sorcerers are mentioned in Egypt, and various forms of witchcraft are forbidden, but there is no real demonology; we find exactly the same thing among the Samaritans, and in all probability this was the case among the Jews in the Pre-Exilic period. The only name known to the Samaritans is that mentioned by them as Belial, who is believed to be the power which caused Eve to disobey the command of God.

But however primitive this angelology and demonology may be, it is the first sign of the recognition of these deeper problems which affect human life. Knowledge of the existence of the spirit generally appears in the development of a nation, and is closely related to the question of the Supreme Power, the manner in which the Divine Power is displayed in the world, and how it manifests itself in the various ways of God with man. The mind does not rest satisfied with the mere knowledge of some facts which are believed to be ascertainable, but tries to fathom the unknown and solve the mysteries of the universe. Speculation about God and man started with the general question of the creation. In what manner did God create the world? What was meant by the allusions made to the appearance of God on Mount Sinai? What should be understood from the description given in Exod. xxiv. 10, that God was seen by the people, and that under His feet 'was as it were a paved work of sapphire stone, as it were the very heaven for clearness'? Among the Jews this was further expounded in the Vision of Ezekiel and in other mystical visions of a more or less pronounced character down to the Visions of Daniel. And yet the text of the Pentateuch alone was the real starting-point for every mystical speculation, for it was the word of God, nay, the very writing of His Finger, and therefore every mystery of heaven and earth had to find its solution in it. From this we get the theory of the Logos, the Creative Word, which, to some extent, explains the stress laid upon the first chapter of Genesis or rather upon the Ten Words contained therein, and their consequent inclusion in the liturgy. According to the Maxims of the Fathers of the Synagogue, the world was created by the Ten Words,[1] and these creative words

[1] Pirke Abot, v. 1.

are not only found in the first chapter of Genesis, but are also scattered throughout the whole text of the Pentateuch. Every word, therefore, contained an open and a hidden meaning, and it was the aim and object of those who followed the speculative training to discover the hidden meaning of the word and thereby acquire the mystical power of creation inherent in it. The most potent of these words was, of course, the very name of God, and so powerful and mysterious was it that it could never be pronounced, at any rate not as it was written. Substitutes were therefore found for it by a combination and permutation of the letters of the alphabet, either to make 42 or 72, which gave adequate expression to the mystical meaning. This matter has been fully discussed by me in the Jewish mystical book, *The Sword of Moses*, and it therefore suffices to state here that the origin of the Kabbalah or the mysticism arising out of the Oral Tradition rests exclusively upon the text of the Pentateuch.

It is very clear that this Kabbalah developed slowly, until it assumed the fantastic character that we find in the literature of the post-Maccabean period, such as the Book of Heavenly Halls (*hekhalot*), Otiot de R. Akiba, Sefer Yeṣira, and others. These must be compared to the Hellenistic literature of a similar syncretistic character, such as is found in the Gnostic Speculations, the Greek Magical Papyri, and the Latin Magical Texts and Conjurations, with their multiplicity of angels and divine names, and with their sentences and letters which are meaningless as they stand, but for which an explanation has been found in the comparative study of the Samaritan mystical literature.

In the Samaritan literature we find exactly the same process in operation. According to them the text of the Pentateuch is a Divine work, and every word in it of Divine origin; it is infallible, and its potency and efficacy immeasurable. It is only a question of knowing how to make use of the secret powers hidden in the text, although the words must not be used for magical purposes since witchcraft is forbidden in Israel. They could therefore never be used for the purpose of producing miracles and wonders, all of which were the actions of wizards and sorcerers. But the Samaritans maintained that the word of God, properly used, might be helpful as a protection, both prophylactic and cathartic. As already remarked before, it was probably the fear of writing the Divine Name which induced Dustan to remove it from the text altogether and to substitute Elohim for it; since it was under no consideration to be pronounced, the temptation to do

Plate 8

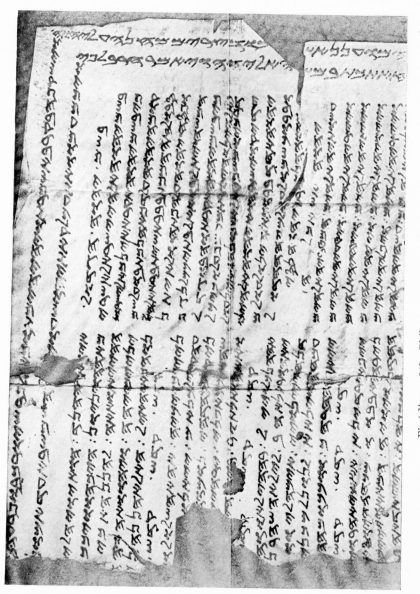

First lines of the Philactery, second or third century

so had to be eliminated. The other Samaritans were not so rigorous, and we find a fuller system of the permutation and combination of letters fully developed. They are preceded by the selection of special verses from the Bible, in which the miracles performed by God, the prayer by which Moses produced healing, or the animadversion against the action of wizards and sorcerers in Egypt and elsewhere are mentioned. All these are put together under various groups, and thus a highly protective amulet is produced having the characteristics of ancient mystical speculations, which acts as a powerful protection against evil, disease, and all physical troubles. The Samaritans call this amulet Shem Hamitfaresh, i.e. the name of God fully set out in detail, and by means of it the key has been found which solves the mystery that has hitherto surrounded the magical literature of ancient times. This amulet has come down to us in both a very elaborate form and also a very reduced form; the contents are practically the same, but whilst in the more elaborate one all the verses quoted from the Samaritan Pentateuch are given in full, in the reduced form they are merely represented by one word selected from each sentence. Thus meaningless words are strung together, which can only be understood if each word is traced back to its original complete verse. The same thing is found in the Greek and Latin Magical Conjurations which have remained unintelligible to this very day, because no one recognized in them portions of long sentences, and endeavours were made to elucidate them by putting together into a sentence words which could not give any meaning at all. Later on these amulets were reduced to a much smaller compass, either to make them more wearable, or else because the material used, i.e. pure parchment, became difficult to obtain: then the initial letters only were used, so that instead of single words we find a large number of letters, vowels and consonants, sometimes whole lines being joined together, as in the Magical Papyri, which no one has been able to fathom. These combinations of letters and vowels have been described as meaningless words or horrible sounds used by the magician for the confusion of the demon he wished to exorcise, or else for the purpose of impressing the hearer. It will now be the task of scholars to try and reconstruct these magical words and letters by tracing them back to full words and then to the complete sentences.

This process is not so difficult with the Samaritan phylacteries, as three separate classes of these amulets have been preserved.

G

Here we not only find a full use of such sentences, words, or letters, all of which are taken from the text of the Pentateuch according to their recension, but also squares made of the letters of the alphabet in as many permutations as there are letters. The Tetragrammaton and Elohim are dissolved into their single letters and placed in innumerable combinations, just as we find them in the fully developed Ḳabbalah of the Jews. The date of the Ḳabbalah is unknown, but it must be much older than has hitherto been supposed, because of the use of the Gematria in the most ancient parts of the Sibylline Oracles and in the compilations of the Gnostic literature. Moreover one of the phylacteries in my possession can be shown on palaeographic grounds to be not later than the first inscription of Emmaus,[1] i.e. probably of the second century, and much of the same speculation is also found in Markaḥ.

It is necessary to remark that the care which is taken to write a correct text of the Pentateuch is scarcely more than the care which is taken to write a correct phylactery or amulet, for the slightest mistake or deviation from the original would be sufficient to destroy its efficacy. It would become absolutely valueless. One is therefore justified in claiming accuracy of tradition and high antiquity for the text found in a phylactery. It is equal evidence, though a collateral one, for the fidelity with which the Samaritan text has been transmitted, and also for the knowledge of it, which had been preserved up to the time of the composition of the amulet. It proves, further, that at the time of the composition of the amulet, the text of the Samaritan Pentateuch was already fixed in its present form and invested with that high character of sanctity which alone would ensure its efficacy in the use to which a phylactery was put.

This very manipulation of words and letters, this endowment of every word and sign with a deeper meaning, opened the door to all kinds of fantastic speculations, and paved the way for those sectarian tendencies and Gnostic influences—although, no doubt, at a later period—which were able to work upon the speculative mind of the Samaritans. Men arose who read a different and deeper meaning into the simple words of the text, and thus claimed for themselves the right of proclaiming a different truth. This very freedom of interpretation, this mystical exegesis and hermeneutics, lies at the basis of all mystical speculations: hence

---

[1] v. *J. R. A. S.* Jan. 1918.

the rise of so many sects on the soil of Palestine. None of them started from abstract systems wholly unconnected with ancient traditions, independent theories by which the problems of the world were solved and the deeper mysteries revealed. Without a book on which to rely whose sanctity was above dispute, no mystic speculation ever had any success. It was in their attempt to find what they believed to be the hidden meaning contained in the text before them, that these various schools were able to evolve their peculiar systems, and it is for the same reason that we find ascribed to one or another of the great sages or philosophers, great masters, or divinely inspired men, the magical books from which all these theosophic systems start or to which they return. This is a point to which sufficient attention has not yet been paid by those who have made ancient magical books the object of their studies. It explains the so-called Hermetic, Orphic, and Gnostic literature of the later schools, both Jewish and Christian, for each of them claimed to possess a sacred book by which they sought to justify their own speculations.

The Greek invasion destroyed the ancient civilization of the East and sapped the fount of faith and life: nations were bewildered in face of the devastation which had overwhelmed them and their literature. A new ferment was thrown into the ancient dough, and many a problem which may have been latent in the minds of the nations now assumed an acute form. All groped about, trying to find a solution to the question of what it meant and whether the world were destined to be continually destroyed by sword or fire; whether sin and wickedness could flourish with impunity, and whether any value were still to be attached to the worship of the gods of old. Their oracles were mute, and they turned this way and that to find an answer. Many of the ancient faiths and cults succumbed, but out of the welter something which would content the mind and satisfy the heart was shaped by that syncretistic activity, so characteristic of the period, starting, one might say, a couple of centuries before and continuing for a couple of centuries after the destruction of the Temple of Jerusalem. It is the period when mysticism flourished, and attempts were made to piece together from the ruins of the old faiths what was believed to be most valuable and most efficacious. A rich literature arose which endeavoured to answer the questions raised; much has been lost, and more has come down to us in a mutilated form, since it was used by the various sects to justify their own claims and dogmatic teachings.

This literature was no man's land, and every one was free to deal
with it as he saw fit.   In my last lecture I shall have occasion to
refer to this literary activity, which may explain some problems
hitherto not solved.   Every sect or school that taught a new
truth or claimed to be able to offer a satisfactory solution to the
problems of the Beginnings and the End, of the spiritual life of
man, of death and immortality, of reward and punishment, and
concomitant with it the idea of a divinely appointed Redeemer or
guide and resurrection, thus either based its claim on a written
book of special revelation, or upon a much older book recognized
as of Divine origin and now used in a different interpretation.
For that reason many apocalyptic writings appeared, and in lieu
of the old Bibles new ones were invented, the old being represented in a somewhat different form, often supplemented by
legendary or apocalyptic matter.   This activity was continued
from that period, i. e. the second century B.C.E., down to the end
of the Middle Ages.   From early times lists of such books pro-
scribed by the Church have been preserved, as well as of others
characteristic of Hellenistic literature.

Jews and Samaritans alike also had to face these problems and
take up a definite position if they were not to be sucked down in
the general whirlpool, and to succumb to the new flood of ideas
and superstitions which at that time swept the world.   Both fell
back upon their Bibles, and endeavoured to find therein the
answers to the new questions, or solutions to the problems which
Hellenism had raised.   But neither Jews nor Samaritans were
entirely impermeable to the new influences.   They were, no doubt,
satisfied with the razing of the ancient idols, but they could not
view with equanimity the erection of new ones; thus they had
to retire within the four corners of their holy Scripture to find
refuge and protection against the danger which threatened, and
to which some of the leading men in their own midst succumbed.
The danger was twofold: the first was to admit all the new ideas
without questioning, and to incorporate them into their own code
of laws and doctrines by assimilating them to their own standards
and principles; in that way they gradually became assimilated
to the strange world of ideas without, with the consequent
loosening of the hold which the Law had upon them.   The other
danger was to try and find a justification for this very process of
undiluted assimilation in the words of the sacred text.   The
former led to apostasy and to the erection of idols in the Temples
of Jerusalem and Sichem: the other to the creation of sects,

some of whom still clung closely to the old faith, but who sub-jected the text to a dissolving exegesis until it assumed that mystical interpretation which we find in the writings of Philo; according to that interpretation the laws have almost completely lost that simple, severe, and unsophisticated meaning which is found in the ancient text. This activity in its turn led either to other peculiar interpretations of an ascetic character or to the mystic speculations of the Gnostic schools, which more or less rose or at least started from an arbitrary interpretation of the word of Scripture, but which took an independent course.

The Jews were less exposed than the Samaritans to this specu-lative activity, as they had a larger basis upon which to rest their doctrines. In addition to the Pentateuch they also had the writings of the prophets, which opened a wider outlook to them and which, in a way, contained answers to the questions raised by the new state of things. The prophets preached the outpourings of the spirit for the benefit of mankind, and a new era was anticipated in which many of the troubles which now beset the world would be finally removed; slowly the figure of a Messiah who would bring peace to the world and unite mankind in the worship of the one God, though at first but dimly perceived, assumed a definite form. The prophecies of Ezekiel and the others who look upon David as the future Ruler became more and more consolidated when the fight between Pharisees and Sadducees led to an open breach between the two parties, and brought these ideals nearer to the mind and heart of the Jews. The recall of Hillel from Babylon, as the representative of these new tenden-cies, was the outward sign that Judaism would not easily be broken up by contradictory sectarian movements. A number of these, however, must have existed on the fringe, for sufficient allusions and indications of an eschatological or soteriological character could be found in Holy Writ which would satisfy all the requirements of the time and answer all the questions raised, questions which were simply the natural evolution of the em-bryonic ideas embodied therein. There is therefore no reason, as has been suggested by modern scholars, to look to outside in-fluences to explain the origin of these new ideas, which, how-ever, have never assumed an absolutely dogmatic character; with the exception of general principles of immortality, resurrection, punishment and reward, and the advent of the Messiah or king, all the details were left in a fluid state. The angelology and demonology never took root and never formed part of the principles of faith, and were only applied to the legendary additions or excrescences of popular lore.

The case was somewhat different with the Samaritans, and their difficulties were greater in attempting to find an answer to, or in satisfying the yearnings of, the people in questions about the Beginnings and the End; they were limited only and solely to the words of the Pentateuch, and in it they had to find all the elements necessary for a satisfactory reply to the deeper stirrings of the soul. They could not claim the moral support of the writings of the prophets with their hopeful or gloomy anticipations of the future. To them the be-all and end-all were the Five Books of Moses, and every word and letter had to be carefully scanned, and conclusions drawn from these words and letters to form a satisfactory basis or be a decisive proof for new and hitherto unexpected beliefs. It was therefore much easier for dissenting voices to be heard among the Samaritans since the basis was much more slender and the tradition uncertain; in these matters neither Jews nor Samaritans could speak with one voice. The turn of events brought these questions to the fore, and the general unrest of the nations also seized upon those who had rested satisfied with the simple doctrines and practices handed down from the past and enshrined in the pages of the Law. Thus we see among the Samaritans the rise of sects which were much more pronounced and much more numerous than among the Jews even on the soil of Palestine. But the traditions are so vague and the nomenclature used for the determining of the special character of these alleged heretical movements so obscure, that it has been difficult to this very day to give a clear exposition of the views propagated by Simon called Magus, or of those ascribed to the somewhat later period of a certain Dusis and his followers. Legend and history have been inextricably interwoven, and very little that is definite can be said about the specific teaching of these schools. They seemed to have assumed a more or less ascetic character and to have proclaimed a new prophet, a matter which is of some importance. As far as their observances and practices are concerned, some of them clung closely to the letter of the text to which they gave their own interpretation and application, while others seem to have strayed farther away. Until further material comes to light, if it ever does, we must be satisfied with the fact that these heretical sects only lasted a few centuries in Palestine, although they found a profound echo in more distant settlements of Jews and Samaritans in the Diaspora.

It would lead me too far from my subject to discuss this point at length, but enough has been said to show the reason why at one time Syria as well as Palestine and the settlements farther north were all rent with sectarian polemics, and by new leaders who found followers among the inhabitants of those countries. Gnosticism, Manichaism, and Mandaism found numerous adherents; how far these doctrines which emanated from Palestine may have influenced Parsism and other dualistic systems, and even assisted in the development of a soteriology akin to that propagated on the soil of Palestine, will be a matter of historical investigation dependent upon such chronological data as can be ascertained with reliability. That much that is taught by Parsism resembles the cult of Judaism, or the cult of Samaritanism as it is called, has been noted by those who have studied the Avesta and the cognate literature. Therefore, instead of being of Iranic origin, much of it may be due to those speculations which had their home outside Iran. This of course is just the reverse of the views which have prevailed hitherto. The existence of numerous Jewish and Samaritan settlements in Persia is attested by Josephus, and the whole history of the Jews in Babylon proves the fact that large numbers of them, and also of course of the Ten Tribes, continued to live there from the time of the First Exile onwards. The dissenting Jews, i.e. the Samaritans, just because they differed from the former would have been the first to develop theories akin to those held by their brethren in faith in Samaria. How far this may have contributed to the spirit of the new doctrine of Christianity and to the rise of the various Christian sects is a matter of speculation ; it might, however, be usefully pursued hereafter when the tenets of the Samaritans can be compared with those held by the primitive Christians.

Now how did the Samaritans evolve their own theories from the Pentateuch, and why could not the Jews find the same proofs from the text? A glance at the Samaritan recension answers these questions. Not a few of the variants in this latter are the pegs on which the Samaritans hang their doctrines. It may be a coincidence, but at any rate it is very curious that in most of these eschatological points the Samaritan text differs slightly from the Jewish. Whether these changes were made in order to find a Biblical reason for these beliefs, or whether these beliefs were found in the text in a form satisfactory enough to be adduced, cannot easily be decided. I have already had occasion to point out that many an ancient Halakhah is based upon or is

justified by the reading peculiar to the Samaritan text. There
again the same question arises whether the text is anterior to the
Halakhah or vice versa, but as it is unlikely that a text would be
altered when the latter has already been put into practice in
order to find *a posteriori* reasons for it, it must be assumed that
the reading is anterior to the interpretation. The same must
therefore be assumed for their application of the text to
eschatological doctrines. Thus the Resurrection is proved from
the reading in Gen. iii. 19. The Massoretic Text reads : ' Dust
thou art and unto dust shalt thou return.' The Samaritan text
reads: 'For dust thou art and unto *thy* dust shalt thou return ', and
they interpret this to mean that Adam and of course every human
being—for the words apply to the whole of the human race—will
return again to live in the same material form in which he was
when he died : man will return to his own dust. An example of
how the Samaritans deduce proof of punishment and reward
after death is the way in which they interpret the verse in
Gen. ix. 5, which differs from the reading of the Massoretic
text, inasmuch as instead of ' wild beast' they put ' living being ',
and explain it as referring of course to the punishment to be
meted out to the man who has committed suicide ; for they insist
that no Divine Law would impose punishment upon a wild
beast for having killed a human being, but would apply it to
a human being who had committed murder or suicide. These
few examples are sufficient to show the manner in which the
Samaritans endeavour to extract from the text of the Bible proof
for those principles which affected human life hereafter. But
they were also greatly affected by the troubles of the time and
never failed to point out the intimate connexion between sin and
punishment as shown in Holy Writ, for it is emphatically stated
in the Pentateuch that disobedience to God's commands would
bring all manner of punishment with it as an inevitable consequence, pestilence, famine, and slavery. The writers of their
historical books always emphasized the lesson that obedience to
God's Law brought the people freedom and happiness, and that
disobedience was always followed by misery and trouble, when
they were subjugated by other nations and finally carried into
exile as a result of their backsliding. This is exemplified in the
story of the lions.

Future punishment and reward is also proved from the verse
in the last grand oration of Moses : Deut. xxxii has become the
very basis of all the eschatological theories of the Samaritans.

By a very ingenious exegesis which, however, does not differ from the ancient halakhic midrash, they are able to evolve from this chapter a whole theory of life after death, of punishment and reward, and of the final events. For example, instead of the reading of the Massoretic text in verse 35, ' Mine is vengeance and recompense ', they read ' On the day of vengeance and recompense ', ליום instead of לי. Altogether this chapter is considered by them as the revelation of the deepest mysteries of the world and of the future, and is fully interpreted in a great work called *The Day of Judgment*, ' Yom al-Din ', and in the *Code of Laws*, 'Hillukh', from which many of the doctrines hitherto discussed have been taken. It is so important in their eyes that the priest reads it at the bedside of the dying. Traces of a similar importance among the Jews is found in the fact that this chapter is recited in the service of the Synagogue on the day of fasting and mourning, while verse 4 is introduced into the prayer for the dead. This expression ' day of vengeance' occurs more than once with an eschatological meaning in the writings of the prophets Isaiah and Jeremiah. Then the prophet Malachi identifies it with the great day of the Lord when the prophet Elijah will reappear.[1] It is necessary to put these points together to show exactly the working of the mind of those who searched the text of the Bible for the basis for a belief which had now become an almost absorbing subject of faith and hope. In the same manner the Samaritans never failed to draw their lessons from the admonitions contained in the Scriptures ; but whilst the Jews drew their hope of a future Ruler from the glowing pictures of the prophets, the Samaritans had to draw that consolation from the few allusions in the Pentateuch itself. Thus they recognized that all the trouble to which they were exposed was the inevitable consequence of the disobeying of God's laws.

The establishment of what they called the false tabernacle and the beginning of the heresy connected with Eli both brought in their train the disappearance of the sacred vessels to which reference has been made before. It was a literal interpretation of the warning given in the Pentateuch, 'I will turn away' : hence they call the subsequent period ' The Period of Fanuta ; the dark, abysmal period, the terrible period of Fanuta.' But according to the Samaritans this will not last for ever ; the hope is held out that by repentance or turning to God, they will again be restored

---

[1] Mal. iii. 23 (iv. 5).

to that favour of God which they had enjoyed previously, 'Rahuta'. This consciousness of being constantly in the period of Fanuta has given to the mind of the Samaritans a kind of morbid introspection ; in their prayers they are continually dwelling upon their sins, weaknesses, backslidings, and falling away. There is scarcely a single song of joy and exaltation. They therefore hope, if possible with greater keenness and desire than the Jews, for the return of the period of Divine favour.

There is nothing really eschatological connected with that period ; it is, in fact, to precede the time when the end of the world will be expected and the fate of mankind finally decided. According to Samaritan computation, which again records some of the most ancient traditions, the world is to subsist for 6,000 years, at the end of which the final doom will take place. No definite period, however, is assigned to the period of Divine favour ; this may come at any time and will take place as soon as the necessary conditions for such an era of happiness have been fulfilled. It must be made perfectly clear that the Samaritans do not expect this period to be one of conquest or great power : it is nothing but absolute freedom and peace, together with the conversion of the Jews to the recognition of the fact that they had been led astray in a strange error by their false prophets, especially by Ezra the Accursed, who had falsified the text and changed the writing. The Samaritans recognize the Divine rule as the supreme one, and no man will represent that Divine rule ; it is nevertheless a period of Divine favour, 'Raṣon' (Deut. xxxiii. 23) (Ar. Riḍvan), and approximates much more closely to the kingdom of Heaven than any other Biblical expression except the Rabbinic form Malkhut Shamayim.[1] A promise of such a time is contained in the Scripture, but it is made dependent on repentance and a return to the strict observance of the ritual law, as well as to the unfailing recognition of all its applications, accompanied no doubt by such outward ceremonies as ablutions, self-chastisement, fasting, and almsgiving, for all these are conducive to a state of repentance which will hasten the period of Divine favour.

Then a man will arise who will be the Restorer, the Taheb or Shaheb. Nothing definite is said about him ; even his character and activity are only indicated in general outlines, and he is just

---

[1] The Jews themselves have retained this word in all formulas of invocation of the Divine grace ; it is always used in the phrase ' Yehi raṣon ', which is not to be translated, as is usually the case, 'May it be the will ', but 'May it be the Divine favour '.

as dim and vague as the whole eschatology of the Samaritans, with the exception of one thing. The Samaritans rest their expectation of the advent of the Restorer on the promise given in their tenth commandment and on Deut. xviii. 15 and 18 : ' The Lord thy God will raise up unto thee a prophet from the midst of thee, of thy brethren, like unto me ; unto him ye shall hearken ', and ' I will raise them up a prophet from among their brethren, like unto thee ; and I will put my words in his mouth, and he shall speak unto them all that I shall command him '. They therefore interpret this promise to mean that out of the tribe of Levi, i.e. Moses's brethren, a prophet will arise like unto Moses ; and as no one can be like unto Moses in all his perfection, they hold that perhaps Moses himself will come to life again and bring them the promised happiness. He will carry the rod of Moses in his hand, and perform all those signs aforementioned, and as further proof that he is the true Restorer, he will discover the hidden vessels of the Temple. After having accomplished these things, he will die and be buried among the ' Pure Ones ' at the foot of Mount Garizim, there probably to await the general resurrection.

In the light of history one can easily understand that the choice of the Samaritans should have fallen upon one of the tribe of Levi. Firstly it is a literal interpretation of the text, and secondly they could under no consideration agree to any other Restorer but one from the House of Moses and Aaron. In opposition to the Jews, they repudiated everything connected with Jerusalem, especially the House of David, nor was their aim to obtain secular power. An obscure passage in Josephus (*Antiq.* xviii. 4 (§§ 1 and 2)), which some scholars have identified with the events connected with the name of Jesus, tells us of a man who went up Mount Garizim and gathered the people round him, promising to discover the hidden vessels of the Temple. Here we have unquestionably the record of such a Taheb, who was more or less contemporary with Jesus. Pilate, the governor of Palestine, is said to have sent an army which massacred the people and killed the leader. As the attack was unprovoked, complaints were lodged at Rome, and in consequence Pilate was removed from his governorship and banished. This incident is sufficient to prove, not only the antiquity of the belief in such a Taheb, but also the reliability of the traditions preserved among the Samaritans from that day on.

In this case the parallelism between Jews and Samaritans runs very close, but it is not identical; the Jews themselves were

conscious of the fact, and endeavoured to conciliate the two
principles by admitting the advent of two messiahs, one called
the Messiah, the Son of Joseph, i.e. a Messiah of the tribe of
Joseph, and the other the 'Messiah, the Son of David'. According to Jewish tradition, the former, however, will die in his
great battle against the nations, when the prophet Elijah will
come and restore them all to life, after which the Messiah, the
Son of David, will appear. The appearance of Elijah and Moses
together on the Mount of the Transfiguration is a question
which I only venture to raise, but which I must leave to others
to decide.

So far there is no trace of that fully developed soteriology of
the Redeemer of the world from sin through self-sacrifice; it was
probably not known to Samaritan or Jew anterior to the period
of the advent of Christianity, and is quite independent of resurrection and the Final Judgement. These ideas stand by themselves and have no direct bearing upon one another, at any rate
not at the time when Samaritans and Jews formulated these con-
ceptions and evolved them from the Book of the Law. It may be
mentioned in connexion therewith that the Samaritans, unlike the
Jews, do not derive the promise of the advent of the Messiah from
the prophecy of Balaam. The Jews, and notably the Pharisees,
were driven to find such a passage if they were to contradict the
Samaritans and fight the teaching of those who claimed the
glory of the future Ruler and Redeemer for the descendant of
the House of Levi. They had to prove that the great ruler was
not specifically from the tribe of Levi, but could easily belong to
one of the other tribes : hence their interpretation of that
verse (Num. xxiv. 17), which they interpreted to refer to the
future Messiah.

It still remains to be stated that the future reward of the
Samaritans is painted in very sober colours, and that their conception of the life in Paradise is of the utmost simplicity ; there
is nothing of the sensuality of the Mohammedan paradise and
nothing approaching the descriptions found in the Apocalyptic
writings of Enoch and the Book of Revelation, nor those visions
of Heaven and Hell found in the Apocalypse of Paul and in the
Jewish visions of Heaven, Hell, and Paradise visited by Moses.
This is also true of their description of Hell, which is subdivided
into several compartments wherein the punishments vary according to the gravity of the sin committed. Curiously enough no
demons appear nor is any satanic power mentioned, and we

therefore see in the Samaritan writings a reflex of that spiritual atmosphere of the period between the first centuries B.C.E. and C.E. How old it may be it would be very difficult to say now, and until the great work on the Day of Judgement has been published a decisive opinion must be withheld. But there can be no doubt that we are dealing with very archaic opinions. Again, no trace can be found of the later developments of eschatological and esoteric speculations, for whatever found no justification in the text of the Pentateuch, or could not be traced back to a sentence or allusion in it, seems to have been strictly barred from the system of Samaritan doctrine and practice.

What we have seen hitherto has been a parallel development among Jews and Samaritans, more or less independent of one another, in the interpretation of the Scriptures which is much older than the Greek translation. It justifies many of the old practices, which slowly crystallized to form a code of law, and used a peculiar exegesis, studying every word and letter of a text which for many centuries must have been the common property of Jews and Samaritans alike, and which was invested with a special character of sanctity and reverence, being considered the direct exposition of the Divine will, nay the very writing of God Himself. No outward influences can be traced upon this development, neither Iranian soteriology nor eschatology ; it is due to the mystical speculations and the slow consolidation of ideas and hopes which owed their existence a great deal to changed political circumstances and economic conditions, but above all to the conscious rivalry between Jews and Samaritans, with its aloofness through hatred while remaining closely akin to one another in spirit and tendency. This can only be explained if we assume both nations to have derived their inspiration from a common source, to have lived under the same spiritual influences, and to have developed under parallel conditions, retaining much that is very archaic, yet each retaining it in a form peculiar to itself. All this is anterior to Christianity, free from Hellenistic influences save for a few Gnostic speculations in the sectarian movements, and certainly quite anterior to Islam, since all these doctrines and practices belong to a period anterior to the destruction of the Temple. What influence these doctrines and practices may have had on primitive Christianity ; how far they can be connected with the birth of Islam ; how far this sectarian movement has contributed to the rise of other sectarian movements in Asia Minor ; the part Samaritans and Jews may have played in the origin and development of Masdaism, Mandaism, Manichaism, and other similar syncretistic movements, must be left to such time when the monuments of the Samaritan literature will all have been made more accessible, and when modern scholarship will have been able to sift the material thus presented and draw such conclusions as will further the claim advanced hitherto : that we have in the Samaritan tradition a most valuable and important contribution to the knowledge of the spiritual forces which have played so large a part in the history of modern civilization.

Having arrived thus far and having drawn all these conclusions, I must guard myself against some possible misunderstandings. Nations are not assumed to live in watertight compartments or to be so profoundly separated from one another, however deep an enmity may be, that some practice, some movements of the spirit, some ideas should not imperceptibly flow from one to the other. I do not mean, therefore, that there has been no communication whatsoever between Jews, Samaritans, and the other nations who lived on the soil of Palestine. The tremendous upheaval which the Greek invasion produced caused a tremor to run through all the institutions of Palestine, and many an old temple and many an old belief felt the effect of the earthquake. The leaders would certainly take steps to avert any impending disaster overtaking the foundations of the buildings. They would not consciously borrow from one another the material necessary for such precautions, but they might unconsciously follow the lines adopted by the others. The common people, however, never felt the differences so acutely, since among the lower forms of faith, superstitious or popular practices travel from one to the other and are unconsciously adopted and assimilated by the lower stratum. These forms would to-day be called the folk-lore common to all these nations. But this latter was a slow process which did not affect the fundamental principles : it merely occasionally caused a small stir in the upper circles. What I have been dealing with here has not been this unconscious assimilation, but the conscious development of doctrines and tendencies, and it is a study of these which has led to the results herein delineated.

One fact of no mean value may be repeated once more, namely, that in strict accordance with the word of Scripture, the High Priest of the Samaritans was never allowed to leave the Sanctuary. No single one in the course of history is known to have travelled unless forced to do so by circumstances over which he had no control, such as being taken into exile. Otherwise that law has been strictly observed, and this alone is a sufficient guarantee for the continuity of tradition and interpretation, and therefore gives to the religious practices of the Samaritans a stability as well as an antiquity which cannot easily be gainsaid.

THIRD LECTURE

LITERATURE

I SHALL now endeavour to give a brief survey of the Samaritan literature as far as I have been able to collect it, which I believe is as complete as any collection found in a European library, and perhaps even richer by some texts which I have been able to obtain from the Samaritans. I shall not attempt to describe that literature in detail, but shall only treat it from the point of view which has been the guiding principle of these lectures, viz. the archaeological. It is of specific importance to try and explain from within the origin of these few fragments of their ancient literature which have been preserved until to-day. A mere description will not be of assistance, for it is my endeavour, as far as it is possible from fragmentary writings, to trace their development, and show how much of the old has come down to us, and how much reliance can be placed on writings of apparently later date, if we are to draw conclusions from them for a state of things belonging to a period 1,000 years or more before the time of these writings.

It must be stated at once that the date of a copy need not necessarily be the date of its composition. There is no MS. of the complete Hebrew Bible which is older than the tenth century, but no one would venture to say that the Bible is therefore a composition of the tenth century : proofs internal as well as external are necessary to decide the antiquity of any ancient composition.

The general character of the Samaritan literature has been determined by that isolation to which reference has already been made before. Cut off from any relation with the West, oppressed and decimated by pagan domination and Christian tyranny and intolerance, scattered all over the East from the south of Egypt to the confines of Persia and India, without coherence, without an extensive literature, without anything from within which could exercise an influence upon their progressive development, the Samaritans developed a literature which was almost exclusively religious. Like the Jews after the

Return, they had no political aspirations; everything centred round their holy writings, their religious observances and their legendary lore, which formed part of the interpretation of the text of the Pentateuch. The misery of the times left an indelible impress upon their minds: they became self-centred and morbid, spending their lives in contemplation of the terrible things through which they had passed. On all sides they saw the darkness of the Fanuta only; they dwelt almost exclusively upon their sins and upon their backslidings through which they had forfeited the favour of God, and their only hope was for a return to a time of peace, free from every persecution, when the Jews would recognize the error of their ways and the superiority of the sacred text held by the Samaritans, and unite once again in the Divine worship as in the time of Divine favour. They had little interest in history, but started their own with the Book of Joshua, and continued it in the form of chronicles throughout the ages. The basis for all their chronicles was the chain of priestly succession from Adam downward, and it served as a connecting link between the various sections which were added in the course of time, the old always being embodied in the new and continued. The consciousness of their rivalry with the Jews gave to their literature a distinctly polemical and apologetic character, for they were at once aggressive and defensive. They endeavoured to show the error of the Jews, and were among the first to accuse the latter of falsifying the text, an accusation which was afterwards repeated by the Christians, heretical sects, and by Mohammed, each time with equal baselessness. They further endeavoured to prove the correctness of their doctrines and practices from the words of the Samaritan recension of the Pentateuch, and later accepted the challenge of Christianity and the Karaites, and, as already remarked before, of those spiritual movements which arose in Palestine from the time of the Persian domination down to the second or third centuries c.e. All this development, however, seems to have been arrested at the beginning or end of the third or fourth century. From that time on, a pall seems to have fallen over the Samaritan literature, and it does not emerge from comparative obscurity and barrenness until the eighth or ninth century or perhaps later.

Precisely the same thing happened to the Jews in Palestine. They also developed an almost exclusively religious literature which started originally in Jerusalem, and was then continued

at one or two of the schools of learning in Galilee, especially
Sepphoris and Tiberias. Of this literature also nothing is known
from the close of the Palestinian Talmud—about the fourth
century—until very late in the eighth or ninth century. Then
both the Samaritans and the Jews of the East began to develop
a literature written in Arabic, and where the conditions were
similar to those under which the Samaritans lived, as before the
literary activities of both often run on parallel lines. But
whereas the Jews expanded under the influence of Arabic
literature, the Samaritans became more restricted and more
conservative. The dominating factor in this change, however,
was the loss of their old vernacular, Aramaic : the people no
longer understood it and easily acquired Arabic, with the result
that the whole Samaritan-Aramaic literature which may have
existed up to that period slowly disappeared, except for what was
indispensable for religious service, such as the Targum and
prayers and the great work of Markah. They could not dispense
with these, but in order to satisfy the people they were translated
into Arabic. As far as I am aware, no religious compilation is
known in which the Arabic stands alone ; it merely accompanies
the original, for the prayers are recited in the original Aramaic
language. The translation was merely added to assist the people
in the better understanding of the original, for neither the
Arabic nor the Targum has ever been substituted for the original :
the Targum has never taken the place of the Hebrew text of the
Pentateuch, nor the Arabic the place of the Aramaic prayers and
hymns. This is a point upon which some stress must be laid, for
it cannot be stated with sufficient emphasis that as far as the
Jewish tradition is concerned, and here it is supplemented by the
Samaritan, the Hebrew original of the Bible and of the prayers
and hymns has never been eliminated from the Divine service
although they may have been translated into other languages ;
the Biblical lesson was always read in the original Hebrew during
the service. This is a cardinal point which has dominated the
spiritual development of Jews and Samaritans, and has remained
uncontaminated in faith and practice ; to this very day throughout Jewry the text is read in Hebrew from the scroll of the Law.
The Samaritans for their part have also continued that practice
unchanged.

The Arabic literature which arose from the ninth century
onwards is to a large extent merely a substitution for that
Aramaic literature which probably perished in consequence. The

Plate 9

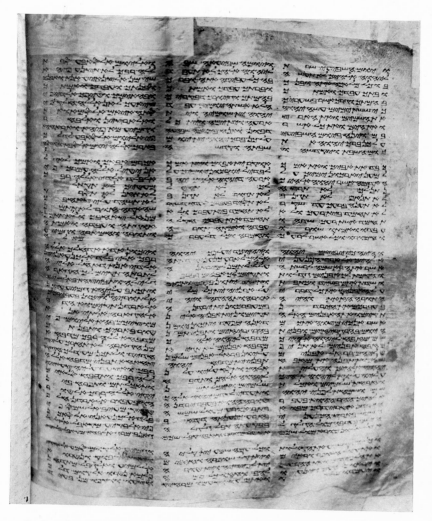

Last section of the Ten Commandments from the Triglot in the British Museum.
Hebrew, Targum, and Arabic, thirteenth or fourteenth century. (Exod. xx.
10-15, with the inclusion of the Samaritan Tenth Commandment)

same doctrines and practices were continually restated by successive writers, who had very little to add that was new, and who only repeated the old in various forms, some more systematically, others less. The so-called revival of the fourteenth century consists of a number of hymns and poems written in a language more akin to Hebrew than the older ones, which are written in pure Aramaic or Samaritan, and the important chronicles, like that of Abul-Fatḥ and others, which, however, were all written in Arabic. The reason why Hebrew was now chosen is obvious from what has preceded, for to write in an obsolete language which the people no longer understood would have been a useless endeavour. The knowledge of Hebrew, however, never vanished entirely, since the weekly lessons and part of the older prayers were sufficient to maintain, at any rate among the priests and scholars, a tolerably good acquaintance with that language; in addition parts of the older literature, starting with the Book of Joshua and including some of the older chronicles mentioned by Abul Fatḥ as well as other compilations which have since disappeared, were written in their Hebrew, and probably contributed to keep the knowledge of that peculiar Hebrew long enough alive to enable poets like Abisha and Pineḥas to write in it.

Let there be no mistake about the character of this Hebrew. It is neither the Jewish Biblical Hebrew nor the Rabbinic Hebrew which developed in Palestine especially in the literature of the Midrash, but is a Hebrew which shows precisely the same characteristics, though with slight differences in grammatical construction, as that found in the Samaritan Pentateuch. It has developed on the lines of that recension and must therefore be of a greater antiquity than the time when the Samaritans used it in the fourteenth century. Moreover it is so characteristic that there cannot be any doubt of its peculiar form. Jewish scholars fully acquainted with the Hebrew grammar have therefore not hesitated to describe it as 'barbarous' Hebrew. If compared with the Hebrew Bible it is certainly a strange form of Hebrew. But a careful study of the Samaritan Hebrew literature proves that this was the form of Hebrew in general use among them from the earliest times down to a comparatively modern age. It is absolutely Samaritan. We find it in the interpolated passages in the Book of Joshua, the antiquity of which cannot be gainsaid, in the letter from the Genizah published by Cowley,[1] and in the

_____
[1] *J. Q. R.*, vol. xvi, 1903, pp. 474 ff.

subsequent letters from the sixteenth century on. It is still more pronounced in the older chronicles and in the hymns found in the oldest portions of the liturgy, such as those ascribed to Moses, Joshua, and the spies or messengers. The same form also occurs in the 'Confession of Faith' (En Sira), though there it is to some extent mixed up with Samaritan prose, and it is the language of the hymns of the period of the revival in the fourteenth and fifteenth centuries. We see the same tradition everywhere, and however artificial or 'barbarous' it may be called, it is none the less *the* Hebrew language of the Samaritans. Pure Hebrew was always more the language of the learned, who thereby maintained an uninterrupted tradition.

There is another curious parallel to this 'barbarous' language in the so-called 'Zadokite' documents. By their own showing their home was Damascus, where the sect had made its head-quarters. A cursory glance over these strange writings will show a surprisingly close affinity with the Samaritan Hebrew in language, style, construction, and the use of Biblical roots; in one place I believe I have found a complete Samaritan form (f. 16^b) which was subjected to violent emendations in order to make sense of some of these obscure words. If read in the light of Samaritan tradition they are perfectly clear, and a Samaritan would have no difficulty in understanding them. He would translate 'the explanation of the sections to another Israelite'. Attention has been drawn to the similarity between some of the leading principles enunciated by those documents and Samaritan traditions; and this must suffice to strengthen the argument adduced for the peculiar 'barbarous' language so characteristic of these documents. The sect, however, is not Samaritan, but, as remarked above, belongs to the numerous class of religious dissenters who flourished in Galilee and Syria, and who endeavoured to create a new order to bring about the era of the Messiah. These documents of the fifth century appear to be an attempt to translate into this artificial Hebrew documents written in another language, in all probability Aramaic.

The oldest monument to which we must now turn is of course the Samaritan Pentateuch. The history of the discovery of that Pentateuch is as romantic as the rediscovery of the Samaritans themselves, which precedes the former by about thirty years only.

The correspondence initiated by Scaliger had borne unexpected fruit. The Christian world was made aware that there were still living descendants of a sect of which mention was found in the writings of the New Testament. From that correspondence the world of scholars also learned that the Samaritans were in possession of the Pentateuch. Then commenced a hunt for that precious book, which, however, seemed to be without result. At last Pietro della Valle, a man versed in the knowledge of the East, started on his travels and spent a year at Constantinople before proceeding to Egypt and thence to the other parts of the Turkish Empire. In Constantinople he met the French ambassador, de Sansy, and was urged by the latter to try and secure a copy of the Samaritan Pentateuch. Della Valle mentions that de Sancy placed 100 scudi at his disposal, which was a very large amount at that time. Faithful to his trust, Della Valle tried to obtain such a copy from the Samaritans he met in Cairo, Gaza, and in Nablus, but all in vain. As we learn from Huntington's correspondence, the Samaritans—at any rate those living in Nablus—would not deliver up so sacred a book to a Gentile. But at last, towards the end of the month of May in 1616, and through the intermediary of a Jew, Della Valle was able to go to the synagogue of the Samaritans in Damascus, which he found to be a much more beautiful building within than it had looked from without. There he found a 'Hakham' and a Samaritan woman willing to part with two MSS., one on parchment containing the Hebrew recension of the Samaritan text of the Pentateuch, and another on paper containing the Targum. The first he sent to the ambassador and the other he retained for himself. He declined to part with it, adding it, as he said, to his own small library of Oriental books, and refused even to send it to the Vatican, for he said that it might be buried among the mass of other Oriental books already there, and thus become inaccessible to scholars.[1]

Howbeit both MSS., the one on parchment containing the text of the Pentateuch and the one on paper containing the Targum, came at length into the possession of the library of the Oratory of Paris, and Morini published both as the fifth volume of the Paris Polyglot.[2] This publication at once created a profound impression in spite of the many faults it contained. It was slightly corrected and amended from other MSS., and reappeared in Walton's Polyglot Bible in London in 1657; in both editions the

---

[1] v. Appendix II.

[2] Contrary to the statement which has been universally accepted and repeated, this volume appeared in 1632 and not in 1645, the latter date being the date of the last volume of the publication.

text was reprinted in the old Samaritan type. As soon as this text appeared, it was discovered that it differed in a large number of words and sometimes in sentences from the Massoretic text of the Jews. Disputes arose, which are not necessary to follow here because other interests became involved in the discussion of the genuineness and antiquity of this Samaritan text. Some started by asserting it to be a forgery, and a clumsy one at that; but this view was soon abandoned when the text was compared with other versions, for it became apparent that there existed some close connexion between the Samaritan recension and the Greek translation. The latter, as is known, differs in a large number of passages from the Massoretic text, and not a few of these are found in the Samaritan text. This, of course, gave rise to the question whether the Samaritan text represented an older and more accurate recension, being, as it were, supported by the Greek in many instances, or whether the Massoretic text retained its value as the more ancient and more reliable of the two recensions. The differences between the Massoretic text and the Samaritan are often of a far more definite character than those between the Massoretic text and the LXX, and the Catholic Church endeavoured to use the Samaritan text as a weapon against the authority and genuineness of the Massoretic text. It was to the interest of the Catholic Church to shake the authority of the latter, for this was the ground on which the battle of the Reformation was fought. The Protestants took their stand on the absolute authority of the Hebrew Bible, and in their zeal not only maintained the absolute infallibility of every letter and word, but even affirmed the same infallibility for all the accents and vowel signs found in the Hebrew text. This war between the two factions assumed a theological character, and the real problem became obscured until in 1816 Gesenius took up the question once more.

By means of a dispassionate analysis of the text, in which he compared the Samaritan with the Massoretic recension, he drew certain conclusions which, to a large extent, were detrimental to the claim of the superior value of the Samaritan over the Massoretic version. He divided the variants into several classes, and endeavoured to show that in a number of instances the readings in the Samaritan text were due to misreadings of the square characters of the Massoretic text. These faults, together with other apparent misunderstandings of a supposed original in square characters, led Gesenius to the conclusion that the Samaritan text was nothing else but a corrupt copy from the Jewish Massoretic recension. So cogent did these conclusions seem, that for some time afterwards they were accepted unquestionably, and the importance attached to the Samaritan text was reduced to vanishing point. It could no longer be claimed to represent an independent and possibly more ancient text of the Pentateuch, and its value for a critical investigation of the Pentateuch was considered negligible. But the matter was not allowed to rest where Gesenius had left it. More MSS. were brought from Samaria to Europe, and a closer examination of this new material helped to establish the fundamental fact that the MS. which had been the basis of Gesenius's investigations and conclusions was of comparatively more recent origin, and full of mistakes which did not exist in more ancient copies. For the moment I will limit myself to the palaeographical aspect of the problem.

A point which has hitherto escaped the notice of the scholars and upon which sufficient emphasis has not been laid is the fact that the Pentateuch has been preserved in two distinct forms, as a scroll and as a book. Of the two the former was treated with special care and reverence, and was the only one used for Divine service. The minister read the lessons from the sacred scroll but never from the book, for the latter was not invested with the same sacred character as that with which the scroll was endowed. Moreover, among the Jews the scroll contained the words of the Pentateuch only and was written with such minute care that no blemish was allowed to pass ; every word and every letter was counted, and special rules were laid down for the columns, lines, and for the internal divisions, all of which had to be observed, a practice which is still followed to-day. None of these rules governed the writing of the Pentateuch in book form, and the scribe had much greater latitude ; to all intents and purposes he was not bound by any rule whatsoever ; diacritical signs were freely introduced, the text was endowed with vowels and accents, and was often surrounded by Massoretic notes and references. There are, of course, model codices in the primitive form, for the text was not allowed to be copied from the scroll, lest by some negligence a blemish might be created in the original. The same thing holds good among the Samaritans. Although they have neither vowels nor accents, some diacritical signs have been discovered by me, and greater liberty is taken when copying the Pentateuch in book form than would be allowed when writing a scroll. Moreover, a definite tradition has been established governing the writing of the scroll, as far as the columns and the sections are concerned, which is typical of the scroll and which is not faithfully followed in the book form. Hitherto, with perhaps but one exception, all the texts of the Samaritan Pentateuch known in Europe are those contained in book form. It was only recently that I was able to take a photograph of one of the oldest scrolls in the possession of the Samaritans, which, according to the date given therein, belongs to the year 1166.

Another peculiarity common to Jews and Samaritans is the fact that the scribes of the sacred scrolls never followed any change of writing which may have crept into the secular literature, but tried to imitate the ancient script as closely as possible. When examining the scrolls of the Law, therefore, it is not easy to determine their age or even their home. There are, of course, general differences between one set of scribes and another, as, for example, the Oriental and Occidental, but apart from that it is sometimes extremely difficult to distinguish between a scroll written in the eighteenth century and one written some four or five centuries previous. Unfortunately the means for such a comparison are scanty, owing to the practice of the Jews of burying such MSS. which had become deteriorated or the writing obliterated in passages containing the Divine Name, for these could not be corrected. It is somewhat easier with the Samaritans, because they have preserved some of their oldest scrolls, even though they are in a mutilated form.

But before mentioning them, a few details may here be given of the extreme care taken by the Samaritans in the writing of the scroll. The whole text is divided up into five portions separated from one another by a certain space, and it is written on specially prepared parchment in identical columns, as far as this is possible. The Samaritans use for this purpose the skins of those animals which have been offered up in the Passover sacrifice, and then only when the ceremony has been performed in absolute Levitical purity. As the ashes of the red heifer were not used after the end of the fifteenth century no scroll of the Bible nor even the book form has been written on parchment since that date. The text is divided again into small sections almost of equal length. The columns always finish with one of these sections, and the writing is sometimes cramped at the end of the

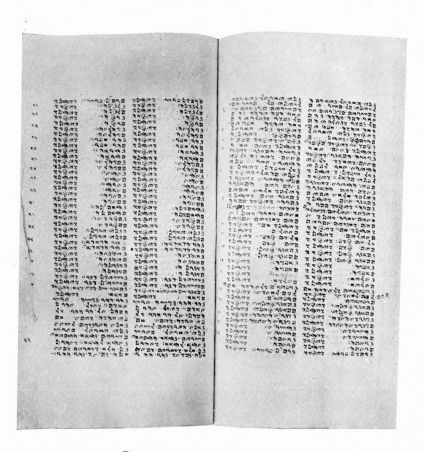

Plate 10

Pentateuch: Symmetric Writing

column to ensure this. As already remarked, the division of the text follows a system which required the skill of scholars. This is not the place to describe that system more fully, but it may be remarked that most of the sections begin with the word 'And he spoke' ויאמר, and as shown by me elsewhere,[1] these divisions seem to agree with some of the divisions of the Hebrew scroll known as open and closed sections. At the same time the Samaritan sections seem to be preserved in the Greek text, which proves a very high antiquity for this kind of division ; but it must be stated again that this is of an independent origin and has not been taken from the Jewish text. The relation between these various forms of division have been discussed elsewhere. Perfect harmony is preserved throughout the scroll and certain portions of the Law are written in a peculiar symmetrical form. The utterances of Bileam are written in the form of poetry, and the two songs of Moses, that in Exodus and that in Deuteronomy, are each written in a way differing from the regular form, both being in two small columns, thus agreeing with the Jews as far as the last song in Deuteronomy is concerned. Besides these there are other details observed in the writing of the blessings of Jacob and the blessings of Moses as well as in the writing of the Ten Commandments. It is obvious that a plan so carefully worked out must be the work of expert scribes, and that it must have taken a very long time before unanimity could have been reached and the whole crystallized in its present shape.

There is also another palaeographic point of no mean importance in determining the antiquity of the Samaritan scroll of the Pentateuch. The smaller divisions are already mentioned in Markah and form the basis of the quotations in the ancient Samaritan phylacteries; they are the headings in the oldest MS. of the Arabic translation, and a list of them is also found elsewhere, which corresponds to the way in which they are quoted in the phylacteries. Reference will be made to this later on in connexion with the traces of a Massorah among the Samaritans. But before the text could be divided it had to be written down, and the use of the ancient Hebrew alphabet must be taken as another proof of very great antiquity. According to Jewish tradition the Bible was originally written in characters similar to those preserved by the Samaritans, and Ezra is credited with the transliteration into an alphabet more akin to the

[1] Gaster's *Studies and Texts*, pp. 503 ff.

Aramaic. The reasons for this change of alphabet have already been given in the first lecture. The Samaritans, however, true to their claim of being the preservers of the ancient text, also preserved the ancient script unchanged. A comparison between the writing of the Samaritans and the alphabet which appears on the Maccabaean coins shows that the Samaritans had an alphabet of their own and were, therefore, absolutely independent of the Jewish form. Jewish tradition maintains further that the so-called final letters by which words were separated were introduced into the sacred text by the later prophets. What is meant thereby is that this change had already taken place before the time when the 'scribes' began their activity, and is relegated to that obscure period which followed immediately after the return from the Exile.

Modern research, however, has shown that the evolution of the final letters took a different course, inasmuch as the present final letters correspond almost exactly to the shape of those letters, whether final or medial, in the Aramaic script, which was the basis of the square letters; what really did take place was that the medial and initial letters were reduced to the size of the others. This retention of the final longer letters was the first attempt at an exegetical interpretation of the text by defining the shape of the words as far as possible, and separating them from each other. The Samaritans, however, had recourse to another device which was much more effective; they separated the words by a dot and thus avoided the possibility of misreading or of joining together words which ought to have been separated. They, however, were not the inventors of this device. Here again we have many more ancient examples which carry us back to centuries before the Exile, as, e.g., the famous Moabite inscription of King Mesha and the inscription found in Zenjirli, not to mention various inscriptions found in Palestine where the words are separated from one another by one or two dots. It is an extremely archaic device which the Samaritans would hardly have invented had they copied their Pentateuch from the Jewish text.

This separation of the words by means of dots is the work of expert scholars and must have been done before the transliteration into square characters took place. The dot and the note line are the two elements out of which all the Massoretic diacritical signs, the vowels and accents, dagesh, &c., have been evolved. When the old Hebrew writing was discarded the dot was discarded as well, with the result that a difference had to be made between

Plate 11

Statement of the late High Priest Jacob concerning the cryptogram in Abisha's Scroll

(*See* Appendix IV, pp. 191 ff.)

the same final and medial letters in order to separate the words. We thus have here four stages of development : first the old Hebrew writing, then some time afterwards the separating dot, then the transliteration of the old Hebrew writing into the square associated with the name of Ezra, and lastly the final evolution of the difference between the final and medial letters. This development of course covers a long period and is probably the work of centuries. The Samaritan scroll shows the period of the separating dot, and thus from the point of view of palaeography has preserved a most archaic form which in all its details is entirely independent of any Jewish or other known influence.

If we examine the writing of the scroll of the Pentateuch of the beginning of the twelfth century, and compare it with a copy made at the end of the nineteenth century, it will require the eye of an expert palaeographer to determine the difference between the writing. That, however, is not the oldest in possession of the Samaritans, for they have preserved another scroll which is separated by a long lapse of years from that of the twelfth century, the colophon of which is given here.[1] I am, of course, referring to the famous scroll ascribed to Abisha.

But before discussing this scroll mention must be made of another fragment, which according to the Samaritans themselves seems to be the oldest in existence, save of course that of Abisha, and which is now in my possession. It has suffered much from age, the edges are all worn away, and the whole is in such a state of frailty that if it be compared with the scroll of the twelfth century it must be unhesitatingly declared to belong to a period some centuries before. And yet very little difference can be discerned between the two as far as the internal arrangement, the division of the text, and other characteristic features like the form of the letters and the style of writing are concerned. This fragment may therefore be considered as filling the gap between the twelfth century and the possible date to be assigned to the Abisha scroll.

Returning now to the scroll of Abisha, it has been my privilege to see it and to satisfy myself of its extreme antiquity. It was naturally to the interest of the Samaritans to preserve their ancient documents, especially the ancient scroll of the Law, since the latter was their justification upon which rested their claim

---

[1] v. Appendix.

of being the keepers of the true, unadulterated text of the Bible. It was therefore unlikely that they would destroy what they possessed, and although they were not of necessity anxious to save their other ancient scrolls from deterioration through use, they still kept this one in whatever state it happened to be. With the Jews any deterioration in a text of the Pentateuch carried with it its elimination from the service and final disappearance. That ancient scroll of Abisha bears all the traces of high antiquity; parts have become illegible, some of the letters have been rewritten, and it consists mainly of a mass of patches, held together by a backing. Altogether it is in such a dilapidated condition that only the utmost care in handling it will preserve it. And yet a close examination of some of the portions still visible has satisfied me that all the subsequent copies which I have seen agree in their outward arrangements with that ancient text down to minute details, both those already mentioned and others to which reference has not yet been made, but of which I have obtained the colophons. The small size of the parchment—for it is written on a kind of parchment, in all probability goatskins—the division into columns, the subdivision of the text into small sections, and even the writing itself are very similar to those preserved in the later documents. It would be impossible to make it later than the first century : it may be older, but it is certainly not later than the date assigned by me. I venture to say that I have seen and closely examined all the existing Samaritan scrolls in addition to all the copies of the Pentateuch in book form found in England, besides photographs of the Barberini Triglot and all the inscriptions as far as they have been published, including those that were in my possession, and it is on the strength of this comparative study that I venture to advance the opinion stated above concerning the date of that Abisha scroll. It is evident at once that I differ entirely from the Samaritans, who date that scroll back to the thirteenth year of the entry of the children of Israel into the land of Canaan. A glance at that document written, I believe, on skins already prepared—for I was not allowed to handle it—must at once destroy the assumption of such a high antiquity as that claimed by the Samaritans.

The Samaritans have evolved a peculiar system of giving the date of a scroll, the name of the writer, and the place where it was written should they so choose. There is no parallel to this system which they have invented, and it is arranged in such a

The oldest Scroll thus far known, with cryptographic date 562 Hedge,
equalling 1167. (Deut. ii. 3–iv. 32)

Plate 12

manner that it cannot be changed or forged. Whatever the first scribe entered into the text must remain so long as the text exists, and it would be an interesting problem to find out whence they have derived this ingenious device of dating their scrolls, which is limited to the scrolls and books of the Bible. The letters which form the names and dates are part and parcel of the text itself, which is divided into two columns, a small empty space being left between. Into that empty space such letters are written that if they are read in a consecutive column from top to bottom they form the name and dates. The letters are taken out of the words of the text; assuming a word consists of five letters, then two letters may be written at the end of the line of one column, the last two letters may begin the opposite line, and the middle letter could be placed in the intervening space. A horizontal stroke after a letter marks the end of each word. This system assures permanency to the date and to the whole inscription ; it cannot be altered, since no substitution is possible. On the one hand, no one can take a letter out of the text and put it within the column without being easily detected owing to the gap created one way or the other ; on the other hand, a letter once written in the middle can never be pushed into either column, because it would mean the complete erasure of the word and a rewriting of the word and the whole of the second column, since no line begins or finishes with half a word. This system might almost be called a cryptogram, although there is nothing cryptic about it.

Now the Abisha scroll has just such an inscription which I have seen myself. As very few people have had access to the Abisha scroll to make a personal inspection thereof, the information concerning it found in Samaritan MSS. and elsewhere seems to vary slightly. I therefore asked the late High Priest, Jacob, the son of Aaron, to let me have an absolutely accurate transcript of that inscription. I am publishing in Appendix IV a facsimile of his communication, together with a full transliteration and translation. It will be seen that this MS. claims to have been written by Abisha, the son of Pineḥas, on the skins of sacrifices at the gate of the Tent of Assembly in the thirteenth year after the occupation of Canaan. The only solution of the problem seems to be that the MS. in question is in all likelihood a copy of a much older one in which this peculiar claim was set forth. There can be no doubt that copies of the Pentateuch were made successively from olden times. According to the Law the king

was commanded to have a copy made, and what held good for the
king held good no doubt for the priests.   In fact the chief
occupation of the Samaritan High Priests was the copying of
Pentateuchs, as is attested by the colophons.   Moreover, if the
latter were the judges who had the care of the community in all
matters of a legal character, they must have had something upon
which to rely.   However few and far between the copies may
have been, copies certainly must have been made; and without
wishing to accept the statement that this scroll was the actual
writing of Abisha, we may be inclined to accept the view held by
the Samaritans that their text rests upon a copy claimed to have
been made by Abisha himself. It may sound fantastic, but the
question may be asked on the other hand whence the Jews
derived their scroll of the Law, if not from copies which
had been made successively in the course of ages from the
old originals handed down from generation to generation.   The
very fact that Ezra was called a Sofer, and that a most important class of authorities immediately after the Return were
called the Soferim or scribes, proves incontestably that they
must have been the men who were entrusted with the making of
such copies, as being the men best qualified for the purpose.
All this presupposes special training, and the study of the
palaeography of the Pentateuch, which has not yet been undertaken, will make that activity more evident, especially if studied
in connexion with the scroll and the history of the Massorah, and
will also lend belief to the fact that model codices must have
existed from very olden times.   As already remarked, the
oldest references to the text presuppose the existence of definite
rules for the writing of the Bible, together with an intensive
occupation with every word and letter of the Pentateuch.
Although the introduction of the six final letters is ascribed to
the time of the Prophets, in addition, various actions of the
Soferim are mentioned which are described as Tiḳḳun and Iṭṭur.
There are also other details found in the Massoretic text which
all point in the same direction.

The constant critical faculty exercised in the creation and
preservation of a standard text of the Pentateuch, purified of all
excrescences and additions of a midrashic character, was continued
almost down to the time of the destruction of the Temple; these
model codices were preserved in the hall of the Temple.   One
example of a somewhat elementary procedure in establishing the
correct reading is seen in the Talmudic reference of the elimina-

tion of one word וְעטוטי by substituting נערי, while others of a similar character often occur.[1] Moreover Josephus refers distinctly to a copy of the Bible in the Temple which differed from that which he followed in his *Antiquities*. He refers to the stanza in the Book of Joshua in which the latter bids the sun and moon stand still (Joshua x. 12).[2] It is important to notice that his version of that passage agrees entirely with the Samaritan Hebrew Book of Joshua, where it is also missing. Again, such action can only be understood if we assume that those who were engaged upon it must have had older authorities upon which to rely. This, to my mind, would solve the problem connected with the Abisha scroll; it would mean that this scroll rests upon an older one which was reputed to be of extreme antiquity. The name of Abisha, however, must not be taken too seriously.

We are no doubt dealing here with hypotheses, but the origin of a text with such a colophon ascribing the archetype to Abisha, son of Pineḥas, may with some safety be connected with the final break in the time of Ezra. In the Jewish literature a tradition appears from time to time, especially in Massoretic notes, in which reference is made to a standard codex named the Codex of Ezra, and some Massoretic annotators of the Bible even down to the fifteenth century refer distinctly to that standard codex as the one used by them for establishing the correct text.[3] No one will contend that a MS. containing a colophon which declared the MS. in question to be the work of Ezra must necessarily be the archetype, but it would be considered more or less as a copy in which, however, the actual colophon from the actual original had been preserved. It was in order to counteract such a text that the Samaritans may have been induced to produce another one ascribed to a much higher antiquity, centuries older than the one proclaimed by Ezra to be the only true and genuine one, or according to their tradition to have been produced by Ezra and falsified by him. It may be that in opposition to the scroll of the Jews to which Ezra appealed, the Samaritans claimed to possess one of a still higher antiquity.

An examination of the various Samaritan scrolls from a purely palaeographical point of view justifies our assumption that the Samaritans have kept most faithfully to the text which was in

---

[1] J. Taan, iv. 68 a ; v. Levi, *Talmud, Wörterbuch*, s.v. זאטוט, vol. i, p. 508.
[2] Josephus, *Antiq.* v. 1. 17 (§ 61).
[3] v. Ginsburg, *Introduction to the Hebrew Bible*, London, 1897, p. 748 f.

their possession. If only minute changes can be shown to have crept in during a period of close upon 2,000 years, we may surely believe that they were in possession of a much older copy, of which the Abisha scroll is the only one which has survived the ravages of time and is a faithful representative.

Other scrolls of the Samaritans were probably also torn up in the time of Antiochus. But a disaster far more radical overtook them in the time of Hadrian, when almost by a miracle this old codex survived the ruthless storms which had as their object the destruction of the Jewish faith and literature as well as that of the Samaritans. Who knows whether better Samaritan scrolls may not also have survived and one day be brought to light?

This conclusion excludes the possibility of the Samaritans having taken over the Pentateuch of the Jews at so late a period as the destruction of the Temple. It further contradicts the statement that the Pentateuch was brought by Manasseh in the time of Nehemiah, *circa* 430, or according to Josephus, *circa* 320 B.C.E. Even if the taunt be true that the Samaritans are the descendants of the proselyte Kuthaeans, the priests who came back so many centuries before and taught them the Law of God and re-established the service must have had some code or some book upon which to rest their claim of being the lawful priests entrusted with the duty of carrying out the Divine Law.

These palaeographic and historical reasons, although resting upon many undoubted facts, may be considered by some as not sufficiently convincing and of rather a hypothetical character, so that the relation between the Jewish and Samaritan recensions of the Pentateuch cannot be definitely settled thereby. I therefore turn now to the Greek translation. For many centuries there existed a doubt whether the Samariticon referred to by the Fathers of the Church during the first centuries meant a Samaritan-Hebrew recension or a Greek translation running parallel to the well-known Greek translation ostensibly made by Jews. The discovery of fragments of the Samariticon, as well as other evidence which has since come to light, has now definitely settled that question, and no doubt exists that the Samaritans also prepared a Greek translation of their recension. What was the object of such a translation? This opens the question of the Greek translation of the Pentateuch. It is generally assumed, mainly on the strength of the Letter of Aristeas, that the work was done in Egypt. Josephus, for his part, repeats the same story with slight variations, and this view has attained almost the value of a dogma. According to Aristeas [1] it was in consequence of the desire of the chief librarian, Demetrius of Phaleron, to enrich the great library established by Ptolemeus, that the king, Ptolemeus II Phila-delphus (283–247 B.C.), was induced to send an invitation to Eleazar, the High Priest of Jerusalem, requesting him to send men expert in the Law, with a knowledge of Hebrew and Greek, who would translate the Pentateuch for him. Eleazar accordingly selected seventy-two elders, six for each tribe, whom he sent to Egypt; there, settled in separate cells, they produced in the space of seventy-two days, not merely the translation required, but in comparing the texts it was found that by an inspiration all had selected the same words and made identical translations. The king was overjoyed with the result, and the text thus pre-pared was placed in the royal library and known as the work of the seventy. Many more exaggerations have been added in the course of time, but for our purpose it is sufficient to have given the general outline of this story. The improbabilities of the record have been recognized in modern times and the whole story relegated to the domain of legends and fables. The great works of Fraenkel,[2] who was best equipped for such an investiga-tion, have been specially valuable in throwing a different light upon the history of the Septuagint (LXX). He pointed out that not even the Pentateuch, not to speak of other books of the Bible, was the work of one man or of one hand. The books were translated by different scholars, some better equipped for the task than others, with the result that there is no trace of unity of authorship, nor can a positive date be assigned to any book. On one or two occasions Aristeas himself refers to translations already in existence. The whole story, therefore, of a translation having been made at the request of the Egyptian king, in order to enrich the Alexandrian library, must be relegated to the domain of legend ; it forms part of the apologetic tendency so characteristic of the whole Hellenistic literature.

There must, however, have been a totally different reason for connecting this Greek text with Ptolemy, and in order to explain the origin of that translation, scholars devised another

---

[1] Cf. whole literature : Stählin, *Geschichte d. griech. Literatur—II. Nach-klassische Periode*, pp. 542 ff., Munich, 1920.

[2] *Vorstudien zur Septuaginta*, Leipzig, 1841 ; *Ueber den Einfluss der palästi-nensischen Exegese auf die alexandrinische Hermeneutik*, Leipzig, 1851.

legend which finds its justification in the rooted idea that
the LXX is of Egyptian origin. The reason adduced was that
the Jews who had emigrated to Egypt had forgotten their
own language, had become so assimilated to the Greek that
they knew none other, and suddenly evinced an unconquerable
desire to have their own sacred Scripture translated into the
vernacular.   In advancing this story two very important
points have been forgotten—the real status of the Jews in
Egypt, and their relation to the Greeks. Leaving aside those
Jewish colonies which were settled in Egypt during the Persian
period or even a little earlier, the mass of the Jews living in
Alexandria were either people settled there by Alexander, *circa*
320, or slaves whom Ptolemy had brought as captives from his
wars in Palestine. In point of fact, Aristeas asked as a favour
from the king, in appreciation of the work done by the elders,
that these slaves should be set free, to which the king agreed,
paying an enormous sum in ransom. On the other hand, there
was an ever-growing enmity between Jews and Greeks, and a
hatred which often flared up and led to violent riots which had
to be suppressed by armed force and great bloodshed. Can any
one imagine that during the few years which had elapsed since
the majority of the people had been carried away as captives
from Palestine and had been living as slaves, they would so easily
have forgotten their mother tongue and have been anxious to have
of all the books the sacred Scripture translated into a tongue
which they hated? Besides, what purpose was this translation
to serve? It was surely not intended to take the place of Hebrew
in the Divine service. However great the ignorance of the
people may have been, and the masses of the Jewish people in
the Diaspora were never great scholars or profoundly versed
in a knowledge of Hebrew, still no one ever dreamed of
replacing the Hebrew of the sacred text by any translation
into any vernacular. A Targum in the popular Aramaic may
have existed in Palestine side by side with the Hebrew, and
after centuries may have been invested with some authority,
but in nothing was it to be compared with the unalterable
Hebrew text of the Pentateuch. Moreover, how much time
must be assumed to have elapsed between the translation of
Philadelphus before, and the period when, such a text could
have claimed any authority and become the basis of Hellenistic
historical and legendary speculation? Demetrius, who was
probably separated from the nominal date of that translation by

only fifty years or so, took this text as a basis for his chronology of the Bible, and introduced into it such legendary or Agadic material as can be traced in other Hebrew writings. The idea of an Egyptian origin will have to be abandoned, in spite of the fact that it afterwards became the property of the Jews of Egypt and endowed with a character of sanctity almost equal to that of the Hebrew original, as can be seen from the writings of Philo. Just because it had become the Bible of the Egyptian Jews, and later on of the Christians, it is not surprising that an Egyptian word or phrase crept in here and there. But the text was corrupted in so many ways that there is no critical justification for drawing conclusions as to the place of composition from a few evident interpolations or corruptions. Now many centuries had elapsed and many important changes had taken place between the date of Philo and the time of the origin of the LXX.

Another reason must be found for this translation and for its connexion with Philadelphus, stripped as far as is possible of its legendary character. One thing may be taken as axiomatic, that the Jews of Palestine would not rely upon anything done by Jews in Egypt or pay any real attention to writings composed there. The temple of Onias and all that happened in Egypt is an example in point. The Jews living there were simply ignored in Jerusalem, if they were not treated as an heretical or seditionary movement. The case, however, would be quite different with any writings produced in Palestine, and carried with the seal of Jerusalem upon them not only to Alexandria but to other parts of the Diaspora; for thus alone were they invested with authority. If therefore a translation, be it Greek or Aramaic, were to be received with respect by the Jews, it had to be of Palestinian origin and not the reverse. On sundry occasions I have pointed out, and even developed at length, the fact that in Palestine a Hebrew text of the Bible had been subjected to a peculiar exegesis in order to base upon it, or to deduce from it, or to justify by it, those practices which formed the Oral Law and for which no definite directions were given in the text as it stood. Fraenkel, who was a master of the subject, had no difficulty in showing the profound impress which Palestinian exegesis had made upon the Alexandrian literature, meaning especially the LXX. He, of course, accepted the view that the LXX was of Egyptian origin, but on almost every page he was able to show how much the Greek translation depended on this midrashic

Palestinian exegesis. Now it would be a sheer miracle if a work of such complexity could have been carried out in Egypt within the space of seventy days by some elders, even if they had come from Jerusalem to make the translation. The native population could not understand the meaning of it, nor would they want to find a justification for such an interpretation by means of an exegesis which rested upon the most subtle understanding of the Hebrew text, for these interpretations were not in the text but had to be read into it. And even if that had been the case, how did those who had come from Jerusalem and no doubt had brought an authentic text with them, free from change and interpolation, produce a translation which differs in hundreds of places from that original? Even Josephus does not seem to pay much attention to the Alexandrian literature; he gives various parallel legends, but they do not agree with those of Eupolemos and Artaphanos concerning the history of Moses. Those religious legends, like the legal prescriptions, originated in Palestine only and were thence carried to Alexandria. The home of the LXX must therefore be sought in Palestine, the reason for its translation being totally different from that hitherto assumed.

The Greek wave which overwhelmed the East threatened to sweep away every national faith and every national literature. Some went under; others, among them the Jews, endeavoured to resist; the Greeks brought material culture, physical enjoyment, loose morality if any, and an immeasurable amount of arrogance and pride. They claimed superiority over all the other nations, and besides their military prowess, pointed to their success in various arts and sciences, and their extraordinary bevy of gods and goddesses. The nations of the East for their part endeavoured to oppose the Greeks by writing their own histories and making them anterior to the beginnings of Greek history by thousands of years, and all attempted to prove that the Greeks were dependent upon the East for whatever they possessed. Thus Sanchuniathon wrote the history of Phoenicia, Berosus that of Assyria and Babylon, commencing their narratives with kings who had ruled tens of thousands of years before their own time. The Jews opposed the Greek claims by pointing to their own history, which was sane, sober, simple, and more reliable than the fantastic histories of the others, besides being full of the highest principles of morality and humanity. Moreover, they carried the war into the enemy's camp by translating their own literature into Greek. Starting with the Bible, the Jewish literature was translated at an early period and exercised a great influence upon the Greek-speaking world. This translation served the purpose of being polemic and apologetic at one and the same time, and nowhere was such action needed more than in Palestine itself. There the Jews stood on their own ground, for they were still masters in their own home; but from the time of Alexander they had to defend their Temple and their service because, in spite of the various wars between the Seleucids and Ptolemies, the people still enjoyed sufficient freedom to follow their own religious practices. Here, however, the danger of Greek influence was greatest; it insinuated itself easily among the upper classes, it led many a Jew to apostasy or at any rate to imitation of Greek sports and pastimes, and priests were accused of taking part in races and combats in the stadium; in fact, this Greek influence grew so powerful that even a High Priest was prevailed upon to abjure his loyalty to his faith and allow a statue of Zeus to be erected in the Temple. This was, therefore, the place and the time for the production of a translation which bears the imprint of the Palestinian spirit and almost unconsciously follows the exegetical interpretation in which the mind of the scribe was soaked at the time. Even if carried elsewhere, it would receive the respect and enjoy the authority which such a work demanded, just because it was a Palestinian production,

The Samaritans were exposed to the same danger and had to fight the same battle. It is unlikely that they would have allowed the Jews to get ahead of them, for in addition they had to prove their own claim of being the true representatives of old Israel and the only keepers of the true faith. They had to justify their claims in the eyes of the Greeks and would therefore have been anxious to translate their Pentateuch into Greek, especially as they had been favoured by Alexander and probably by his successors as well, seeing that a large number had settled in Egypt. Hence the old translation known as the Samariticon. Now in what relation does this stand to the story of Philadelphus? If we combine Josephus, the various Jewish traditions, and some portions of the Aristeas legend on the one hand, and the Samaritan traditions on the other, an answer to the question may perhaps be forthcoming. Each individual account may be biased, but if they be studied together they neutralize one another, and some true facts may be gleaned from these con-tradictory reports.

The rivalry between Jews and Samaritans did not end at the

boundary of Palestine.   Josephus records[1] a virulent fight between the Jews and Samaritans in Egypt, the cause being the mutual antagonistic claims whither the gifts and vows should be sent, the one contending for Jerusalem and the other for Garizim. The fight was so violent that the king's intervention was sought. This dispute does not seem to refer to individual gifts which every one was free to send as he chose, but probably to the royal gifts, for the kings used to send gifts to some central sanctuary from time to time as a mark of royal favour, and also to win the allegiance of those subjects whose sanctuary they honoured.   The question therefore arose whither these royal gifts should be sent, whether to Jerusalem as the Jews contended, or to Samaria as the Samaritans contended.   Josephus continues the story and tells of a dispute which took place before King Philometor, when Jews and Samaritans were called upon to prove their claim of possessing the true Bible, the vanquished being punishable with death.   The Jews appeared bringing their sacred Scriptures with them and—let it be noted—a list of the genealogies of their priests, in order to prove their claim that they were in possession of an uninterrupted and therefore reliable tradition. It not only rested on the authority of the Scripture, but on the genealogical chain of the High Priests as well.   The Samaritans also sent two delegates, Sabbeus and Theodosius, who carried with them their own Scripture.   According to the Samaritan statement the Jews were vanquished, the king declaring the Samaritan text to be the authentic one ; according to Josephus the result was just the reverse, the Samaritans paying for their audacity with their lives.   Thus far the bare outline of these incidents. Here, however, we find the real historical substratum for the whole Aristeas legend.

It was neither the enriching of the Alexandrian library nor the welfare of his Jewish subjects that caused Philadelphus to show any interest in the Greek translation of the Bible.   It was brought before him in consequence of the intense rivalry between Jews and Samaritans who appealed to him to settle their disputes. In reply he summoned representative leaders of both parties to appear before him.   Now when these two delegations came before the king, they must have brought with them Greek translations of the Bibles which were already in their possession, if the exhibition of their texts were the proof of their claims.

---

[1] *Antiq.* xiii. 3. 4 (§§ 74 ff.).

They surely did not come with a Hebrew text to be translated, for the king understood no Hebrew, but with a text already translated long before. In all probability Philadelphus decided in favour of the Jewish recension, with the result that this became the 'authorized' version and therefore recognized and adopted as such by the Jews of Alexandria. It became canonical, i.e. it was henceforth the canon for the Greek translation of the Scripture.

We must remember that when Demetrius of Phaleron tried to collect the books for the Alexandrian Library he was faced with a very great literary problem. In their endeavour to show that they possessed books on every subject and of high antiquity, the Greeks had not hesitated to affix ancient and great names to a large number of forged writings : it was their vanity which created the whole pseudepigraphic literature. The problem which beset the librarian was to separate the true from the false, and he was therefore the first to introduce the idea of a canon, a rule, a standard by which to measure these spurious writings. Those which came up to the standard became the canon or canonical, while the others were relegated to a second place as pseudepigraphic or spurious. The same thing happened to the Greek translations of the Bible ; the 'authorized' text became the canon, while the rest were relegated to the pseudepigrapha.[1]

The origin of the LXX will now also find a better explanation, since every legend must have some kernel of truth. The idea of the LXX is not wholly the result of a pious fiction. It so happened that at the end of one or two of the MSS. of the Samaritan Pentateuch in book form I found a peculiar colophon. Among others reference is made to the '70', and in many of their writings, especially the Book of the Laws which will be described hereafter, it is distinctly stated that the text of the Bible in their possession is the one which they received as an 'ancient tradition' from the seventy elders. These were the seventy elders chosen by Moses in the wilderness to whom he had entrusted a copy of the Law. According to their statements, the text which the Samaritans exhibited before King Ptolemy Philadelphus was a text which rested upon the authority of the seventy elders. These were the '70' who were responsible

---

[1] It must be remarked in this connexion that the words 'canon, canonical, and uncanonical' have been applied exclusively to the Greek translation of the Scriptures. No such word or anything approximating it or representing it is found in the Hebrew language. But this is a subject which lies outside the sphere of the present investigation.

for the text and later for the translation which was made from that text. The same tradition has also been preserved by the Jews, although curiously enough it has been entirely overlooked. The Maxims of the Fathers of the Synagogue begin with the following words : ' Moses received the Law from Sinai, and he handed it over to Joshua, and Joshua to the elders, and the elders to the prophets.' Here the elders are placed immediately after Joshua, to whom the Law, both Written and Oral, had been handed. Thus we have the same elders as the holders of the Law and witnesses for the authenticity of the text. The rise of the scribes and the development of the Massorah among the Jews contributed to obliterate entirely the meaning and importance of that tradition. This, I submit, is the historical kernel for Aristeas and Josephus, and explains the origin of the canon as well as that of the LXX, and at the same time dispenses with the legend of the Egyptian origin of the Greek translation. In Jewish Talmudic literature, which by the way was written down centuries after the event, there are various traditions concerning the Greek versions. The word העתיקו used in one place has been wrongly understood. It does not mean 'they have translated', but merely 'they have made a copy from an older original'. It is stated further that the seventy introduced a number of changes into their work. Of these only two or three are found in our Greek text.[1] If the seventy elders had really been sent by the High Priest Eleazar, and were the translators and were responsible for the Greek text, why should all these alterations have disappeared? In another variant in the Talmud only five elders are mentioned as having undertaken that charge,[2] and again in a third place,[3] which has been completely misunderstood hitherto, the real fundamental word has been mistranslated altogether. It says there that on a certain day when the Greek ' translation ' was made, there was darkness in the world for three days, and totally unfounded deductions have been adduced from this alleged mourning over the translation. The Hebrew words used here are כתבו יוונית, which mean 'they wrote in Greek', i. e. they transliterated the Hebrew characters into the Greek alphabet, which was rightly considered by the Jews as a grievous calamity. This is, by the way, another proof of the fact that the Hebrew text alone

[1] v. Fraenkel, *Vorstudien zur Septuaginta*, Leipzig, 1841, pp. 25 ff.
[2] v. Gaster, *Exempla of the Rabbis*, No. 61, pp. 60 and 197.
[3] Ibid.

Plate 13

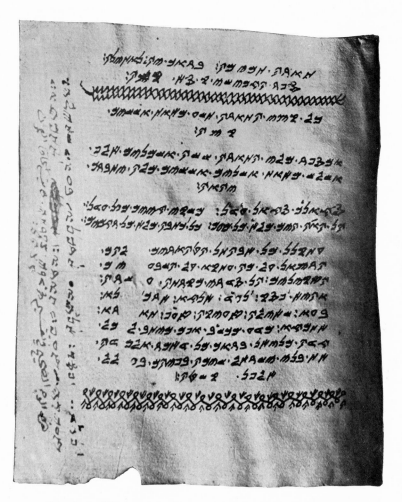

Colophon of Pentateuch with reference to the Seventy Elders

was the sacred one and that not even a transliteration was to be tolerated.

There is, however, a problem connected with this transliteration which, as far as I am aware, has not yet been touched. How old is that transliteration, what purpose did it serve, and in what relation does it stand to the ancient 'Koine' and the LXX? It must unquestionably be of high antiquity if Origenes found it important enough to insert into his Hexapla. It is certainly not his own work and there was no reason for him to insert it, unless he saw in it a very old tradition which in some form or another was connected with the Hebrew text of the Pentateuch, and with its translation. To transliterate it merely to show the character of the translation was a superfluous task, since the translator of course could read the Hebrew text, and those for whom the Hexapla was intended were expected to be thoroughly acquainted with the Hebrew letters and the Hebrew language, if they were to appreciate the differences of the various translations.

If that be the case, then what purpose did the transliteration serve? Evidently at some time or other it was the text in the hands of Jews who had forgotten the Hebrew characters, but who were interested in following the reading of the text during the service. It must be stated again—and this transliteration proves it—that the Biblical lessons as part of the service were never read in any other language but Hebrew. A similar phenomenon occurs many centuries later among the Karaites, who probably for the same reason transliterated the Hebrew text into Arabic characters. No one acquainted with Karaite traditions would for one moment believe that the sect which pinned its faith to the word of the written text in contradistinction to the Oral Law, and who at one time were credited with being the inventors of the Massorah because of Anan's strict injunction ' to search the Law ', should have substituted a transliteration for the Hebrew text. And yet numerous fragments of such transliterations are extant, most of which are in the British Museum ; [1] in this case even the vowels and accents have been added to the text. Here we have a 'Koine' of the period when the people were acquainted with Arabic characters in their daily life, just as in olden times the people were acquainted with the Greek characters in their daily life.

The main importance of this transliteration, therefore, lies in

---

[1] v. Hoerning, R., *Karaite MSS. in the British Museum,* London, 1889.

its relation to that ancient text which I presuppose as the basis
for the Greek translations. Although the existing fragments are
very small, there can be no doubt of the definite relation between
the transliterated text of the Hexapla and that which lies at the
basis of the LXX, both of which approximate more or less to the
primitive text of the Samaritans. I believe that the text before
us is a representative of that ancient 'Koine', and if that assumption proves correct the problems of the origin of the LXX may
be satisfactorily solved. I must, however, refrain from entering
into further details, as these could only fittingly be the subject of
a detailed investigation. Suffice this brief reference to a subject
which may prove of great value. A portion of the old transliteration has been preserved to us in Origenes' Hexapla.

A glance at the Hellenistic literature furthermore contributes
to postulate an older date for the Greek translation of the
Pentateuch. Demetrios, 'Eupolemos', Malchos, and the other
known Samaritans, so dexterously discovered by Freudenthal, and
even Artaphanos up to a point, contain such a mass of legendary
matter which has grown out of the simple narrative of the
Bible, that a long time must have elapsed before it could have
assumed the form in which it appears in these writings. It has
already been remarked that the exegesis of the Bible moved in
two directions, the legal and the legendary, the Halakhah and
Agadah, both of which were evolved through the midrash of the
text. Such an evolution required a great lapse of time after the
text had been definitely formulated and fixed. The LXX represents both these tendencies in a more embryonic form, while the
Hellenistic writers show them in full growth; the simple
translation must therefore have preceded the latter by some
length of time. If in addition to the writers mentioned above
we also find distinct traces of similar influences in the oldest
portions of the Sibylline Oracles, as will be shown by me in the
publication of the Asatir, then the fact can no longer be doubted
that Jews and Samaritans possessed a Greek translation long
before the time of Ptolemy Philadelphus, i. e. towards the end of
the fourth and the beginning of the third century B.C.E., or
latest about a hundred years after Alexander, that being sufficient
time for such a work to be produced. Most of these Hellenistic
writers are just as likely to be Palestinian as Egyptian, and if, as
will be shown, we also have close parallels in the Samaritan
literature, not only to these Hellenistic writings and to the
Sibylline Oracles, but also a key to some of the sources of

Josephus' *Antiquities,* then I think there can be little doubt that the Palestinian origin of the LXX is definitely proved.

We can now go one step farther. The existence of the Samariticon, i. e. a Greek translation of the Samaritan recension, may now be considered as established. It must be of the same antiquity as the Jewish version, for if both were produced before Philadelphus, they must at least be of contemporary origin. What is more, Fraenkel himself, who stoutly denies any authenticity or antiquity to the Samaritan recension of the text of the Pentateuch,[1] suggests on one or two occasions that readings from the Samariticon may have crept into the LXX, especially in that famous passage after the commandment in Exod. xxiii. 19 : 'Thou shalt not seethe the kid in its mother's milk.' Such a reading could not have been introduced at a later date, so that the two translations must be coeval and may have influenced each other in their oldest form. On the other hand, in the Samaritan literature, Biblical legends are found in the Asatir and in other subsequent writings which agree with and yet are distinct from the Jewish parallels. If the Samaritans already possessed in the fourth or third century a Greek translation of the Bible and subsequently other Hellenistic writings resting upon the Bible, and if we remember the constant opposition to and objection of the Jews, it is hardly possible for borrowing to have taken place. Thus we come once more to the conclusion that the Samaritan Hebrew original must belong to a very high antiquity.

The next problem which arises from this comparison is the relation of the Greek text to the Massoretic or Jewish recension on the one hand and to the Samaritan on the other, which carries us back to the very problem of the Samaritan Hebrew original itself.

A critical examination of the Greek text of the Bible differs entirely from a similar investigation of any other ancient writing. The Bible was not like a secular book written for a narrow circle of readers who were interested in a certain subject, be it historical, poetical, or philosophical, which left the masses unaffected, and which had on the whole a very small circulation. Such works are not invested with any special character nor are they indispensable for the spiritual life of a nation. Not so the Bible. As already pointed out, it was first and foremost an answer to Greek pretensions; it was a source of pride to the nation which

---

[1] *Einfluss d. palästinensischen Exegese,* pp. 237 ff.

drew from it its knowledge and all its inspiration; it was a practical guide in all matters affecting the material and the spiritual life; it gave the record of the past and the hope for the future, and at the same time the necessary strength to withstand the temptations and allurements of what claimed to be a superior civilization. By its very nature it was a popular book in the sense that it belonged to the masses, for the Law and its practice had to be made known to the people week by week, and in comparison with other literatures it offered all the information of which the people stood in need. It was not a book reserved for a separate class like the priests, but passed from hand to hand, since every reader and teacher had to read from it and interpret it to the people assembled for worship. Every synagogue possessed one or more copies, and its study was not limited to a few; on the contrary, it was part of the general education. As it was the basis of the legal life, the book no doubt obtained a special character from very ancient times without thereby ever losing its popular character.

Now a work which was in constant circulation and which was copied generation after generation by many hands and in many lands, was exposed to at least a threefold danger of alteration and adulteration. Firstly, there are the mistakes inherent in all human work; every copyist was liable to make mistakes, and unless a standard had been established which served as a model from which the scribe could not deviate under the penalty of destroying the validity of the copy, it was only natural that almost every copy would have had one or more blemishes; and if one of these copies had obtained the reputation of being the most accurate, the mistakes found therein would thereby have been perpetuated and increased. This is one class of mistakes. The second class is specially characteristic of the Bible; a number of alterations, interpolations, and additions occur which serve the special purpose of smoothing out apparent difficulties and explaining away apparent contradictions, or of adding smaller or larger interpolations in order to justify the interpretation and practical application of the passage in question. This sometimes served the purpose of drawing a legendary interpretation or development from the text. The diorthotes and kataskeuast exercised their function to the full in the preparation of a text of the Bible which would give satisfaction to the masses, and these are the starting-points for the more fully developed midrash which finds its expression in the work of the meturgeman or interpreter in the vernacular.   The latter assisted the reader during the recital of the Biblical lessons on Sabbath and festivals, and thus the Word of God was made known to the people in conformity with the ancient tradition of the historical development of the Oral Law.

The third danger to which the text of the Bible was subjected was the result of its use for sectarian purposes.   Whilst the other two were more or less unavoidable and indispensable for a proper understanding of the text, this last was the arbitrary work of various sections, who so manipulated the text that they found in it a full justification for their own claims.   These are deliberate alterations and changes.   The Samaritans charged the Jews with having done so and the Jews had no hesitation in returning the charge against the Samaritans.   ' You have falsified the Law ' is the charge made against the Samaritans by some of the prominent Rabbis of the first and second centuries c.e.[1] It was, and is, the usual form of polemics employed by sects against one another.

If we now examine the Greek text from this threefold point of view we shall find all of them borne out in detail.   Any one who is conversant with the history of the Greek text and who has glanced at the critical edition by Swete knows how unreliable is the text which is now in our hands.   Already as far back as the second century Origenes found the text in such a deplorable state that he attempted to establish a more correct text and marked the various readings by peculiar signs.   The later scribes took no notice of these signs, with the result that the number of variants in the text were multiplied without being recognized as such.   It is unnecessary to remark that there are a number of scribes' errors. The second class of change I must leave for later consideration as I would now deal with the third.

The Christians who first appealed to the Jews in the Diaspora, and then from the Jews to the Gentiles, took their stand on the Greek Bible. and a number of interpolations and alterations are due to their propaganda activity.   So much was this the case that during the time of Akiba (*c.* 130 c.e.) and before, the Jews of Palestine felt there was no more reliance upon the accuracy of the Greek text then in circulation.   A number of new translations were therefore undertaken to bring the Greek text into closer proximity to the Hebrew verity ; Aquilas, Theodotion, Sym-

[1] Palestinian Talmud, Soṭah, vii. 21[c] ; T. Bab. Soṭah, f. 33[b] ; T. Bab. Sanhedrin, f. 90[b].

machus, and other unknown authors worked at the new translation which has been preserved to us in the Hexapla, and we find there the remnants of these various attempts to correct the Greek text.

I now come to the second class of mistakes, which is the most important from our point of view. If we eliminate the mistakes and interpolations due to the shortcomings of scribes and the deliberate alterations owing to sectarian interests, a mass of readings still remains which requires most careful consideration. They are to a large extent due to that desire of making the text stylistically smoother, and of toning down and slightly modifying some expressions in the Bible which was intended for the masses and had therefore to be adjusted to their understanding. The authors of the translation, such as we have it, endeavoured to follow the Hebrew original slavishly. At the time when the translation was made, the people had become conscious that they were dealing with a Divine work; it was the Word of God which they were asked to transfer from one language to another without violating the meaning and spirit of the original. The sentences are often couched in the style of the Hebrew Bible, and great care was taken to reproduce the most minute particles whenever possible; for thereby hung either a legend or a law. We must assume therefore that whatever is found in the Greek text is, as far as possible, a perfect copy of the Hebrew original from which they made the translation.

If we compare this Greek translation with the Hebrew of the Massoretic text, we shall find a great mass of such additional or changed matter. Many a particle, word, or verse has been added or changed. No one can for a moment believe that the authors of the translation took upon themselves to alter the text deliberately. What then was the original from which they made the translation? Here the Samaritan text takes its place, for curiously enough a large number of those additions and changes which appear in the Greek are also found in the Samaritan text. How is this to be explained? It is incredible that the authors of the Greek translation, all of whom were Jews and anxious to defend the last particle of their text, would have deliberately taken the Samaritan text as the basis for their translation. The Greek text in their possession was the very one used in their disputes with the Samaritans before Ptolemy. They must, therefore, have had a Hebrew text which somehow approximated to the text of the Samaritan. From the above the solution is not far to seek: they used the 'popular Bible', or rather a 'Koine', as I should call it, for the translation. They did not intend to give an absolute replica of the Massoretic text, since that would have helped neither Greek nor Jew to understand the real meaning of the text. The Greek translation therefore represents the first step towards the Targum ; it was intended for the masses and never for use in the Divine service, as, in fact, it never has been used. In the synagogue Hebrew alone was used, though the meturgeman made a kind of running commentary which, however, he did not read ; he interpreted freely and was helped in that interpretation by the indications found in the Bible prepared for popular use. I must repeat again here that all the differences between the Jewish and Samaritan recensions of the Pentateuch upon which stress has been laid, and to which reference has been made over and over again in the course of these lectures, always excluding the dogmatic portions, are on the whole of comparatively small importance. They are of course of value from the midrashic point of view, where every letter and word is of consequence, but as far as the contents of the books are concerned the differences are mostly of a very insignificant character. They do not alter the sense much, nor do they intro-duce or contain any serious modifications of the historical or legislative parts of the Pentateuch. But just because these differences are comparatively minute they are of special value, for they throw a light upon the origin of the LXX and show us the beginning of a development which took place at a later time, when for definite reasons the popular Bible or 'Koine' was eliminated from the service, and the general use of the standard original text alone was sanctioned for such purposes. The void thus created was filled by the Targum, which gradually replaced the popular Bible, and which reproduced and developed more fully those little additions found in the popular Hebrew text. The small beginnings of legends or allusions to legendary interpretation were fully elaborated in the Targum, while the practice of the Oral Law found expression in a popular manner and in the Aramaic language best understood by the people.

The Hebrew Bible became less and less intelligible to the latter, and the purpose which it had originally served was now more fully satisfied by the Targum. A large literature arose which is represented by the Halakhic and Agadic midrashim, in which every word and sentence of the Bible became the subject of long and elaborate discussion, and so vast was the material already accumulated during the first century before and after the common era, that such works as Mekhilta, Sifra, Sifre, Pesiḳta, &c., could be compiled by a man of that period. The old popular Bible fell into desuetude and was entirely forgotten. This, however, is the Bible which the Samaritans have preserved. They also acted under the same influences. With them the Bible was also the popular book ; from it they read their lessons ; from it they drew all the substance of their prayers ; upon it they rested all their religious life and the priesthood its claim. In competition with the Jews they also translated the Pentateuch into Greek ; they had the same interests to defend as the Jews, and they appealed to the outer world in the same way as did their rivals. In both cases it was a question of giving to the world a copy of the sacred book which they possessed, and in both cases it was so translated in such a manner as to preserve its popular character, so that it might be read by Greek and Samaritan or Jew alike. With the Samaritans the diorthotes went a step farther. Apparent lacunae in the Biblical narrative were filled up by the insertion of other Biblical passages, difficulties were smoothed down in many ways, and pegs prepared on which to hang legends and laws. The existence of a Samariticon was known in early times, and it was quoted by some of the Fathers of the Church, but when the world forgot the existence of the Samaritans and the Samaritan Hebrew Bible it also lost every trace of the Greek translation. The discovery of the Samariticon proves that at the time when the Jews undertook the work the Samaritans did likewise. This activity runs parallel to that of the Jews, and the question has not yet been answered how far the one translation may have influenced the other, and how much of what is found in the Jewish version of the LXX is due to interpolation from the Samariticon. It is, however, a curious fact that in the Hexapla (ed. Field) we find the specific addition of the tenth commandment of the Samaritans, which is so decisive for their dogma. True, it is marked by an asterisk, showing thereby that it was missing from the Hebrew text, yet it had found a place in the old recension. There is, however, no remark to the effect that it is of Samaritan origin, as Origenes often does when he adds Samaritan glosses to the text. In this case, then, he evidently did not realize that it was of Samaritan origin. Surely this could only be due to the Samaritan Greek translation influencing the LXX. This proof of the actual existence of such a Samariticon, of course, disposes of the hypothesis advanced by some scholars that the Samaritan Hebrew recension was modelled and altered after the Greek version of the LXX had been made. It also proves that the translation of the Samaritan Pentateuch must be at least as old as the Jewish translation into Greek.

Now if we assume, as is generally accepted, that these translations were made towards the end of the fourth century, *circa* 300 or even 250 B.C.E., i. e. a short century before the Maccabees, then the original text from which the LXX was taken must have been very much older, for the translators must have looked upon it as sufficiently authoritative to form a basis for their work, even though they considered it necessary to present the masses of the Greek public with a slightly sophisticated translation.

Like the Jews the Samaritans introduced similar slight alterations for legal or dogmatic reasons. Now whilst the translator of the Massoretic Book of Joshua does not hesitate to change Sichem into Shiloh because he feels that the former would favour Samaritan claims, he never alters anything in the Pentateuch. The Pentateuch, therefore, which he had before him, must have contained the slight additions and interpolations which we find in his translation. The Samaritans also introduced additions into their text, but in this case the differences between Jews and Samaritans commenced with the activity of the Jewish scribes. These evidently watched over the accuracy of the official text, and with them begins what is henceforth known as the Massorah.

The men at the helm began to recognize that unless a check were made the text of the Jewish Bible would be so altered and enlarged that it would become unrecognizable, and look almost like the Palestinian Targum. But there was also another reason which actuated the scribes and authorities of the time in eliminating all the additional elements which might have crept in during the course of ages. As already remarked many of these are due to the legal interpretation, and owe their origin to the priesthood or the Ṣadoḳites, who were the guardians and interpreters of the Law. It was to their interest that their prerogatives should not be diminished, and that their absolute authority in the interpretation and handling of the Law should remain unaffected. The Pharisees chiefly concentrated their activity in diminishing that authority and in claiming for themselves the right of interpreting and applying the Law. It was, therefore, their first duty to clear the text of all the additional elements by means of a standard copy of a specific sacred character, which was in their possession, especially as they disagreed with a number of them. Thus the necessity arose to establish a fence round the Law, on the one hand to protect it from interpolations, and on the other to eliminate all the strange matter which might have found a place therein. Moreover, the rigidity of the interpretation could become more flexible if it formed a part of the text itself. Thus the process of elimination and purification continued and the scroll was saved from becoming the vastly changed popular book it had threatened to become.

In the same opening chapter of the Maxims of the Fathers, which is so invaluable for the understanding of the period in question, there is a somewhat mysterious sentence which requires elucidation, and which is ascribed to the men of the Great Assembly. The maxims are : ' Be circumspect in judgement,' which must be interpreted : ' Be circumspect in the way in which you deduce legal consequences and decisions from the word of the Law,' for surely every judge is expected to be circumspect in judgement. The next is the recommendation of the appointment of many pupils, which must be interpreted : ' Spread this interpretation by a number of pupils : make propaganda for this kind of interpretation.' And finally : ' Make a fence round the Torah.'. This cannot be understood otherwise than as a reference to the establishment of a Massorah, a fence round the Torah, to protect it from inroads and from being influenced by the other recensions or by other traditions. The only fence which can be considered is the use of graphic signs or marks which would emphasize and critically establish, as it were, the readings found in the Hebrew Massoretic text down to the most minute particle. Later an occasion will present itself to return to this last very important class. The beginnings of the Massorah are very obscure, but if we consider the state of the text as now disclosed by a comparison of the Greek, Samaritan, and Hebrew recensions, we can easily understand the importance attached to this injunction; without it the text would never have been preserved in the form in which we now have it. Previous to that time the interpolations and additions were not looked upon with the same critical eye. Nobody thought that by inserting a word here or a sentence there he would vitiate the character of the book ; on the contrary, he thought he would enhance its value by removing difficulties, making it clearer, and by certain readings justifying their practice of the laws and the holding of beliefs which were slowly crystallizing in their midst, especially those of an eschatological character.

If we now turn to the Samaritans, we find that this process of elimination and purification was never undertaken because, un-like the Jews, opposing forces never appeared amongst them. They never had reason to eliminate anything, and as they never had a Massorah in the strict sense as practised by the Jews, alterations and corruptions crept in much more easily. The power of the hierarchy was never questioned : they were and still are the first and last exponents of the Law ; there were no parties like Pharisees and Sadducees disputing with one another for the supreme power, and therefore anything that might improve the text or any gloss which was found inserted therein from olden times was left untouched and unchallenged. Because of this the changes which had been made for dogmatic reasons and were found therein were not touched. If in addition they corroborated the differences between them and the Jews, they were of equal value with all the other changes and interpolations which had been handed down from olden times and which were due to the same motive of giving the text a special character; by removing difficulties and by inserting words and forms they made the basis for their practical application of the Law and for their eschatological beliefs. We have now in the Samaritan Pentateuch a most striking example of that fossilization which has overtaken Samaritan literature, to which reference has been made through-out these lectures. They stopped short at a certain period, and they have thus preserved to us forms and traditions which go back to a very high antiquity, and of which only a few traces can be found in the parallel Jewish literature. These slight additions and interpolations—always excepting the dogmatic portions for which a much higher antiquity must be claimed— go back to a period older by centuries than the Greek translation, and lead us to the conclusion that at a very early period the popular Bible or 'Koine' among the Jews must have assumed a character which was similar to that of the Samaritan recension. The popular Bible mentioned here always refers to the text in the hands of the people, i.e. the 'Koine'; otherwise the appear-ance of these changes in the Greek translation would be abso-lutely inexplicable. That 'Koine' must have enjoyed the reputa-tion of being the real representative of Holy Writ, not only to justify the almost literal translation when rendered into Greek, but also to explain the origin of the Hellenistic literature. This, as is well known, is also of high antiquity, and goes back to the third century B.C.E. It contains a mass of chronicles and legendary matter, the origin of which must be sought in such a popular text. As will be shown by me in my publication of the Asatir, at the time of the birth of the Hellenistic literature the text of the Pentateuch had already been expanded by additional glosses, from which grew a mass of legendary lore. Among the Jews this tendency developed later and divided into two large streams. Special writings were devoted to this explanation and interpretation, the one dealing with the Halakhah, the Law ('the way'), and the other dealing with the Agadah, the legend as mentioned before. It will now be shown that this agadic development is also of very high antiquity among the Samaritans. Its parallelism with Sadducean and ancient Pharisean traditions and practices has been discussed more fully in the previous pages, but will be more evident from a full examination of Samaritan writings.

The existence of the popular Bible in the hands of the masses must be assumed if the relations between the Samaritan, Greek, and Massoretic recensions are to be reconciled at all. Josephus, in spite of his hatred of the Samaritans, shows many parallel traits in his writings which cannot be explained except by the existence of such an 'historiated' Bible, from which he drew his material. The existence of such a Bible will also explain some apparent anomalies in the citations found in the New Testament.

The elimination of this popular Bible from the service and the reintroduction of the old unadulterated text are coincident with the success of the Maccabees and with the rise of the two political parties whose differences, though of a purely political character, still rested upon the text of the Bible. We read in 1 Macc. i. 56: 'And when they had rent in pieces the books of the law which they found, they burnt them with fire.' After cleansing the Temple and handing it over to the priests, the first duty of the scribes must have been to collect the remnants of the books of the Law and to piece them together as far as possible. This is the starting-point for the critical activity in connexion with the Book of the Law and for the application of such a Massorah as they possessed at the time, for of course the chief work of the Massorah consisted in preserving the text from all the interpolations which had crept in, while the activity of the Soferim was directed either towards removing such additions from the text or else eliminating entirely such copies from the service in the synagogue. This coincides with the rise of the two parties, and at the same time is the turning-point in the history of Holy Writ. All literary activity had come to a violent end during the persecution of Antiochus; automatically a breach had been created between the past and the future, the result of which was of a more far-reaching character than has hitherto been recognized. Closely connected therewith is, I believe, the close of the books forming Holy Writ, which in the Greek recension was afterwards called the canon, but for which no word exists in Hebrew. It seems that everything which existed before the Greek persecution was invested with a special character of its own, and that whatever was written after the Maccabean victory was no longer joined on to it. These were considered as popular tales, and popular books did not share in that character of sanctity accorded to the older writings. The close of the Bible was not premeditated, nor was it the result of any decision by any authority; it was simply the result of the terrible persecution which brought literary activity to an end for a whole generation and sufficed to draw a line between those books which had existed before the revolt and those that came after.

Whether the Samaritans underwent similar persecution or not it is difficult to say; according to an allegation of a later time, they simulated the worship of an idol or dove in order to avert the wrath of Antiochus. This allegation is, of course, strongly repudiated by the Samaritans, and they refer to the same period as one of dire distress. For the reasons already advanced, the copy of the Pentateuch at that time in their hands remained for the most part unchanged, but for the same reason there arose no Massorah and no protection for the text against the intrusion of other elements. It suffered no doubt from the hands of successive scribes, and thus many mistakes in spelling and many additional words must slowly have found their way into the text and contributed to a corruption against which there existed no check.

Reference may be made here to the statement found in Gesenius, that many a word now in the Samaritan text is due to a misunderstanding of Hebrew, for he alleged that the Samaritan text was copied. The palaeographic investigation of the shape and form of the old Hebrew writing, however, has shown that many of the letters mentioned by Gesenius are very much alike; the Samaritan scribe, who was not always the most learned, wrote mechanically and could easily have mistaken one letter for another, even in the old Samaritan script. It must also be remembered that in olden times scribes often did not write from an original, but from dictation. The Samaritan pronunciation of certain letters was a question of differentiation between gutturals, while other peculiar forms of pronunciation which they shared with the Galileans, and which are already mentioned in the later Jewish writings, could easily explain many of the mistakes found in the Samaritan text; so that the later the copy the greater the number of mistakes. As there was no model copy for comparison, the old mistakes were taken over and new ones added, especially in the book form. It can therefore readily be understood how the Samaritan text came to be corrupted in such a manner. Most, if not all, of the points raised by Gesenius could thus easily be disposed of.

There is, however, one more point to consider in connexion with this problem. Did the Samaritans know the Jewish recension and, vice versa, did the Jews know the Samaritan recension? No one has yet raised that question except by the suggestion that the Samaritans copied their Pentateuch from the Jewish recension. Before I answer this question, however, I must turn to another book which it was my good fortune to discover; I am referring to the Samaritan Book of Joshua. I do not wish to traverse the same ground as that occupied by my first publication, as I am preparing a new critical edition on the basis of all the MSS. and recensions which have since come to hand; nor will I refer here to the would-be criticism brought against the authenticity of the book discovered by me. I would, however, mention one point here to dispose of a legend which has found credence even among scholars. A certain Ab Sakhuah or Murjan the Danafite has been credited with being the author of this Hebrew text. At my request the Samaritans sent me a list of all the MSS. which he left behind after his death, which I have since purchased from his son Saad; in vain have I searched for a trace of this Book of Joshua, of which he would doubtless have kept one copy; but I have found among his papers his Samaritan translation of the Arabic paraphrase, which differs entirely from the Hebrew text, with which it has only small portions in common, and merely shows that use has been made of that Hebrew version discovered by me for some of the corresponding passages appearing in the Arabic version. Having disposed of this and other allegations connected therewith, I turn to the book itself. Without entering into any details which would be out of place, I will limit myself to the question of the relation between the two recensions, the Jewish and Samaritan, and to the question whether the Samaritans knew anything of the Hebrew Bible, since these problems are intimately connected with one another.

No one has hitherto doubted the existence of a certain code of laws among the tribes in the north similar to that in the possession of the southern tribes; these have been respectively designated by Higher Criticism by the letter 'E', Ephraimite or Elohistic, and 'J', Judean or Jehovistic. The question which Higher Criticism attempted to settle was the character and extent of each of these supposedly independent recensions of the Pentateuch, which at one period or another were assumed to have been blended together by an editor, who also added to these primitive codes the supposed later Book of Deuteronomy, which was alleged to have been compiled in the time of Josiah and to have been discovered by Ḥilḳiah. Now Josiah made war against the people in Samaria, and went up and destroyed the altar, i.e. the Temple.[1] Long before that time the Samaritan priest had returned from the Exile at the request of the colonists and had rebuilt their temple. It is necessary to point out that only the altar is mentioned as having been destroyed in Samaria; if the people were indeed foreign colonists who followed pagan worship, there would have been more than one altar in existence and Josiah could not have claimed any merit for having destroyed altars erected to heathen gods by strange peoples. The only altar for the destruction of which he could claim merit was one erected outside Jerusalem by his own kinsfolk who worshipped or claimed to worship the same God. If this be so, it would be more than passing strange that the Samaritans or Israelites who were living there should have accepted and incorporated into their Holy Writ a book which, as is now alleged, had only then been discovered or rather written in the time of Josiah himself, and which had made such an impression upon him when read, that he rent his clothes and showed signs of deep contrition.

But I do not wish to discuss these theories which give us neither the date, nor the age, nor form of the Pentateuch as we have it. A simple comparison with the Samaritan, especially with the Joshua, leads us to quite different conclusions. The Massoretic Book of Joshua is quoted by some of the oldest prophets, and its high antiquity has never been doubted.

We find in the Massoretic Bible an ancient sign wrongly called a Pasek, but more correctly a note line, which stands vertically between the words. In an excellent monograph, *The Note Line*

[1] 2 Kings xxiii. 15.

in Hebrew, Professor Kennedy has proved conclusively that this sign belongs to a period long before the introduction of the Massorah of vowels and accents, even before the Ķeri and Ketib, and that far from being an accent it serves a critical purpose; further that it belongs to the very beginnings of the activity usually connected with the scribes (pp. 10 and 19). He has examined exhaustively the manifold uses to which this ancient sign has been put, which by its simplicity and primitive origin lent itself to many diverse purposes. This fact alone proves its high antiquity, for as soon as other more complicated signs were invented its original meaning was entirely forgotten. If we hold fast to the results thus obtained, we see that this note line or Pasek has a critical value.

In preparing the new edition of the Book of Joshua, in which I am assisted by one of my sons and in which all the problems connected with its genuineness and antiquity will be fully discussed, I have made a discovery which I believe to be of momentous importance. It not only corroborates the results obtained by Professor Kennedy, but it amplifies them and strengthens them to an extent hitherto unsuspected. To put it briefly, we examined all the passages in the Massoretic text in which this line was found, and compared them with the corresponding portions preserved in the Samaritan. It may be noted here that only a number of chapters are found in the Samaritan which correspond to the Hebrew. In every one of these cases we found that wherever the note line occurred in the Massoretic text a word or passage differed in the Samaritan, though the latter often agreed with the LXX. This fact cannot be due to mere coincidence, but allows us a glimpse into the methods of the ancient editor of the Hebrew Bible; he must have compared the Hebrew with the Samaritan or, to put it differently, the authorized with the popular version; and whenever the passage differed he marked it, to emphasize to the subsequent copyist or reader that this reading was the correct one. It is like ' *sic* ', which is often inserted in model editions to show the reader that this is the proper form, without reference to the fact whether it be found correct or incorrect by others. This is the real beginning of that Massorah which ' put a hedge ' round the text, and by marginal notes and glosses directed the scribe and the reader to the fact that the form in which the respective word was found was the correct one and should be maintained even though it appeared strange or inexplicable.

Plate 14

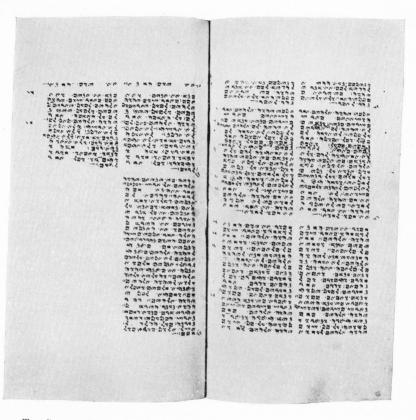

Ten Commandments in Parallel Bible : Jewish and Samaritan Recension

This alone is sufficient proof to establish the high antiquity and genuineness of that Samaritan Joshua, which, as already mentioned, will be corroborated to the full by the minute comparison of that recension with the Massoretic text and with the other versions. If, then, the editor of the Massoretic Joshua found it necessary and advisable to compare it with the Samaritan version, the book must have had in his eyes the value of a very old and authentic text of sufficient importance to take decided notice of it. Again, the Book of Joshua as found among the Samaritans differs in extent and arrangement from the Massoretic text, being smaller and in some details differently arranged. The Book of Joshua is no longer a sacred book to the Samaritans. It is neither treated with the same veneration as that accorded to the Pentateuch, nor is it the basis for any legal practices; it is simply the first book of their chronicles. Their history begins with the entry of Joshua into Canaan and is continued as far as possible down to the present day. And yet in spite of its simple secular character the Samaritans seem to have preserved it with very little change and alteration. A comparison with the LXX brings furthermore to light the very close approximation between the Greek and the Samaritan recensions. The Greek stands much closer to the Samaritan than the Hebrew, and in many passages the Samaritan corroborates some additional matter or variant found in the LXX. This is also the case when we compare generally the contents of the Samaritan Book of Joshua with the corresponding portion in Josephus' *Antiquities*. A peculiar parallelism runs through all three, which can only be explained if we assume for this Samaritan Book of Joshua the same high antiquity and popular character as that claimed for their Pentateuch. The Jews must have been fully acquainted with the Samaritan recension and vice versa; think of the disputations, of which we hear more in the Samaritan than in the Jewish literature, and which all turned round the authenticity of the text held by each section; a thorough acquaintance of the rival text was absolutely essential for such a dispute. Round it turned that disputation before Ptolemy which decided the fate of the Greek version, and, as already stated, the Rabbis at a later period were fully acquainted with the Samaritan text.

The Samaritans, for their part, not only knew the Pentateuch but all the historical Jewish writings. There is in existence in the Kinsha an old MS. on parchment, probably of the tenth century, which I have seen, containing the two recensions of the Pentateuch side by side, and a copy of it made by the late High Priest Aaron is now in my possession. In my MS. the differences between the one and the other are clearly marked, and a facsimile is given here. Besides many more codices there is one which contains a special treatise on the different readings between Samaritans and Jews, and all their writings on the Law refer constantly to the various readings. Finally at the end of the Book of Joshua and in another MS. in my possession, the author has preserved what I believe to be a slightly different recension of the first chapters of Judges, and refers to other historical books. Their very chronicles, with their constant references to Jewish history, prove their accurate knowledge of the Massoretic Hebrew Bible and more especially of the historical books of that recension.

There is now another section of the Samaritan Book of Joshua which must also be briefly dealt with since it leads us to a further problem. The division of the land among the tribes, and the boundaries granted to each, is described in the Samaritan Book of Joshua in a manner differing entirely from the very confused and elaborate description found in the Massoretic text. In the former it is a very brief, succinct narrative, in which the whole land is taken as a parallelogram with the Jordan as the boundary in the east and the sea in the west; the enumeration proceeds from south to north, one tribe succeeding another, and the portion for each tribe being bounded by the Jordan and the sea with one exception. Dan is described as having his portion in the south; his western boundary is the sea, while the eastern runs parallel to the western boundary of Benjamin, whose eastern boundary is the Jordan. This was the real historical position of the tribe of Dan down to the time of Samson and even at a later period, for only a portion of the tribe emigrated to the north and settled there.

If we now turn to Josephus' *Antiquities* (v. 1. 1, 22 (§§ 80 ff.)) we find precisely the same geographical division of the land, with some minor differences in the names of places. But a profound difference exists in the allocation of Dan; Josephus knew of the emigration towards the north and he put them in the north, thus representing the later tradition. Important as this fact may be for ascertaining the probable date of the Samaritan Joshua, the parallelism between the geographical disposition in the Samaritan Joshua and that found in the prophet Ezekiel is still more important (ch. xlvii. 15 ff.). Ezekiel takes precisely the

Plate 15

Book of Joshua: Division of Land

same boundaries for Palestine—on the east the Jordan, on the west the sea—and he divides the land into portions one after the other from north to south, following almost the same lines of demarcation as those found in the Samaritan Joshua, with the difference that as he has to place twelve tribes instead of nine and a half, he transfers Reuben and Gad to the south and adds Issachar also, whilst Dan is northernmost.[1] It is not likely that this similarity is a mere coincidence, and it is not at all improbable that the prophet Ezekiel repeated the division of the land actually made by Joshua when he delineated a repetition of that action.

One more point remains to be elucidated. As the Book of Joshua was not considered Holy Writ it was treated by the Samaritans with greater freedom, but on lines precisely similar to those followed in the Book of the Law. In the Pentateuch they only inserted small words and verses, but here they added larger portions. The Targumist held sway and the midrashic element which had grown up out of the later history (the first period of the Judges) was introduced wholesale. Here again the same distinguishing features can be recognized. On the one hand we have a pure Hebrew such as is found in the Bible in general, and on the other whole interpolations and additions which are written in the peculiar Hebrew which has been stigmatized as barbarous and already found in the interpolations of the Pentateuch. Whatever its character may be it was not an artificial invention, but must have been the language understood by those who used it, and they in their turn must have been more familiar with it than with the pure Hebrew; otherwise there is no reason why any of these interpolations should not have been couched in the same language as the rest. If a deliberate falsification had been intended this was the worst means to be employed, since it would be recognized at first glance as a strange interpolation introduced by a different hand. It must therefore be assumed that this was the popular language in use at the time when these changes and additions were made, at least in all the provinces of Samaria, and known and understood wherever Samaritans lived in the Diaspora. These interpolations therefore show the transition from the literary to the popular language, and from the Hebrew to the Aramaic. They occupy, as it were, a place on the border and have a character of their own which for that

---

[1] In the Appendix I am giving the portion of the Samaritan Joshua containing the geographical division.

reason need not be styled barbarous. Moreover, the tradition and knowledge of this language must have continued from very olden times down to the most recent.

A careful examination of the syntax and peculiar grammatical forms shows how closely the language of the last chapters of Ezekiel as well as some parallel expressions in Ezra, Nehemiah, and Chronicles correspond to the ' barbarisms' so characteristic of the Samaritan Pentateuch. We therefore have here the language of the period of the Exile, which of course did not originate then, but had found its way into literature by that time. It must have been the language used by the people a long while before that period, if the prophets and learned scribes became so deeply influenced by it that they used it in their own writings. As this, however, belongs to the problem connected with the Book of Joshua it is in that edition that these problems will be discussed in detail, and the parallelism shown between the Samaritan Hebrew and the popular Hebrew of the time of the Exile.

I will now turn to the literature which has grown out of the Bible through that peculiar midrashic interpretation to which reference has constantly been made here. The people were not satisfied with the mere text and desired to have fuller information concerning many aspects of Biblical history. As already mentioned, a large number of legends grew up among the Jews, and the same thing took place among the Samaritans. Here again the same parallelism can be observed, without, however, assuming the direct borrowing of one from the other. At the same time we are entering upon the origin of the Hellenistic literature. Unfortunately the latter has been preserved in a very fragmentary state ; still, sufficient has come down to us to enable us to deduce connexions and parallels which throw important light on the literature which grew up in that dim period known as the Post-Exilic.

I have dwelt on it and on the Bible itself at some length because the value to be attached to the Samaritan literature depends entirely upon a proper understanding and interpretation of these problems, and on an attempt at their solution. Here, the first to be mentioned is the Asatir Mosheh, or the ' Secrets of Moses', which belongs to that series of writings known as pseudepigraphic and apocryphal, which occupy so prominent a position during that period. It is a kind of legendary supplement to the Bible. The complete edition of this text discovered by me, which is to be published under the auspices of the Royal

Asiatic Society, will furnish all the material required for the elucidation of the question of its antiquity and importance. Here I must restrict myself to the results obtained after a careful examination of all the material available in the Jewish, Samaritan, Hellenistic, and other literatures. It is written in the Samaritan language, and contains the oldest traditions found in Eupolemos, Artaphanos, and Demetrios. Some of the older portions of the Sibylline Oracles (Book III) find their proper explanation through comparison with the Asatir, and, what is still more important, many of the legendary elements in Josephus' *Antiquities* find their source or parallels in this old Samaritan writing. In the main it agrees with these traditions, and yet it presents an independent character which shows it to be anterior to and probably the source of the forms preserved in the other writings just mentioned and not dependent on them. No one would admit that Josephus borrowed from the Samaritans; throughout his writings his bias against them is undisguised, and he misses no opportunity of saying something unfavourable about them. But if we find close parallels in the Asatir, the Palestinian Targum, and Josephus, we are justified in concluding that the Samaritan Asatir as well as the Palestinian Targum and Josephus go back to a more ancient source from which all had drawn, each one representing the legend or story in his own way, or amplifying the records of the Bible in his own peculiar manner. It would be difficult to determine the period to which that ancient source may belong; it is certainly much older than the Sibylline and the oldest of the Hellenistic writings, and if, as Frankel surmises, traces of a Targum can be shown in the LXX, the existence of such a Targum or popular elaborate commentary of the Bible written for the purpose of edification and use in the synagogues and schools must be of much greater antiquity than has hitherto been surmised. The period between the Return and that in which this literature comes to full light was not a vacuum, and if the Jews and Samaritans had been living in peace under the sway of the Persian kings for centuries, it is not difficult to suggest that much of that literature was created and developed under these favourable circumstances. It is quite possible that the first questions of an eschatological character may have been mooted at that time, for we already find in the Asatir the term set for the existence of the world, although the ideas of the Taheb are very vague and embryonic. We are told in that writing there will be a 'return' to a time and period of definite 'favour' after great troubles, and after a series of kings have arisen and fallen ; then the Jews will be converted to the belief of the Samaritans, recognizing the accuracy of the Samaritan tradition and the Samaritan Bible, and all will live henceforth in peace and happiness.   Reference is also made to the fire from which those are saved who have been buried within a certain distance of Mount Garizim, and certain divinities are mentioned, embodiments of the elements which were worshipped by Bileam. Thus we find in this very small treatise points of contact with many of the problems which later on acquired such great prominence.

Closely connected with this Asatir is the Molad Mosheh, or 'Birth of Moses', containing practically the same legend about the birth of Moses as that found in the Asatir, but greatly elaborated.   No date is given anywhere for the origin of that work, which in its structure and form reminds one very forcibly of some of the apocryphal gospels of the Nativity.   The form in which this book has been preserved seems to me to remind us of the writings of Markah of the third or fourth century c.e., if not earlier, who is universally recognized as the oldest liturgical poet and the most important writer of the Samaritans.   There is no service in which some of his poems are not recited, and poems are sometimes wrongly ascribed to him when the name of the real writer has been forgotten.   He wrote in the Samaritan language, and the great compilation of which he was the author is at the same time the greatest monument thus far preserved among the Samaritans.   It is of no small interest to add here briefly that in his style, and in the repetition of phrases in the hymn, he very closely resembles the Apocryphal Acts, especially of Thomas, which seems to show that Markah and the author of these Acts must have lived almost at the same time and followed similar principles.   This, of course, carries us back to the second century c.e.   His great work has been falsely described by all who have written about it as a commentary on Exodus.   It is, however, nothing of the kind, but a poem in a number of cantos on Moses, the Exodus, and the vicissitudes of the people during that period, finishing with the death of Moses.   This latter to a large extent resembles the description found in Josephus, though in a Samaritan MS. in my possession we find still another variant of the same theme which will appear together with the Asatir, and which is also of the same semi-apocalyptic character.

We see in Marḳaḥ a parallel to that great poem on Moses by Ezekiel,[1] the Hellenistic poet of whom fragments have been preserved by Eusebius.

It is difficult to say whether Ezekiel worked up an older Hebrew-Samaritan poem, or whether, following Greek example, he took his material and inspiration direct from the text of the Bible. It is, however, a remarkable coincidence that Marḳaḥ should have chosen the same material for his great epic poem, which in certain passages looks as if it were in the form of a drama. Angels appear praising God in precisely the way as we find them in Ezekiel, while the historical and geographical background is the same in both, and altogether both seem to have drawn their inspiration from a common source. It is not unlikely that Marḳaḥ and Ezekiel lived under the same legendary traditions, and that each of them worked them up in his own way, one as a drama and the other as an epic, both keeping strictly to the Biblical narrative, but each embellishing it according to his own genius. It looks, therefore, as if the first cantos of Marḳaḥ which have disappeared are represented by the Molad Mosheh, or else that the latter is the source from which Marḳaḥ has drawn.

The semi-legendary character of the Molad agrees with the same legendary character of the last chapter of Marḳaḥ, which is on the death of Moses. It is therefore not at all improbable that the first chapters were like the Molad Mosheh, especially as we find similar legends in Ezekiel and other Hellenistic writers as well as in the Jewish literature. Quippe seems to have proved quite satisfactorily that Ezekiel may have been a Samaritan. The whole problem of the Samaritan participation in Hellenistic literature will have to be carefully investigated in view of the fact that Samaria was more open to Greek influence than Judea. There was no Maccabean revolt and no complete break with Greek influence and Greek literature, while Galilee became the centre of numerous Greek settlements. It is therefore not at all improbable that Ezekiel should have written his drama in Greek, especially when we remember that other Samaritan authors like Cleodemus, Malchos, Pseudo-Artapanos, and others also contributed to Hellenistic literature.

There also exists among the Samaritans a collection of Biblical legends of which nothing has hitherto been known. It is arranged in the form of questions and answers and contains

---

[1] v. Stählin, *Griechische Literatur*, pp. 607 ff.

a mass of similar traditions. If, as I have endeavoured to show throughout these lectures, the Samaritan traditions be independent of the Jewish, though both may have a common origin, having developed independently, and if they be much older than any of the writings of the Christian and Mohammedan periods, the date of the compilation in which any of these legends or stories may be found among the Samaritans is of no consequence in establishing their antiquity. The very isolation in which the Samaritans lived, cut off as they were from the rest of the world, was the cause of their intact preservation throughout the ages. They cannot be new, and it is only a question of determining how old they can be. If, therefore, Markaḥ of the third or fourth century should have already developed some of these traditions in his own way, and if we find them in other writings among both Jews and Samaritans, the presumption is that they are very old and go back at least a few centuries before the common era. Moreover, we find Ezekiel and Theodotos using the same material, both of whom are anterior to the second century B.C.E., and probably Kleodemos (Malchos) as well. The Samaritans must have been in possession of these traditions from very early times, for they could not possibly have obtained them from later sources, as all traces of these traditions had by then disappeared, while the ancient Greek literature was certainly unknown to them.

Besides these writings in the vernacular, the Samaritans, like the Jews, have a Targum, a literal translation of the text of the Pentateuch. I have been able to discover two recensions which differ slightly from one another in the words used and in some details of translation. It has been alleged that the Samaritan Targum agrees to a large extent with the Jewish Targum ascribed to Onkelos. This is not the place to discuss the origin of or the form in which the latter is now extant; it is, however, not Palestinian but Babylonian, and in its primitive state probably went back to the school of Aḳiba, under whose direction the proselyte Aquilas also made a new Greek translation, which differed in many ways from the LXX. This was the attempt to substitute a literal translation of the textus receptus for a text which differed from the Hebrew verity by those additions and changes often referred to, which are found in the Greek and Samaritan. The new Greek translation was produced against the current LXX, not, as has hitherto been surmised, because the latter had become the Bible of the Christians. At that time the Christian sect was of no consequence, and no one among the

Jews would have paid any attention to the fact that the Gentile Christians had accepted the Greek text of the Bible as their sacred Scripture. This, in fact, was not the case, as is shown by the work of Origenes, who was anxious to obtain a correct text, as well as by the activity of Jerome, who always went back to the Hebrew original. Aḳiba's opposition to the old Greek version was the same as was the opposition of the scribes to the contaminated or popular version. In the same way the Aramaic Targum was an attempt to eliminate the very elaborate Targum in the vernacular, which was full of legendary matter and of legal interpretations which had either become obsolete or had been contradicted by the later school of sages. Moreover, the homily had taken the place of the Targum, and the only thing now required for the people was a simple literal translation of the text. Even here various tendencies manifested themselves, like the avoidance of anthropomorphisms and other allegorical translations of poetical passages.

The original Aramaic translation was subjected to revision in the Babylonian schools, with the result that the Targum Onkelos differs somewhat in language and tendency from the old Palestinian Targum. But its principal object was and remained for centuries to be read with the Hebrew text as a commentary and explanation for the masses.

As mentioned before the Samaritans have a similar Targum, and from the information which I have been able to gather from them, the practice of reading the Targum together with the original Hebrew during the service was continued until a couple of centuries ago. This was the privilege of a special family or specially appointed man called the ' Haftawi ', but as the people have forgotten Aramaic and now only speak Arabic, it has been discontinued. So popular was this translation that in time Arabic words were substituted for older Aramaic words which had become obsolete or unintelligible ; in the course of centuries these Arabic words were so mutilated and transformed that many scholars could not trace their origin and believed them to be of Kuthean or another ancient unknown origin. It was the merit of Kohn[1] to have unravelled the mystery and to have shown that they were merely corrupt forms of Arabic words. But there is not the slightest doubt that the Targum is much older than Marḳaḥ, and it is a most important monument of the Samaritan language.

[1] Kohn, S., *Zur Sprache, Literatur u. Dogmatik der Samaritaner*, Leipzig, 1876, pp. 96 ff.

It is, in fact, believed to be coeval with the original Jewish Targum. This, of course, creates the new problem of the relation between the two. That the Samaritans should have borrowed from the Jews is just as unlikely as the reverse, and from the actual state of the Samaritan Targum it is not easy to determine whether it represents an older form, whilst the Jewish Targum is a later modification of a more ancient form. The alleged similarity, however, is only superficial; since both aim at a literal translation, the translation must be similar. In many essential points they differ from one another, especially in those characteristic features which are typical of the Onkelos. The Samaritan is a different translation and represents the Samaritan recension only. It is difficult to determine its date, and as it is independent of the Onkelos it may be of much higher antiquity than is generally assumed. The date hitherto assigned to it is the second century, though no reason has been given. In point of fact, however, no date has yet been determined for any of the Targumim.

The next chapter in the history of the Samaritan literature is occupied by the liturgy, of which a brief sketch may now be given. It is not intended to describe the contents of each of the twelve volumes which contain the liturgy for the year, but merely to give the outlines of some of the principal features which belong to higher antiquity. The framework of the liturgy has already been described, a number of prayers have been mentioned and their character defined, the recitation of passages from the Bible, the first chapter of Genesis single verses, and a florilegium (Ḳatef); these were introduced by a confession of faith which contains the principal doctrines, and were closed by the priestly blessing. Mention has also been made of the Biblical lessons which follow the seasons of the year. Prayers are recited on special occasions, like birth, circumcision, weddings, and death, all of which are more or less akin to the practices of the Jews, and resemble those known to have existed in the time of the Temple. A number of hymns are added to these prayers, some of which are very old. The time when hymns were introduced into the service is a question which has not yet been answered either for Jews or Samaritans; but in both cases they probably followed the practice of the Temples of Jerusalem and Sichem; hymns, no doubt, accompanied prayers of the primitive Christians, while the practices of other sects show that hymns formed an essential portion of the Divine service. The oldest among the Samaritan are probably those ascribed to Moses, Joshua, and the messengers; in fact all that are written in the Samaritan language probably belong to the oldest period. Many of these have alphabetical acrostics, which are well known from Biblical psalms; while an attempt at rhythm and rhyme is to be found even in the oldest. They are often divided into stanzas of an equal number of lines, and are recited in an antiphonal manner. The oldest MS. of the Samaritan prayers is the MS. of the thirteenth century, 1265, in the British Museum. In this codex we find that the old Samaritan prayers have already been translated into Arabic. Most, if not all, of the oldest prayers and hymns have been gathered together in the Kenosh or collection, and that Kenosh forms the stem upon which the other prayers were grafted later on. Among the oldest hymn-writers mention may be made of Amram Dara and of course of Markaḥ, both of whom are believed to have flourished in the third or fourth century, but may be earlier. So popular did their works become that, as already mentioned, anonymous poems were often indiscriminately ascribed to Markaḥ, whilst those called Duran were ascribed to Dara. It would be of interest to compare the form and contents of these ancient Samaritan hymns with the oldest Syriac ones, since they differ completely from the hymns of Jewish poets, although very few ancient hymns have been preserved in the Jewish literature. They were not considered essential to the service, and almost each generation and each great poet contributed his quota; in time they became so numerous that selections had to be made, and the later ones often supplanted the older. The same has happened to the Samaritans. The character of the Samaritan hymns is almost always one of morbid consciousness of sinfulness. The revival which took place in the fourteenth century only marks a new stage in the production of poems which were destined to supplant the older ones.

Many factors seem to have contributed to what seems now to have been a poetic and literary revival. In the first place the Samaritans enjoyed great freedom at that period, and then the influx of the vigorous element of Samaritans from Damascus and other parts stirred the sluggish minds of the people of Sichem. Their interests widened a little, especially during the time of the High Priests Pineḥas and Abisha, who by their own productions and by the impulse which they gave stimulated the Samaritans to fresh literary output. The latter had forgotten their own old Aramaic language to such an extent that, as already remarked, most of the ancient prayers had been translated into Arabic. Nothing really new was produced, but as the people no longer understood how to use the old Samaritan Aramaic properly, the writers from that period downwards mostly used Hebrew ; they were to a large extent familiar with the language of the Pentateuch, and must unquestionably have possessed not only the Hebrew recension of the Book of Joshua, but many chronicles and other compositions as well, which gave them the vocabulary and style which we find in the poems of Pineḥas, Abisha, and their successors. The subject-matter, however, was precisely the same as that found in the oldest writings. The legendary history of Moses, the paraphrase of the Creation, the allusions to the Taheb, and the everlasting repetition of confession of sin with the longing hope for the return of the Divine favour are the staple elements of these new liturgical hymns. But they greatly enriched the old smaller form of prayer, with the result that no less than twelve volumes are barely sufficient to contain all the hymns, poems, and prayers used by the Samaritans. Actually only portions of the poems recited are introduced, for the longer ones are divided up into smaller sections, and as they are often acrostichic, the reference to the initial letter is sufficient to indicate the portion to be inserted on one or another occasion. It must be repeated, however, that though the whole is of a stereotyped character, it shows no trace of any outside influence, neither Christian, Mohammedan, nor any other ; nor can the remotest parallelism be traced between the Samaritan liturgy and that of the Karaites. One point more must be added, namely, that the historical element is often very prominent in the liturgical hymns of this revival period. Many poets arose from the fourteenth century onwards, and in modern times some of the Samaritans, among them the High Priests Tabyah, Amram, as well as Pineḥas and many members of the Danafite family, have left a considerable number of hymns, which are used on special occasions. Cowley's Samaritan Liturgy is the most complete of its kind, far superseding in richness of material and accuracy of reproduction all previous publications, including that of Heidenheim. It is now for the scholar interested in this matter to examine this vast material more closely, and to draw from it all the conclusions possible bearing on historical, linguistic, poetic, and dogmatic problems. One thing, however, is certain : the latest shows no progress over the oldest, with the slight difference that in

modern times there are recrudescences of a better knowledge and
a freer use of the old Samaritan language in the liturgy.

The mystical literature is closely connected with the liturgy,
although not outwardly so, for mystical elements are sometimes
introduced into the prayers, or rather forms of prayer are used
for mystical and magical purposes. The formulas are always pro-
pitiatory or prophylactic, and the prayers become an amulet. I
have dealt with this literature at great length in my edition of
the Samaritan Phylacteries,[1] and in my previous lecture I have
endeavoured to trace the origin and rise of mysticism among
the Samaritans. It is as old as any that can be traced in
Jewish and non-Jewish magical or mystical literature, when
special use has been made of the text of the Bible. As
shown before, all these theoretical speculations turn round the
Tetragrammaton, the permutations and combinations of the Holy
Names of God, and the value attached to the alphabet as figures
and ciphers, all of which agree and yet disagree with the theory
and practice of the Jewish Ḳabbalah. In both we not only find
abstract speculations, but also their practical application in the
form of amulets, phylacteries, Ḳameot, &c. The Samaritans call
such a phylactery Shem Hamitfaresh, which corresponds to the
Jewish Shem Hameforash, concerning the Divine Name and its
pronunciation and permutation. The Samaritans themselves
have evolved a peculiar kind of phylactery, which, as shown elsewhere by me, must belong at latest to the first century, if it is not
older ; moreover, it contains the key to the formula of the Magical
Papyri and other Greek and Latin incantations and charms. It
agrees in its general form with some of the oldest Samaritan
inscriptions, but it rests upon the exclusive use of verses and
words from the Bible. At the time of its compilation the
Samaritan Pentateuch must already have been divided into small
sections or Ḳiṣṣim, and the Bible itself must have assumed such
a character of holiness that the mere reference to or the repetition of a verse from the Bible, written on a piece of parchment,
was sufficient to give to the wearer of it the much-desired protection against all kinds of evil ; the Name of God is invoked in
every possible form, and the whole symmetrically disposed so as
to form a well-thought-out phylacteric document. The mystical
problems, however, were not confined to these phylacteries or
amulets, for we already find permutations of the Divine Name in

---

[1] Proceedings of the Society of Biblical Archaeology, March 1915–Feb. 1917.

the Asatir, which thus carries us back to the second or third century B.C.E. It is fully developed in Markaḥ's epic poem, while the very same speculations, permutations, and changes occur in the prayers of Abisha of the fourteenth century. Abraham Ḳabaṣi, one of the great leaders of the Samaritans, who was originally from Damascus, compiled a commentary in Arabic on Deut. xxxii. 2–3, and devoted a chapter to the explanation and interpretation of the Ineffable Name of God. It would be easy to find traces throughout the literature testifying to the existence of fully developed mystical speculations and magical practices among the Samaritans.

Here again the same parallelism can be observed. The Samaritans use the same verses from the Bible, especially Exod. xiv. 19–21, as those which played such a prominent role in the ḳabbalistic speculations of the Jews, with their whole system of permutations and substitution of letters. They all seem to belong to a period before the first century, up to which time both Jews and Samaritans worked on the same common tradition. It was then that the Samaritans struck a different line in the use of Ḳiṣṣim, the initial letters and other details, which they afterwards elaborated independently.

Very little if anything has been preserved in its original form concerning the Oral Law and its practices. As a rule, these traditions are only written down when the responsible men begin to realize the danger of their being forgotten. As long as they are living and thriving, no one thinks of writing them down; it was in fact forbidden among the Jews to write down the Oral Law so that it might not obtain a definite fixed character; its fluidity had to be retained so long as the people were still practising it freely. But when, either through persecution or else through profound changes in the political or social life, the people began to turn away, then, and with difficulty, permission was granted to write down in a definite form the legal practices then in use. Thus the Mishnah arose among the Jews. Whether such a book was ever compiled among the Samaritans must remain an open question. But they must certainly have written down those points in which their practices differed from those of the Jews, together with the reason why they differed and the justification of those differences from the text of the Samaritan Pentateuch. The various polemics in which they were engaged must have forced them to such a course, and we therefore find full descriptions of these practices in their oldest

Arabic compilations which were destined for the use of the people. There is no reason to believe that they changed in the course of centuries ; what was sacred to them in olden times as a religious duty and practice was zealously guarded against change or contamination, for their very existence depended upon rigorously maintaining the religious practices in which they were born.

I must confine myself henceforth to a brief delineation of the Samaritan literature preserved chiefly in the Arabic language, for a fuller description of it, as well as of the influence on Islam exercised by the Samaritans, will be found in the article on Samaritan Arabic Literature which is now appearing in the pages of the *Encyclopaedia of Islam*. Here I can only deal with it in a summary manner, merely selecting the chief monuments.

One of the oldest writings dealing with these practices is the Sefer al-Ṭabaḥ, which may mean 'The Book of Slaughtering', or 'The Book of the Cook' (according to legal prescriptions), and which is ascribed to Abul Hassan al-Ṣuri, who in all probability belongs to the eleventh century. A brief summary of part of its contents will best describe the character of this compilation. It consists of seventy-seven chapters, some larger, some smaller, all comparatively short, which are strung together without any connexion, without any system, and without any order. The book looks more like a collection of notes haphazardly put together. The author does not explain anything, but simply jots down what evidently seemed to strike his fancy at the moment ; he also seems to have put down the practices as known to him, which in all probability he took from older writings. Compilations in the Samaritan language must have existed long before for the guidance of the people, but, like all the authors who have written since that time, he merely translates or paraphrases the older writings in the language then better known to the people. In this collection we find everything with which I have been dealing hitherto—traditional practices, Oral Law, eschatological problems ; polemics against Jews, Christians, Karaites, and Mohammedans ; the traditions about the Second Kingdom and the Taheb ; the allegorical interpretation of the last chapters of Deuteronomy, and similar matter of a mystic or legal character. He writes about the privileges of the priesthood, the accuracy of the pedigree of the Samaritan priests being the true descendants from Pineḥas as against the claim of the Jews, the Ten Commandments, the laws of slaughter, the clean and unclean animals, on the punishment by fire, the Last Judgement, a very detailed description of the service and the sacrifice of the Pasaḥ, marriage laws, the calendar as against those of the Jews and Karaites, on the observance of the festivals, divorce, the choice of the messenger, and the law forbidding the additions or diminutions of the Torah. Thus far the contents of this work.

Before mentioning other books on Laws, I would add that the Samaritans, like all other Oriental writers, did not hesitate to copy the older writings and then circulate them as their own. This was not considered plagiarism, inasmuch as it was a universal custom, and every one knew that the material contained in such compilations could not be the original work of the author, but merely the presentation of old material in a new form. This explains the almost complete uniformity of contents found in all these writings.

An exception must, however, be made of the work of Jusuf al-Askari, called Al-Kafi. He happily gave the year 1042 as the year in which he wrote his book, which consists of thirty-six chapters. It is a curious fact that Jusuf never mentions the work of Hassan nor vice versa; they evidently did not know of one another at the time when they wrote, and it is therefore very difficult to decide which is the earlier and which the later. The probability is, however, that Hassan lived before the time of Jusuf.

In accordance with the above remarks the contents of the two books are in many points very similar, despite the fact that in the Kafi the matter is better arranged and treated in a more systematic manner. This is due to the skill of the author, and as one does not seem to know the other, the only conclusion to be drawn is that both have taken their material from an older source common to both. Here we have an example of how the same process has been continued throughout the Samaritan literature.

The book begins with a panegyric on the excellence of the choice of the priesthood, and then describes the order of washing, priestly purity, prayer, clean and unclean animals, birds and fishes, i. e. fit and unfit for food, skin diseases, purification, pilgrimage, the Nazarite, marriage, divorce, purchase of slaves, pledges, interest, murder, dedication, slaughter, and the Sabbath. In this compilation we have a plain and simple code without any polemics or eschatology.

In the Paris library there is another Arabic compilation called

Plate 16

Picture of leading Samaritans from second half of the nineteenth century

the Book of Laws; it may, however, be identical with or the origin and source of a more recent compilation, i. e. the Hillukh, which contains the laws of the Samaritans, and of which the following is a summary. It is arranged systematically, carefully worked out, all the points of difference are very clearly given, and in every way it is the best representative of Samaritan traditions and practices. Although the copy in my possession is a modern one in Arabic and Samaritan and a modern writer may claim to be the author, I am still inclined to believe that it dates from a much older time.

The first chapter contains a brief sketch of the history of the Samaritans, and Aleppo, Damascus, Egypt, and Gaza are mentioned as places where they are still dwelling. It is known, however, that the Samaritans had disappeared from most of these places at least two or three centuries ago. The only reference to Samaritans in Aleppo which I can trace is in an Arabic translation of the Pentateuch of 1328; at the time of Scaliger at the end of the sixteenth century, Samaritans were only to be found in Damascus, Cairo, and Gaza outside Nablus, and according to Della Valle they had been reduced to a handful in Damascus. The author of this compilation, however, knows of Samaritan communities in Aleppo, so that this therefore must refer to a time about the middle of the sixteenth, or latest, beginning of the seventeenth century. There was no reason, if the author lived recently, to refer to communities long ago extinct.

I have prepared a critical edition with an English translation, because it is, I repeat, the best summary of Samaritan faith and practice. Moreover, it contains the differences between Jews and Samaritans together with the reasons for these differences, which are based on the readings of the Bible. The book finishes with a long chapter on death, punishment, and resurrection.

Throughout the Samaritan literature reference is constantly made to these eschatological problems, and I have since discovered among them the existence of a very elaborate compilation called Yom al-Din, written in Arabic and ascribed to Pineḥas (d. 1898), in which the whole of the Samaritan doctrine is very fully and carefully set out with all possible details. It of course rests upon old traditions, and if it really be a new compilation then it is nothing more than a summary of what has been the constant belief of the Samaritans from very ancient times. The Samaritan version of this book has also been prepared by me for publication.

Reference may also be made to the polemical anti-Jewish writings of Munadja of the twelfth century, which are of interest inasmuch as they corroborate the contents of the other Samaritan writings dealing with the same subject, and show how little new has been added in the course of centuries. The antagonism to Jewish principles is just as strong to-day as it was in olden times.

If we pass over to another section of the literature, a glance may be cast at the rudiments of grammatical knowledge found in one of the old writings of the eleventh century, the author of which shows knowledge of the whole Massoretic Hebrew Bible. More interesting, however, are the Hebrew-Arabic glossaries made by the Samaritans, for their value consists in the insight which they afford us into the manner in which the Samaritans understood the Hebrew language. It must be remembered that our knowledge of Hebrew rests upon one single tradition only; it is the Jewish tradition alone which is reflected in the various translations, Greek, Aramaic, and Latin, and from it we have derived all our knowledge and understanding of the Hebrew language. There is, however, a possibility that in one point or another a different meaning may have been attached to words of the Pentateuch whose use was not frequent. The Samaritans for their part, no doubt, must have tried to understand the Bible, and it is therefore of no small importance both from a philological and exegetical view to learn their interpretation of the sacred Scripture. Herein also lies the value of the few commentaries possessed by the Samaritans, which are very voluminous, and contain a mass of old traditions not found elsewhere. There is a short commentary to the whole of the Pentateuch ascribed to Tabyah or Gazal ibn Surur of the thirteenth century; then a separate one on Genesis by Meshalma of the end of the seventeenth century, which was afterwards rewritten and completed by Ibrahim the Danafite; one on Exodus by Tabyah ibn Doweik, completed by others. These are now preserved in Arabic only, but they are not the work of one man nor of one age. Portions of the Bible have also been commented, such as the song of Moses, the blessings of Jacob, and the prophecy of Bileam by Abu Said. Those on Genesis and Exodus, which I have carefully examined, contain a mass of ancient legendary matter which they could not have derived from the Jews in the form in which we find them, and which differ completely from similar legends found in the pseudepigraphic literature and in the Arabic traditions. If found in the latter, they are unquestionably borrowed from the Samaritans and Jews, and not vice versa. Much information can still be gathered from them, and they are of the highest interest from every point of view ; nothing, however, has hitherto been done towards their publication or translation. In these commentaries we see the old exegesis standing fully revealed, for the authors often state that what they say or write is in accordance with the traditions which have been handed down from their sages in the past. With the exception of Geiger,[1] who just examined one, no detailed study has been made of their contents, although these commentaries are really a mine of information which has not yet been quarried. Here lies the work for the future.

Last, but not least, a few words may be said about the Samaritan historical literature. Here again the same practice prevailed. The later writer simply copied or introduced into his work the complete text of the preceding author. To a certain extent this was also the practice of the medieval chroniclers of the Western world. They simply incorporated the work of their predecessors verbatim, and then added the new portion without thereby thinking that they were committing any wrong or plagiarism. They took it for granted that the older portion belonged to an older author, and that no one would be deceived by finding older material in a new chronicle. The oldest Samaritan chronicle thus preserved is the Chain of Priests, published by me in the *J. R. A. S.*, April 1909, which is a bald enumeration of priests with very few notes. All the High Priests from Adam are mentioned, and the list is continued down to the days of the late High Priest Jacob, the son of Aaron. Adam of course is considered as the first High Priest. In my edition the three eras used by the Samaritans are given, so that it is possible to determine more or less accurately the time of each of the High Priests mentioned therein. I have already drawn attention to the fact that the Samaritans, like the Jews, were in possession of such genealogical lists, since they were of the utmost importance in support of their claims. Use was made of them in the dispute before Ptolemy, and no doubt also in the time of Ezra and Nehemiah, as mentioned in my first lecture, and these lists have always been most carefully preserved. In the Ṭabaḥ reference is made to the dispute between Jews and Samaritans on the accuracy of this genealogy or descent. Later, in the tenth or twelfth century, this

---

[1] *Z. D. M. G.*, vol. xxii, 1868, pp. 528 ff.

Shelshelah, or 'Chain', was further elaborated into the Tolidah ; more historical notes were added, and the old Shelshelah greatly enlarged.   Chronicles of an elaborate character must have existed, for their real history begins with the Book of Joshua, which contains a description of the events since the time of Joshua and is continued down to a more recent period.   Later, this ancient chronicle, together with other old Samaritan works, was also translated and paraphrased into Arabic at some time in the twelfth or thirteenth century, and all the subsequent Samaritan chronicles in Arabic begin with this paraphrase called the Book of Joshua.

These paraphrases were afterwards the starting-point for the great chronicle of Abul Fath, which was due to the inspiration of the same priests, Pinehas and Eleazar, who were instrumental in bringing about the whole revival.   It may be mentioned here that curiously enough the Jews lack any real book of Chronicles down to the same period.   The old genealogies were preserved as far as they were contained in Holy Writ.   The High Priests had special lists, for Josephus refers to them explicitly although he does not reproduce them ; these references are, however, sufficient to prove their existence.   With the disappearance of the priests and their interest in the genealogy, these ancient lists disappeared also, and it was not until the second century that R. Jose is supposed to have compiled the Seder Olam, a kind of Biblical chronology on the data given in the Bible.   But from the close of the Biblical period down to the ninth century nothing is known of an historical book among the Jews.   With the extinction of the political life there was nothing to recount, and the subsequent history of the Jews is merely the history of the scholars, a kind of Tolidah.

The Samaritans were more concentrated and could describe the vicissitudes through which they had passed during the centuries, and the sufferings to which they had been exposed, especially in Palestine.   The Jews were scattered over the whole of the known world, and could therefore not write such a history then, and its beginnings belong to the much later period of the fifteenth century.

In 1355 Abul Fath specifically states in his introduction that he made use of a number of old chronicles, some in Arabic and some in Samaritan or Hebrew, and he carries the history from Adam down to his own time.   His work was continued by others, mostly anonymous writers, who did not hesitate to embody Abul Fath's chronicle in their own compilations, just as Abul Faṭḥ had compiled his own by excerpting more ancient chronicles. Some were satisfied to continue the history where Abul Faṭḥ had left it, but others recast it and made of it a much more elaborate compilation called the Tarikh. Two such different compilations of uncertain date and authorship are now in my possession, of which one is in Arabic and the other in Samaritan, but none of them seems to be known. They often differ in the representation of facts and in the elaboration of details, and one has carried the history of Abul Faṭḥ down to the present day. We therefore have a continuous descriptive history of the Samaritans, more especially of those dwelling in Nablus. One continuation of the work of Abul Faṭḥ is claimed by Jacob, the late High Priest, while the Tarikh is ascribed first to Tabyah and then to Pineḥas.

I have thus reached the end of the sketch of the history of the literature and life of the Samaritans as far as it can be traced from the oldest period down to our own days, and as far as it bears on the subject before us. Their history is tragic, and it is not an easy matter to reconstruct their spiritual life, their inner development, nor the causes which have contributed to the decay and fossilization of the old tradition. They had no impulses from without and no driving force from within which could compel them to productivity. Harassed on all sides, they were satisfied to remain on the defensive and to preserve the little that had been handed down to them from their fathers. Dwindling in numbers, they lost heart, and their outlook became more and more circumscribed. Yet they clung with desperate hope to their old sanctuary and to the old faith. They have followed in their development a course parallel to that of the Jews, and if we were able to follow the stream to its primitive source, which lies far back in hoar antiquity, we might be able to acquire a different interpretation of many of the phenomena hitherto known through Jewish tradition only. Even now, much that seems incomplete becomes completed, many incoherent details become coherent, much that has been obscure becomes clear, and we learn to understand much better many of the allusions in Holy Writ, together with some of the forces which moulded the life of the Jews during those centuries which we only know through the pages of the Bible. Again, many of the problems connected with the history of the Bible may now be solved in the light of these investigations, and the history of the Bible itself may perhaps be placed on a basis free from many of the hypotheses which now hold sway. A better appreciation of the origin of the LXX, of the sources of the Hellenistic literature, and the traditions embodied in Josephus may be won from the pages of the Samaritan literature, while the gain for the history of the development of the Oral Law is immeasurable. What is set forth briefly here rests upon a careful study of all the writings still in existence among the Samaritans; no important work, nay not even a smaller work, has been passed over; and these have been studied from within, entering into the very spirit of the Samaritan literature and tradition. I venture to think, therefore, that a better perspective has been obtained and wider conclusions have been drawn from the rich material which has now been utilized for the first time.

The road to the top of Mount Garizim is strewn with ruins which testify to the ancient glory and show the broken stones of the old Temple. The sun of the Samaritans is setting fast, and I consider myself fortunate that it has been granted to me to catch a few of the rays which still light up the holy Mount Garizim.

Plate 17

Present High Priest and other Samaritans

APPENDIX I

SAMARITAN CORRESPONDENCE

Anent Correspondence of the Samaritans with European scholars.

I AM endeavouring to supplement and complete the information about the correspondence which ensued between European scholars and the Samaritans. Much has been written about it, for up to comparatively recent times it has been the only source from which the scholars of the West were able to draw their information about the faith and the practices of the Samaritans. Scanty as that material was, still it proved of great value. It revived the interest in the Samaritans, whose existence had been forgotten for many centuries, and it had almost as a direct consequence the discovery of the Samaritan recension of the Hebrew Pentateuch as well as of the Samaritan Targum by Della Valle. An abstract of his book, giving the full report of his discovery, appears here farther on as Appendix II in the Italian original as well as in an English translation.

I do not intend giving here a detailed account of that correspondence found principally in the great work of Sylvestre de Sacy and ably summarized by Montgomery in his book on the Samaritans. The first letter, however, which has obtained such a very wide circulation was that received by Huntington, and copies of the letters received by him passed from hand to hand, transcribed in Hebrew characters, and often translated into Latin, French (Basnage), and English.[1] One of such copies is now in the British Museum, of which more later on. Now to this some one has added a copy of the letter sent by Huntington to Pocock, giving his own narrative of the discovery which he made. I have not been able to trace the original source of this covering letter. It is written in a very fine hand at the end of the seventeenth or in the beginning of the eighteenth century, in very minute characters, and as this copy has seen much service and is in a somewhat thumbed condition the reading is anything but easy. Yet it is of such importance that I have made a transcript which I believe is as faithful as can be done, and I am publishing it here as far as I believe for the first time. It reads as follows:

Mr. Huntington's letter to Dr. Pocock.

At Nablouse formerly Sechem, I enquired after the Samaritans who live only in that place scarce 30 families in all and met with a more

[1] A copy of the English version of this letter I owe to the kindness of Sir Herman Gollancz.

intelligent person than ordinary who hearing me enquire after their customs and religions and holy Mount Garizim, et cetera, was apprehensive I must know something now of them and upon my offer (? wish) to read a letter of their character and language concluded I could not possibly have it but from some (? ; indistinct) of their brethren hereupon he brings 4 or 5 (one who came out of Portugal) and they make further enquiries and tryall of w^t (what) I knew (con)cerning their brethren (for by this time they were undoubtedly such) in the (? my) country. And we all of us using the word Hebrew w^ch (which) they arrogate to themselves and that of Israelites where they make the name of Jew to be contradistinct to those of their profession, we mistoke one another so long till at last they would not be prevailed upon that twas a mistake—so that I was obliged to continue it. And upon this account they gave an old Hebrew Samaritan Pentateuch to send to those in England to see it whether it agreed with their Law and I desired one more perfect (which they would not part with) at last that they would write an exact relation of their faith and worship by which the others might gather whether or no they were of one and the same opinion. This they did very accurately according to direction sent two copies to me to Jerusalem the beginning of 7 Ber last which I first looked upon about a month since. They begin with the acknowledgment of the true God and his general names then their Law given by Moses whom they much reverence and also Eldard & Modad, Joshuah the son of Nun and Phinehas (the last of their Prophets). This Phinehas they told me, wrote an history which they now have in Arabic though I could not get a sight of it and his son Abisha they write transcribed a copy of the Law (which they now have) in the 13th year of their possession of the land of Canaan. Then they speak of their Sabbath and Solemn feasts and how they are observed in contradistinction to the Jews, of their computation and reckoning and are mighty serious for an answer and to receive a satisfactory letter from you—(with some of their Number if it might be) but by no means to be sent by a Jew because they are all their enemies so eternal is the old feud betwixt them. The first of these copies designed for England is by a man of war which will depart about 40 days hence the other shall with all possible speed be despatched by the first of the merchant ships. I have sent this intelligence before hand that I might the sooner hear what speciality to enquire further after and how to improve this occasion and whether I am not to disabuse them (for 'tis a cause of confidence) which possibly may be best done from England and whether any advantage may accrew to Xty (Christianity) from this (?) way and nature of it. To personate their brethren will undoubtedly gain from them what they are able to impart, but I think neither religion nor learning mt. (might) allow of any such helps. Pious friends (?) may have the approbation of your polititian but hardly of the honest man. I would have payed them for their law and have since ordered this satisfaction for anything they shall further send and withall acquainted had not yet received their history, but would by your first opportunity, accordingly they should hear further from you (?) about . or . weeks.

This letter speaks for itself.

It is of unquestionable interest to find that the correspondent of Huntington was no one else than the famous Orientalist of Oxford. The success of Scaliger was to yield still greater results than he had anticipated. Once the Samaritans having been discovered others would follow and amplify the first results achieved. This covering letter of Huntington, which as far as I am aware has never yet been published, throws a flood of light on many points connected with the Huntington letters which have hitherto remained obscure. It explains the mistake of the Samaritans who were unconsciously led to believe in the existence of large Samaritan colonies in the West. According to their chronicles large numbers of Samaritans have from time to time been led away captive into strange and distant lands. So more especially under the Byzantine rule. These were to come back at the appointed time when the Rahuta would succeed to the present Fanuta and the Taheb would lead the released captives back to the land of Promise and to the Holy Mountain. The Samaritans now call themselves consistently Israelites in sharp contradistinction to the Yahudayim. Huntington spoke to his Samaritan interlocutors also of Israelites, and as he was able to read their script, what further proof was needed to convince them of the existence of their brethren in foreign lands? They knew from their intercourse with the real Jews that the latter did not know the Samaritan alphabet and did not call themselves Israelites. Hence the misunderstanding which Huntington could not correct. He did not know of the strong belief in the existence of Samaritans elsewhere which formed part of the creed and hope of the Samaritans. He finally acquiesced in that pious fraud although he realized that it was a fraud. But, and therein lies to my mind an additional important point in the details given by this letter, Huntington himself already hints at the possibility of taking advantage of that misconception and fraud for proselytizing purposes. He feels that it would not be quite a proper moral action, still it may be used as a means for the conversion of the Samaritans. The subsequent correspondence which led to its apparent drying up, and for which Marshall was then solely responsible, turns out now to have been merely an attempt at putting into practice the very suggestion made by Huntington himself. It fell in England on fertile ground, but it failed in the result which was expected.

M

Incidentally we also learn from this letter the way in which the Samaritan original travelled in order to reach England. It was carried by mail in the charge of a person to whom it had been handed over directly, and this explains also the duplicate and triplicate for such missives. They were sent in more than one copy lest one or the other be lost in the transit. Such letters were entrusted to envoys who charged themselves with the regular transmission. It is noteworthy that they did not object to making use of Jews for such purposes, especially in the correspondence with Ludolf, of which more anon, although they distrusted them, and when they were sure of another way of sending the letter they did not conceal the old inveterate distrust and hatred.

The practice, however, of writing letters in two or more copies for fear that the one might be lost on the way explains the discrepancies observed in such copies when they reached Europe, as a good many have done. Here they were transliterated and circulated among the band of international scholars deeply interested in that literature. It was the period of the great Hebraists, and their appetite had been keenly whetted by the sparse information in the letters to Scaliger, of which by then not one had yet appeared in print. They were accessible only in writing. De Sacy, who had obtained the copies both in the Samaritan as well as in the Hebrew script, the latter being copies made in Europe, pointed out both these discrepancies. They are also due to the Samaritan originals not being always faithfully reproduced by the transcriber here in Europe. It is also evident from this fact that the Samaritans kept the original drafts among their archives. They indeed referred to them in their subsequent correspondence. The present copy in the British Museum does not seem to have been known by de Sacy. It may perhaps be the copy once in the possession of Schnurrer, which he mentions in the foot-note on p. 11, but must have been made at a much earlier time than Schnurrer, and in all likelihood it is the work of an English scholar almost contemporary with Huntington and Pocock, who had access to the correspondence between them and was allowed to take a copy of the letter to Pocock. Paper and writing are of the end of the seventeenth or beginning of the eighteenth century. The MS. shows traces of rough handling. The edges are frayed and the bottom lines somewhat mutilated. The character of the Hebrew letters agrees in the general outline with the writing of the copy of the letter to Ludolf found bound next to it in the British Museum MS. It is similar, yet not identical, and only proves it to belong to the same time and to have been in the possession of a scholar deeply interested in the Samaritans and in the correspondence with them.

The thread of the correspondence, interrupted through the conversionist activity of Marshall, was then taken up, and with greater success, by the great Ethiopic scholar of Frankfort, Ludolf. He took advantage of the presence in that town of a Jewish traveller from the Holy Land who had come to Europe on a collecting tour. He charged him with a message to the Samaritans which he faithfully delivered. In good time answers came to Ludolf from Sichem, and the correspondence was then continued for some time, probably to the end of Ludolf's life. This correspondence was the first published, and reached wider circles than those reached by the former correspondence of Scaliger and Huntington, which had to wait to the end of the eighteenth century before it saw the light of day in print, thanks to the zeal of Schnurrer[1] and de Sacy,[2] but more notably of the latter, who published the *magnum opus* in 1834. This, however, is not complete, inasmuch as de Sacy omitted the letters to Scaliger, the most noteworthy of the whole series. It seemed also from this collection that the correspondence had ceased at the beginning of the eighteenth century until it was resumed by de Sacy early in the nineteenth. Such, however, has not been the case. I have in my possession what I believe to be an old copy of such a letter. It had been obtained from the Samaritans in Sichem, and is extremely interesting besides being absolutely unknown. It is written on a sheet of foolscap on both sides. It is in a bold hand, and happily the name of the scribe is given at the end of the letter. This will help us to fix the date, which is otherwise missing. Internal evidence will strengthen the conclusion to be arrived at. It had been folded in four, in consequence of which the middle part of the letter had been broken, but happily the tear had not affected the writing, which is a fine specimen of big Samaritan uncial writing. Even in the greatly reduced facsimile here reproduced the writing is easily legible as far as the letters of the alphabet are concerned. The text offers some technical difficulties upon which I may dilate later on. They are principally textual difficulties due to the carelessness of the scribe : dialectic forms and direct omissions due probably to homoio-teleuton, the usual pitfall of copyists.

Far more interesting are the contents of the letter. Whosoever has read the correspondence with the Samaritans will agree that the replies are of a somewhat monotonous character, in keeping in a uniform manner with the questions put to them. Every one who writes to them asks almost the same questions, and it is enough for the Samaritans slightly to vary the older replies in order to answer the new questioner. Some of them are brief and concise, others a little more elaborate, but in the

[1] Eichhorn's Repertorium, ix (8) ; *vide* Montgomery, *Samaritans*, p. 117, note 14.

[2] *Correspondance des Samaritains de Naplouse* in *Notices et Extraits*, vol. xii, Paris.

main they reproduce one and the same original. Yet in spite of the main feature being the same there are smaller details which give to each of these letters a peculiarity of its own. Such is now the case with the present document. It is that portion which refers to the history of this letter, and the personal details, which make it so characteristic of the writer and the circumstances under which that letter was written. We learn thus from the somewhat enigmatic introduction, the substance of the reply that the queries had been brought by a Christian, and the writer goes on to warn the recipient against the Jews who harboured unfriendly feelings towards the Samaritans and are charged with evil intentions. Though the language is guarded the old animosity and distrust of the Jews is clearly visible. In the dogmatic part there is the reference to the present High Priest, who is no longer a descendant of the house of Aaron, but a Levite. And finally the name of the scribe is given here in full : Abraham, the son of Jacob, of the sons of Danaftah, of the tribe of Ephraim. There we have the autograph of one of the most important scholars among the Samaritans of the first half of the eighteenth century. He was the one who completed the great Commentary on Genesis by Meshalma. He was the author of a book on the theory and practice of the Samaritan calendar, and altogether one of the most prominent scholars among them. He was also a great liturgical poet and amongst the copyists of the text of the Pentateuch. Considering that the High Priests in their answers to various correspondents made use of the best-known writers and scribes among the Samaritans, it is obvious that the writer of the present epistle cannot be any other than that well-known poet, writer, and scholar. With this identification agrees also the fact that he mentions the High Priest being of Levite origin. The last High Priest of the house of Aaron died in 1623-4, since when the High Priests were recruited from among the surviving Levites.

I believe that I am in a position to identify that Christian messenger to whom the writer of the epistle alludes. It is in all probability none other than *Henry Maundrell*, whose *Journey from Aleppo to Jerusalem* is still, by the way, a most readable and entertaining book. On the occasion of his visit to the Samaritan High Priest he writes as follows : ' I had an opportunity to go and visit the chief priest of the Samaritans in order to discourse with him on this and some other difficulties occurring in the Pentateuch, which were recommended to me to be enquired about by the learned monsieur Job *Ludolphus*, author of the *Aethiopic History*, when I visited him at Frankfort in my passage through Germany' (London, 1810, p. 80). The journey was undertaken in the year 1697, and the day on which he visited the Samaritans was Wednesday, the 24th of March. If now this identification be correct, then the date of this epistle cannot be much later than the end of the seventeenth century, or at latest the beginning of the eighteenth, and it would seem to be the oldest of the letters which were destined for Ludolf and which had either not reached him or had remained unknown. It is much more probable that he never received it, and then he made use of the Jewish traveller to come into touch with the Samaritans. It is not likely that Huntington is referred to, for the answer he got from the Samaritans differs from this.

If it were not for the fact that the writer mentions a Levite High Priest one might be inclined to see in it, not the copy of a letter written at the time of the copyist, but the copy of a much older letter adapted to altered circumstances. This would be in perfect harmony with the Samaritan literary practice. They are loath to compose something anew when they can copy an older original. They have also faithfully followed such practice in their correspondence. Though written at divers times and by different men, the letters resemble one another so closely as to show their inner relationship and the interdependence of one upon the other. This epistle resembles most closely the short epistle from Egypt which reached Scaliger. I feel almost inclined to see in it the copy of a text of the lost letter from Sichem. This community had also been approached by Scaliger, but it is not known that any answer had come from Sichem. Of course that would be the old archetype, closely followed and adapted to later times by the new correspondent. Be it as it may, it is a further contribution to that peculiar literature which had helped so much to revive the interest in that small community, so little known at the time. I give now in the first place a faithful transcript of the Samaritan, to be followed by a literal translation and a few explanatory notes, such as the text and the contents demand.

1809 :

ברוך יהוה אלהונו :. ואלהי אביתינו :. אברהם ויצחק
ויעקב הזכאים ארשינו :. ויוסף ואדונן משה נבינו :.
ואהרן ובניו כהנינו :. ובתר נתן אמרי שופר שלם :.
עליכם אה עם רם דמן זרע ישראל קם :. על משמר
5 ספר שלם :. דקבלו משה בן עמרם :. וביר את החקים
ואת התורות לשמר את כל דברי התורה הזאת אמת
כמימר יהוה אלהינו :. לא תוסיפו עליו ולא
תגרעו ממנו : ישיב יהוה מבראכתו עלינן ועליכון
ועל כל הקהל בכל הארצות :. בברית האבות :. ועתה
10 נגיד לכם אה אחינו בני ישראל אן בזבנה הזה
אתו מפאתכם אנשים ערלים סחרים ואגידו
לנו בעבורכם ועריכם הרחוקה (!) ממנו :. ואן אתם
שמרים כמונו :. ויפג הלב כי לא נאמן להם
בעבור היהודהים המכסים דברינו : וגם

15 דבריכם עלינו: • וערלים דזכרנו דרשו זה מכתבנו: •

ערבו לנו: • אן ישיגו אתו לכם וישיבו אתנו

דבר את הדרך אשר תלכו בה ואת המעשה אשר

תעשון ונדע האמת א... ונשמח רב בכם אם בחקות

כי תשלחו לנו מכתב גדיל: • (!) והייתם נקוים מיהוה ומישראל: •

20 אלה תלכו ואתו תעבדו ובו תדבקו: • כאשר נעשה: • (!!)

כל אשר דבר יהוה על יד עבדו משה: • נשמר השבת

ברית עולם: • ושבעה מועדים אות היא לעולם: •

מועד הפסח וניכל הקרבן צלי אש על מצות ומרורים

ויום שביעי חג המצות נחג ראש שלש רגלים

25 וממחרת השבת ספירות חמשים יום עד ממחרת

השבת נחג ביום הבכודים ו[בחד]ש השביעי באחד

לחדש: • שבתון זכרון תרועה מקרא קדש: • אך בעשור

לחדש השביעי הזה יום כפורים הוא מקרא

קדש יהיה לנו: • ובו נעני נפשותינו: • בליל

30 זרעינו: • מלבד הטף דינק מן אמו בערב מערב

עד ערב נפרש התשבחן למקדשה ובחמשה עשר

יום לחדש השביעי הזה חג הסכות: • ונקח מן פרי

עץ הדר כפות תמרים וענפי עץ עבות וערבי נחל

ונשמח לפני יהוה שבעת ימים וביום השמיני עצרת

35 תהיה לכל העדה: • ומועדינו השבעה כמו השבת לא נעשה

בון כל מלבת רק מקראי קדש יתקרו: • ואש

בון לא נבעירו: • מלבד אש קרבן הפסח המשמרון

מתודע מן חשבן קשטו הגדל: • דבו יורו משפטיך

ליעקב ותורותיך לישראל: • וחקותינו רבה

40 מן אדני: • וערל זכר אשר לא ימול את בשר ערלתו

ביום השמיני: • והילדת לזכר תטמא כמה זכר: •

ולנקבה עורי (!) כאשר אמר בקצת זאת תורת

הוב והמשפט הזה תמיד ניקמו: • ולא נבשל גדי

בחלב אמו: • וכל טמא לא ניכל ממו: • וכל אשר

45 יגע בו הטמא יטמא ויכבס בגדיו ורחיץ במים

וטמא עד הערב ועמנו כהנים מבני לוי דאמר עליון

כי בם בחר יהוה אלהיך לשרתו ולברך בשמו

ואתנו מכתב גדול משתמר בבית הכנשה בגירת

חלקת השדה דקנה אבינו יעקב במאה קשיטה

50 ויצב שמה מזבח: • ואנן צלאים קראים בו

בערב ובבקר בשלום עיר שכם תחת משפט

בני ישמעאל בשמה ובטוב ובטוב לבב מרב ועמנו

בבית כנשתה מקום בו משתמר השם הגדול

וסביבותינו קברות אדונינן יוסף דעמד עליו

55 ואני נתתי לך שכם אחת על אחיך ואלעזר
ואיתמר ופינחס דלו ברית כהנת עולם ולא
נסגד אלא אל יהוה פני הרגריזיים בית אל
ונסיד ליום נקם ושלם קשט לעולם לית אלה
אלא אחד וברוך אלהינו לעולם וברוך שמו
60 לעולם :•.

מכתב אברהם בן יעקב
דמבני דנפתה מן
שבט אפרים למטה
יוסף :•.

Codex Gaster—Samaritan

Translation.

1. Blessed be the Lord our God and the God of our fathers, Abraham and Isaac

2. and Jacob, the meritorious ones,—our forefathers and Joseph, and our master Moses our prophet,

3. and Aaron and his children, our Priests, and after having given the pleasant words of peace,

4. peace be upon you, O exalted nation which has arisen from the seed of Israel, to keep

5. the perfect book which was received by Moses the son of Amram. He copied the statutes

6. and the laws so that we should keep all the words of this law faithfully,

7. according to the word of the Lord our God : ' Ye shall not add unto it and ye shall not

8. Diminish aught of it.'   May the Lord turn his blessing upon us and upon you

9. and upon every congregation in all the countries that are of the covenant of the fathers.   And now

10. we tell you, O our brethren the children of Israel, that this time

11. came from your countries men uncircumcised,—merchants, and they told

12. us concerning you and your towns that are so far away from us, and that you

13. are also Samaritans like as we are, and our heart doubted, for we did not believe them

14. because of the Jews who cover up our words and also

15. your words unto us.   And the uncircumcised whom we have mentioned asked for this our letter ;

16. they pledged themselves unto us that they would carry it unto you and they would bring back word to us

17. of your walk of life and the manner of your performance that we may know the truth therefrom.

18-21. And we shall rejoice greatly in you if you will send us a long letter saying that you walk in the statutes of the Lord according to all that the Lord has commanded by the hand of his servant Moses, and that you serve him and that you cleave to him as do we ; then you shall be blameless before God and Israel.[1]

21. We keep the Sabbath,—

22. —an everlasting covenant, and seven festivals,—a symbol for ever.

23. On the Feast of Pesaḥ we eat the Sacrifice roasted in fire upon unleavened bread and bitter herbs,

24. and the seventh day of the feast of unleavened bread we keep as the first of the three festivals of pilgrimage.

25. And on the day after the Sabbath (starts) the counting of the fifty days until the day following

26-27. the (last) Sabbath. We go up in the pilgrimage on the day of the first-fruits. On the first of the seventh month there is the Sabbath of the Memorial of the blowing of trumpets, a holy convocation, but on the tenth

28. of this seventh month is the day of Atonement,

29. a holy convocation unto us ; and on it we chastise our souls, even all

30. our seed with the exception of the babe that is suckled by its mother, in the evening from the evening

31. until the evening we recite our praises to him that sanctified it. And on the fifteenth

32. day of this seventh month is the feast of Tabernacles ; we take of the beautiful fruit

33. of a tree, leaves of palms, the leaf of thick boughs and the willows of the brook

34. and we rejoice before the Lord seven days ; and on the eighth day is ' Aṣeret[2]

35. for the whole congregation '. And our seven festivals are like unto the Sabbath ; we do not perform

36. on them any manner of work—holy convocations (proclamations) are they called, and fire

37-38. on them we do not kindle, except the fire of the Sacrifice on Pesaḥ. And the keeping of them is known unto us from the true great Calculation (calendar) through which ' they shall teach thy judgements

---

[1] I have endeavoured to readjust here the confused passages.

[2] The Samaritans take this word to mean the conclusion. I have, therefore, transliterated it.

Plate 18

Worship on Mount Garizim during Passover

39. unto Jacob and thy laws unto Israel '. Our statutes are too numerous for my Lord (to tell).

40. A male uncircumcised is he who does not circumcise the flesh of his foreskin

41. on the eighth day. And the woman who gives birth to a male child is defiled like a male,

42. Although for a female it is different, as is said in the section ' This is the law

43. for the Zab '. And this law we keep perpetually. And we do not seethe the kid

44. in the milk of its mother, neither do we eat anything that is unclean. And he who

45. touches such a thing becomes thoroughly unclean and must wash his garments and bathe in water,

46. and he remains unclean until the even. And we have priests (Cohanim) of the children of Levi, concerning whom it is said :

47. ' The Lord thy God has chosen them to minister unto him and to bless in his Name.'

48. And we have the great Writ which is preserved in the House of the Kinsha. Near by is

49. the Portion of the Field which our father Jacob purchased for 100 kesitah.

50. He erected there an altar ; and we pray and read there

51. in the evening and in the morning for the peace of the town of Sichem which is under the rule

52. of the Children of Ishmael, with rejoicing and with great gladness of heart. And we have with us

53. in the House of the Kinsha a place where is kept the Great Name.

54. Round about us there are the graves of our master Joseph, concerning whom it is said :

55. ' And I have given thee one portion (Sichem) above thy brethren,' and of Eleazar

56. And of Itamar and of Pinehas, to whom belong the covenant of everlasting priesthood. And we

57. worship none but the Lord, whilst turning towards Mount Garizim Beth El.

58. And we trust in (believe in) the Day of Requital and Reward. It is a truth for ever. There is no God

59. But one, and blessed be our God for ever and blessed be his Name

60. for ever.

61. The writing of Abraham the son of Jacob,

62. Of the sons of Danaftah of

63. The tribe of Ephraim the tribe of Joseph.[1]

At the left-hand top corner there is written the following apographon :
' If you will send us a letter then you will be (free, or) guiltless before
God and before Israel.' (Biblical quotation.)

In addition to this letter, hitherto unknown, there exists another only
partly known. It is the longest of its kind and more full of details
than any other. It follows the same pattern and shows the uniformity
of this correspondence. The original has evidently been lost, but the
Samaritans, as mentioned before, have kept a copy. From this, no
doubt, another copy has been made, which has been added to a collection
of prayers. The MS. is now in the British Museum (Add. 19791, folio
84 ff.). Heidenheim has published this letter in Samaritan script in
his *Vierteljahrschrift*, i, pp. 78 ff. and 88–103, with an introduction and
German translation. Unfortunately this publication of this Samaritan
text, like all the Samaritan texts published by him, is vitiated by
innumerable mistakes. Besides, Heidenheim evidently did not know
Arabic, for otherwise he would not have lost himself in empty speculations as to the date of this letter. This Samaritan text has an Arabic
heading and an Arabic Colophon which give us the date of the
composition as well as the date of the copy, the name, or the address
rather, to which this letter was sent, and the name of the copyist of
this letter. The letter was addressed to the Samaritans in 'Ingelterra',
i. e. England, and was written in the year 1147 Hg. (1734), and was
copied by Meshalma ben Murjan, i. e. Ab Sakhuah the Danafite, six years
afterwards—1153 (1740). It shows unmistakably that the Samaritans
continued to send letters to England to their reputed brethren in exile.
I am therefore giving it anew with a correct translation and the
properly corrected text.

The real significance of this letter lies in the fact that it evidently
had been copied by no less a personage than Meshalma, the son of
Ab Sakhuah (in Arabic called Murjan) the Danafite, the author of the great
Commentary on Genesis to which I have already drawn attention for
its high importance for Samaritan exegesis. It assists us also in
determining the time when Meshalma lived, i. e. the first half of the
eighteenth century, thus corroborating the views expressed before as to
the date when Meshalma lived, but the new detail contained in this
letter is that he lived in Tyre and not in Sichem. It is his Commentary
which the writer of the previous letter, Ibrahim the son of Jacob,
afterwards completed. It is remarkable that both emphasize their

---

[1] The writer uses another word for the English ' tribe '. This use of the word
makes it much clearer, inasmuch as Shebet could therefore be translated ' the
branch ' and Matteh ' the rod ', Ephraim being the branch out of the rod of
Joseph.

Ephraimite origin so much so that in some manuscripts Ibrahim is known merely as the Ephraimite. It gives us a clue to the origin of the Danafite family, who did not belong to the priestly class, but who took a very important part in the literary development of the Samaritans ever since the time of Abul Fath in the fourteenth century down to Ab Sakhuah Murjan, who died a few years ago.

B.M. MSS. Add. 19791. My No. 893[a] of Photographic facsimiles.

אז החל לקרא בשם יהוה בדברותי ואשירו
באמירותי : והרים אליו צעקותי ואדרשנו בכל
לבבי : ובכל נפשי בצרעותי :•• כי הוא האל העני
אתי ביום צרתי : ויהי עמדי בדרך אשר
5 הלכתי : והוא המלך (sic) הגאל אתי : מכל רעותי
לישועתו קויתי : אן ישיג אל מכתבי הזה
עם דברותי לקהל ישראל ערתי המתקרים
שמרים מן זרע עבראותי :•• איה הם ממצאים
מן הפאתי : ויענו אתי : ויאמרו טוב הדבר
10 אשד דברתי : כי לדבריהם נכספותי : ואשאלו בנביות
מן אמר עליו נאמן על כל ביתי אן :
ישים להם מה באֹרו בקדש תורותי אם יהיה
נדחך בקצה השמים משם יקבצך יהוה אלהיך :
ומשם יקחך : והביאך (sic) יהוה אלהיך אל הארץ
15 אשר ירשו אבותיך : וירשתה והרבך מאבותיך :
ומל יהוה אלהיך את לבבך : ואת לבב זרעך
לאהבה את יהוה אלהיך בכל לבבך ובכל נפשך
למען חייך : ונתן יהוה אלהיך את כל האלות
חאלה על איביך ועל שנאיך ואשר רדפוך
20 ואתה תשוב : ושמעת בקול יהוה אלהיך ועשית
את כל מצותיו אשר אנכי מצוך היום :
ואחדי כן נשלח שלום יהוה ורחמיו
וברכאתו עליכם : אה אחינו בני ישראל
המתקרים שמרים : יהוה ישמרכם : וירבי מספריכם)
25 כמימרו בקדש ספריכם : יהוה אלהי אבותיכם :
יסף עליכם : ככם אלף פעמים : ויברך אתכם
כאשר דבר לכם :•• ויקבץ בינן ובינכם על
ראש הרגריים בית אל : אחד ההרים המקום
המבחר : אשר הוא לשמים שער : ונקריב עליו
30 חקרבנים ונשמח אנן ואבם אמן אמן : ונגיד
אתכם אה אחינו : כי בא אלינו איש יהודה
והודיע אתנו אן אחד מאחיו : בידע אתכם

ובא אל עריכם : וזכר לו אן אתם שמרים כמונו
ואן אתם שאלתם אתו עלינו : ועל דברינו : ועל
שכם ערינו ואמר לנו : זה האיש אן כתבתם
להם מכתב אני אשיגו להם : והביא לכם מהם
דבר : ובעת שמענו ממו זה הדבר : שמחנו
שמח רב : וכתבנו לכם זה המכתב עד יהי עמכם
דבר אמת בדברינו ואולי תענו אתנו : ותשלחנו
40 לנו דבר צדק יודיע אתנו בצדיק : דבריכם
אן ההיתם שמרים כמונו : ותשמרו התורה כמה
נשמרה : ותגידו לנו מה שם עריכם אשר אתם
יושבים בהם : כי היה מטרם יביא לנו מכתבים
ודברים מן אנשים שמרים : ובא לנו מהם תורה
45 תמימה : והכרתו הדברים מבינינן : מקץ חמשים
שנה : מבלתי מן ישיג המכתבים ועתה נשבע
עליכם ביהוה ובמשה עבדו ונאמן ביתו אן
תשלחו לנו מכתב ותודיעו אתנו בצדיק
דבריכם על האמת : אן ההיתם שמרים כמונו :
50 איך תקרו התורה הקדושה ואיך תכתבו
אתה : כי אנחנו נכתבה כמו זה חמכתב
ואיך תשמרו מצוותה וחקותה ואיך תעשו
המועדים : ולא תסתירו מנן דבר : כי אנחנו
נתקרי שמרים מן בני ישראל : מן שבט אפרים
55 ומנשה שכונים בעיר שכם : מול הרגריזים
בית אל : נשמר התורה הקדושה : ונעשה כל אשר
צוה יהוה בה : מן מצות ומשפטות וחקות :
על האמת לא נוסף עליו : ולא נגרע ממנו :
ונטהר מן כל הטמאות ונרחץ במים מן קרי
60 לילה : ושכבת זרע : האיש והאשה ומה יגע
אחד בכל כלי מן מיני הטמאות אלא ויכבס
בגדיו וירחץ את בשרו במים : ויטמא עד
הערב : וכל אשר צוהו (sic) יהוה בתורה בעד הטמאות
נשמרו ונעשהו על האמת : ונמול ערלת הילד הזכר
65 ביום השמיני : מן מולדו לא נקדמו ולא נאחרו
ונשמר יום השבת : ולא נצא בו מן מקום אל
מקום : אלא אל מקום הצלות
ולא לנו בו מלאכה :
אלא הצלות והמקרא : בתורה הקדושה : והשירות
70 והתהללות ליהוה אלהינו : ונשמרו מערב עד
ערב : ולא נעשה בו מאום מן מיני המלאכה : ולא
נבעיר בו אש : ולא נשכב בו עם האשה : וכל יום

נצלי בערב ובבקר : כאשר אמר יהוה בעד
הקרבנים את הכבש האחד תעשה בבקר :
75 ואת הכבש השני תעשה בין הערבים : ונעבד
את יהוה ובצלותינו נקד ארצה ונשתחו
ליהוה פני הרגרייים בית אל : ונשמר
שבע המועדים בעתם : על מחשב חשבן האמת
חשבן השמש והירח : ונדע מן מחשבו ראש
80 כל חדש בחדשו : ולנו על צדיקות חשבנו
עדים והם כספות השמש והירח : בנדע
אתם : מן חשבנן : ונעשה המועדים על השבנן
ראשם מועד הפסח : ובו נקריב קרבן הפסח
מן הכשבים ומן העזים : בהרגרייים בית אל
85 בחדש האביב : בארבע עשר יום מן חדש הראישון
בין הערבים נזבח אתו : כאשר אמר יהוה : ושחטו
אתו כל קהל ישראל בין הערבים ונאכל אתו
בחצי הלילה צלי אש : על מצות ומרורים :
ראשו על כרעיו ועל קרבו ולא נותר ממנו עד
90 בקר : והנותר ממנו נשרפהו באש ולא נעשה
המועד הזוכיר אלא אן ישיג חדש האביב
שבעת יומי המצות ולו אחד יום : ונאכל
המצות שבעת ימים : ויום השביעי הוא מועד
חג המצות : ובו ליהוה נעלה נחג על
95 הרגרייים בית אל : נלך במקרא מן העיר אל
המקום : ונצלי בו על המזבחות אשר בו : ונתיצב
בתוך גבעת עולם : ונוסף מן השירות והתפילות
ותשרי עלינו הברכות : ובזה המועדים השנים
לא נעשה בהם מלאכה מלבד עשות קרבן הפסח
100 ולא נשבת בהם ⸱⸱ המלאכה אלא ביום הראישׁן :
וביום השביעי : ונספר חמשים יום ממחרת
השבת : אשר הוא ⸱⸱ן שבעת יומי המצות : עד
ממחרת השבת השבעית : ויהי החלם יום האחד
ואחרם יום האחד ואחרם הוא יום חג
105 הקציר : ואתקרי שמו חג השבעות ויום
הבכורים : והוא המועד השלישי ובו נחג ליה
אל ראש הרגרייים בית אל : כמו חג המצות
ובו נשבת מכל המלאכה : ומועד הרביעי הוא
יום ראש החדש השביעי : אשר אמר עליו יהוה בחדש
110 השביעי באחד לחדש יהיה לכם שבתון זכרון
תרועה מקרא קדש כל מלאכת עבדה לא תעשו :
והעשירי ממו המועד החמישי : והוא יום הכפורים

ובו נענה נפשותינו מערב עד ערב :

האנשים והנשים והילדים הגדלים והקט[נים]

115 מלבד הטף הינק יינק מן שדים אמו לבד :

וארך זה היום והלילה לא נשבת מן מקרא

התורה הקדושה : ומן הצלות והשירות

והתפלות ליהוה אלהינו : ואלהיל אבותינו :

אלהי אברהם ויצחק ויעקב : ובחמשה עשר

120 יום מן החדש השביעי : המועד הששי והוא

מועד חג הסכות : ובו נחג ליהוה אל ראש

הרגריזים בית אל : כמו חג המצות

וחג הקציר : כאשר אמר יהוה : בכתבו

הקדש : שלש רגלים תחג לי בשנה ונעשה

125 הסכות כאשר צוה יהוה : ונקח מן פרי

עץ הדר כפות תמרים וענפי עץ עבות

וערבי נחל : וכל האזרח בישראל ישב

בו שבעת ימים : ובל יום מן שבעת הימים

נעמד בתחת הרגריזים בית אל

130 ונצלי בערב ובבקר בשמח וטוב לבב . ולא נשבת מן

המלאכה בשבעת הימים : אלא ביום הראישון

ויום השמיני מהם הוא שביע (!) המוערים :

אשר אתקרא שמו עצרת : והוא חתמת מוערי

יהוה : אשר אמר עליהם בתורה הקדושה :

135 וידבר משה את מועדי יהוה לבני ישראל

ובכל המועדים בשבעת נשבת מכל עבדה :

ולא נבעיר בהם אש כמו יום השבת ולא

נעשה מאום אלא על משפט התורה חקה

אחת ומישפט אחד : הוא לנו : ודעו אה אחינו

140 בני ישראל כי ממצא עמנו

השם יהוה הגדול במקום רב : וממצא

עמנו ספר תורה תמימה משתמרה מן

ימי משכן הקדש : מכתבה בעורות מן זבח

השלמים : בפתח אהל מועד : ואשר כתבה

145 כתוב בתוכה : אני אבישע בן פינחס בן

אלעזר בן אהרן הכהן להם רצון יהוה

וכבודו כתבתי ספר התורה הקדושה בפתח

אהל מועד בהרגריזים בית אל : בשנת שלשה

עשר למושב בני ישראל ארץ כנען

150 לגבלותיה סביב : אודה את יהוה : ועתה

זה ספר משתמר בבית הצלות ביד גדול

כהני בני לוי : ויוציאו לנו ביומי מועדינו :

ועתה נדרש מכם : ונשבע עליכם ביהוה ובמשה

עבדו : אן הייתם שמרים כמונו : וקרובים

155 מיהוה ולכם נכספות לבית יהוה וקרבן יהוה

תשלחו לנו מכם : שנים או שלשה אנשים : יהיו

חכמים ונבונים וידעים : ואן אמרתם מה תובלו כולה תעשו

תשיגו לנו בעבור השבת האמת אתכם ואולם

לכם (ת)[א]הבה(sic) ותלכו בה : כאשר תדרשו : וכתורתו עשיתם

160 כאשר צוה יהוה על יד עבדו משה : לשכינו (!) ו

תדרשו ויביאו עמם מן המעשר והנדר והנדבה

כאשר אמר יהוה כי ירחק ממך המקום אשר

בחר יהוה אלהיך לשכן את שמו שם : כי

יברכך יהוה אלהיך ונתתה בכסף וסרת

165 הכסף בידך והלכת אל המקום אשר בחר

יהוה אלהיך בו : ואנחנו לא נדע מקומכם

ונמצא לנו דרך אתינו אליכם : וידענו

אתכם : אתם השיבו לנו דבר את הדדך אשר

נעלה בה ואת הערים אשר נבוא עליהם וייטב

170 בעיני הדבר ואן לא תשלחו אנשים תשלחו

לנו מכתב : ותשימו בתוכו צדק דבריכם

על האמת לא תוסיפו עליו ולא תגרעו :

ותגידו לנו אן חיה (!) עמכם כהנים גדולים

מן בני אהרן וכהנים מן בני לוי : ואנחנו

175 בעיר שכם קרובים מן הרגריזים בית אל :

וקרוב מנן קבר אדונן יוסף בן פרת

אשר אמר עליו ואני נתתי לך שכם אחת

(!)אל אחיך : וקרוב מן קברות אדונינן אלעזר

ואיתמר ופינחם הכהנים והשבעים

180 הזקינים וקברות יחושע וכלב : כלם

סביבת עיר שכם : ובתוכה חלקת השדה :

אשר אמר עליה : ויבא יעקב שלם עיר שכם

אשר בארץ כנען בבאו מפדן ארם : ויחן

את פני העיר ויקן את חלקת השדה :

185 ועמנו כהנים מן בני לוי : ונתן להם מן

הזבח הזרוע והלחם(!) והקבה : והכהנים

לא יגלחו שער ראשם וערינו במשפט

שליט בני ישמעאל ולהם עלינו בכל שנה

על כל איש שנים זהב : ולא ידרשו מנן

190 אחרם ולא יאונו אתנו ולא יעשו עמנו :

אלא הטוב : ונעשה קרבנינו ומועדינו

בעיניהם ולא מא מהם : ומנ אנשים

שכונים בעיר עזה כפתרים ואנשים

שכונים על שפת ים פלשתים : ותשלחו

195 מכתבים אל המקומם(!) הזוכירים ואנחנו

לא נאמן אלא ביהוה ובמשה בן עמרם

עבדו : ובתורה הקדושה ובהרגרייים בית

אל : וביום נקם ושלם : ואחר דברינו ברוך

אלהינו לעולם : וברוך שמו לעולם : ושלום

200 על אדונן משה בן עמרם הנבי הצדיק

התמים הטהור הנאמן הנקיא מכל

מום : ואני כתובו העבד הדל משלמה בן

אב סכוה : הדנפי מן שבט אפרים יהוה

יכפר לי כל פישעי וחטאי ועוני אמן

205 בעמל משה הנאמן אמן :

Translation of Codex 1708[a]

Letter of Meshalma, son of Ab Sakhuah.

(Folio 84[b].) I begin with calling upon the name of the Lord with my words, and I praise him with my speeches. And I lift up unto him my cries, and I seek him with all my heart and with all my soul in my trouble, for he is the God who answers me in the time of my distress and he is with me on the road in which I walk, and he is the angel who redeems me from all my evils, for in his help do I hope, so that this, my letter, with my words may reach the community of the Israelites, the congregation that is called the Samaritans the faithful (i.e. who faithfully observe the Law) of the seed of the Hebrews wherever they be found in whatever corners, and that they may answer me and say, good is the word which I have spoken, for I am longing for their words, and I pray for them by the prophecy of him concerning whom he said, ' He is faithful over all my house ', that he should fulfil (unto them) that word he copied in his holy law, ' If thy scattering be to the end of the heavens, thence the Lord thy God will gather thee, and thence will he take thee, and the Lord thy God will bring thee to the land which thy fathers have possessed, and thou shalt possess it, and he will multiply thee more than thy fathers, and the Lord thy God will circumcise thy heart and the heart of thy seed to love the Lord thy God with all thy heart and with all thy soul so that thou mayest live, and the Lord thy God will give all these curses on thine enemies and those that hate thee and those that persecute thee.

(85.) And thou shalt return and hearken to the voice of the Lord thy God, and thou shalt do all his commandments which I command thee this day.' And after this we send the peace of the Lord and his mercy and his blessing upon you. Oh! our brethren the children of Israel, who are called the observers of the Lord, may the Lord guard you, and may he multiply your number according to his word in your holy book. ' May the Lord, the God of your fathers, add unto you as you are a thousand times, and bless you as he has spoken unto you.' And may he gather us and you upon the top of Mount Garizim Beth El on the One of the mountains the Chosen Spot which is the gate of heaven, and may we sacrifice upon it the sacrifices, and we rejoice with you, Amen and Amen.

And we will tell you now, O our brothers, that there came to us a Jewish man and told us that there was one of his brethren who knew you and had come into your towns, and he mentioned unto him that you were Samaritans like us and that you had asked about us and about our affairs and about our town of Sichem, and this man told us, ' If you write to them a letter I will forward it to them and bring you their answer '. And when we heard from him this thing we greatly rejoiced and we write to you this letter that you should have a truthful word from us, for you might then answer us also and tell us in truth and faith whether you are also Samaritans as we are, and whether you keep the Law as we do. You will tell us the name of your city wherein you dwell. For some time ago came to us letters and messages from Samaritans and also a complete copy of the Law.[1] Fifty years have elapsed since we received those letters. We adjure you now by the Name of the Lord and by the name of his servant Moses, his faithful steward, that ye write to us and send us faithful and reliable news, and that ye tell us in truth whether ye are Samaritans as we are, how you are reading and writing the Law, for we write it with the same characters as this letter, and how you observe the laws and commandments, and how you keep the festivals. Do not hide anything from us, for we call ourselves the Shamerin, (i. e. the Faithful Observers of the Law), of the children of Israel, from the tribe of Ephraim and Manasseh and we are living in Sichem opposite the Mount of Garizim Beth El, we observe the holy Law and keep all the commandments which he hath commanded therein, the statutes and the ordinances according to the truth, we neither add nor subtract anything of it. We purify ourselves from all impurities . . ., and wash our clothes as soon as we touch any vessel that contains any of the various impure objects and we wash our body as well in water and are unclean until the evening. . . . We circumcise the male child eight days after birth, we neither prolong the time nor do we shorten it. We observe the Sabbath and we do not go from one place to the other except to the place of prayer. We perform no manner of work thereon ; we only have prayers and reading out of the holy Law and songs and hymns to the Lord our God. And we keep it from eve to eve,

[1] Probably the copy of the Walton Polyglot which they still have in Sichem, as I have been told by the High Priest Isaac b. Amram. It is, however, the Polyglot or the Samaritan text published by Morini in the Paris Polyglot.

and perform no manner of work during all that time, we kindle no fire and (lie not with our wives). On every day we pray twice, once in the evening and once in the morning, just as God had said concerning the sacrifices : 'One lamb ye shall bring in the morning and the second you shall bring in the evening.' And we worship the Lord. In our prayers we bow down and prostrate ourselves facing Mount Garizim Beth El. We observe the seven festivals in their proper season by means of the true calculation, the calculation of the sun and of the moon, and we know the new moon through our calculations, and as witnesses for the accuracy of our calculations there are the eclipses of sun and moon which we know by our calculations. We keep our Festivals according to our calculations. The first is the Pesaḥ festival ; on it we bring the sacrifice of the Pesaḥ, from the lambs and the goats on Mount Garizim Beth El ; in the month of Abib on the fourteenth day of the first month at twilight do we sacrifice it according to the command of the Lord, 'And the whole congregation of Israel is to slay it at twilight', and we eat it, by the middle of the night, roasted on fire, with unleavened bread and bitter herbs, and the head with the legs the entrails all together, and nothing left until the morning and whatever remains until the morning must be burnt in the fire. We keep the festival (of unleavened bread) only when the month of Abib has come, not one day but seven days do we eat unleavened bread. On the seventh day is the festive day of the unleavened bread ; on this day we make a pilgrimage to the Lord. We ascend the mountain Garizim Beth El, we go out of the town reading the holy Law and we pray there on the Chosen Spot, close to the altars that are erected there, and we stand in the midst of the 'everlasting Hill', say our prayers adding songs and hymns, and the blessings rest upon us. On these two Festivals we do no manner of work except the sacrifice of the Pesaḥ Lamb, and we desist from work only on the first and seventh day. We then count fifty days from the day after the Sabbath that happens to be in the festival to the morning after the seventh Sabbath. We thus begin their counting with the first day (i. e. Sunday) and finish with the first day (Sunday), and this last day is the feast of reaping the corn harvest ; it is also called the feast of weeks, and the feast of the first-fruits. This is the third festival. We make a pilgrimage on it to the top of Mount Garizim before the Lord, as on the feast of unleavened bread. We cease from all manner of work. The fourth festival is the beginning of the seventh month, of which the Lord said : 'On the seventh month, on the first day of the month shall be unto you a Sabbath, the memorial of blowing the trumpets, a holy convocation, you shall do no manner of work.' On the tenth of that month is the fifth festival, that is the Day of Atonement ; in it we chastise our souls from evening to evening, men as well as women and children, big and small, except the babes that are sucking at the mothers' breasts. And all night we read the sacred Law, and all along that day and night we continually pray and recite hymns and songs to the God of our fathers, Abraham, Isaac, and Jacob. On the fifteenth of the seventh month is the sixth festival, the feast of tabernacles. Therein we make a pilgrimage unto the Lord to the top of Mount Garizim Beth El, as on the feast of unleavened bread and the feast of Harvest of which he commanded us in his sacred Law: 'Three times in the year shalt thou make a pilgrimage unto me.' On the feast of Tabernacles we do make booths as the Lord hath commanded us, we take the beautiful fruit of the tree, and palm-branches, and the leaves of the thick tree, and willows of the brook, and every inborn in Israel shall dwell therein for seven days. And on each of these seven days we stand at the foot of the Mount Garizim Beth El and pray with joy, and with a joyful heart morning and evening. We do not cease from work during these seven days except on the first day and on the eighth day which is the seventh festival and is called Aṣereth, and it is the conclusion of the feasts of the Lord which God commanded Moses, saying in the holy Law: 'And Moses told the feasts of the Lord to the children of Israel.' On all these seven festivals we rest from all manner of work, we kindle thereon no fire, just as on Sabbath, and do no kind of labour, but according to the holy Law we have one law and one statute.

Know ye also, O our brothers, the house of Israel, that we possess among us, in an exalted place, the great Name of the Lord, and we possess also a perfect copy of the scroll of the Law, preserved since the time of the Holy Tabernacle upon the skins of the peace offerings at the entrance to the tent of the covenant, and the following is written therein: 'I, Abisha, son of Pineḥas, son of Eleazar, son of Aaron the priest, may the favour and glory of the Lord rest upon them, have written this Holy Scroll at the entrance of the Tent of Assembly upon Mount Garizim Beth El in the thirteenth year of the Settlement of the Children of Israel in the land of Canaan. I thank the Lord.' This copy is kept in the house of prayer by the High Priest, the son of Levi, and he brings it out only on the great festivals.

We would ask you now, and we adjure you by the Name of God, and by the name of his servant Moses, that if you are Samaritans as we are, and drawing near to the Lord, and you are longing for the house of the Lord and for the sacrifice of the Lord, you shall send unto us two or three men from among you, men of wisdom and discernment and understanding. If you ask what good you can do for us, you may inform us as to the way of keeping the true Sabbath. [1]For you may have a true way of keeping it, but if you have the desire of walking in it, so as to seek

---

[1] This passage is somewhat corrupt in the text, and the rendering here is tentative.

the Lord, and you do according to the Law, as the Lord hath commanded through his servant Moses, saying ' Ye shall seek for the place of his dwelling, and they shall bring with them the tithe and the free gifts, and offerings and vows as the Lord hath said : and if the place be too far from thee where the Lord thy God shall choose to set his Name when the Lord thy God blesses thee : then shalt thou turn it into money, and bind up the money in thine hand, and shalt go unto the place which the Lord thy God shall choose '. But we do not know your place, so that we may find the way for you to us, so that we may learn to know you. Answer us therefore, and tell us the way in which we may come to you, and the countries through which we have to pass, and it will be pleasing in our eyes. But if you do not send men send us at least a letter, and put therein the truthful statement of your words, neither adding nor diminishing anything of it. Tell us whether you have still High Priests among you from the children of Aaron, and priests of the sons of Levi. We are living in the town of Sichem, close to the Mount of Garizim Beth El, and here is the grave of our lord Joseph, ' ben Porath ', of whom he had said : ' I have given thee one Portion (Sichem) above thy brethren.' We are also not far from the graves of our lords Eleazar, and Ithamar, and Pinehas the priests, and the seventy Elders ; the graves of Joshua and Kaleb are also not far from the town of Sichem, and therein is ' the Portion of the Field ' of which it is said : ' And Jacob came in peace to the city of Sichem which is in the land of Canaan, when he came from Paddan Aram, and he encamped before the city, and he bought the Portion of the Field.' We have priests from among the sons of Levi, and we give them from the sacrifice, the shoulder and the cheeks and the maw, and the priests do not shave the hair of their head. Our cities stand under the dominion of the Ishmaelites, to whom we pay annually a capitation tax of two gold pieces, and they do not ask for anything more, and they do not harm us, and are only kind to us. We perform our sacrifices and observe festivals before their eyes, and there is none who hinders us. Some of our people are living in Azza of the Kaphtorites, and others at the coast of the Philistean sea, and you can send your reply to these places here mentioned.

We believe only in God and in Moses the son of Amram his servant, and in his sacred Law, and in the Mount Garizim Beth El, and in the day of punishment and reward.

And the end of our words is, blessed be our Lord for ever and ever, and blessed be his Name, and peace be upon our Master Moses the son of Amram the prophet, the pious, the perfect, the pure, the faithful, free from all blemish.

And I wrote it, the poor slave (servant) Meshalma son of Ab Sakhuah the Danafite (of Tyre) from the tribe of Ephraim. May the Lord forgive me all my trespasses and my sins and my wrongdoings. Amen for the sake of the faithful Moses. Amen.

APPENDIX II

THE REPORT OF PIETRO DELLA VALLE ON HIS DISCOVERY OF THE SAMARITAN PENTATEUCH AND TARGUM IN DAMASCUS

CONSTANT reference is made to the report of Pietro della Valle of his discovery of the Samaritan Pentateuch in Damascus in the year 1616. Few, however, seem to have seen the original, and thus the references often differ and produce a wrong impression as to the state of the Samaritans in that city and the size and form of their Synagogue. This is a complete misrepresentation of the actual state of things seen and described by Della Valle. He always adds some further details which are of no small importance. They agree entirely with a similar institution seen by me in Nablus, another proof of the uniformity and tenacity with which the Samaritans cling to their ceremonies and traditions. The passage here reproduced is found in the *Viaggi di Pietro della Valle Il Pellegrino* . . . Roma, MDCL, pp. 604-8.

Io poi, di tutti i guai hauuti per questa infermità, mi consolai in vna sola mattina; perche condotto dal Padre Michele, e da vn'Ebreo mio amico & interprete, a veder fuori della città ne i giardini alcune poche case che vi sono di Ebrei Samaritani; oltra del gusto che hebbi di vedere i giardini, e quelle case, che dentro trouai galantissime (benche di fuori fossero di mala apparenza) messe tutte ad oro, con pittura, e con lettere loro Samaritane intagliate, e miniate in più luoghi, e così ancora la loro Sinagoga; hebbi anco grandissimo contento di vedere in casa di vn de'loro Chachàm, o Sauij, quattro libri Seferthorà, di quella scrittura Samaritana, che io tanto cercaua. Erano questi libri, antichissimi; scritti tutti con lettere Samaritane in pergameno grande; e trè di lingua puramente Ebraica, & vno con aggiun|ta di certe esplicationi in Arabico; perche la lingua Araba parlano in Damasco al presente questi Semrì, ò Samaritani. Ne vidi anche degli altri di altra sorte, in mano di costui, e d'altre persone. In conclusione, tanto feci con vn poco di denari, e con la diligenza dell'Ebreo mio interprete, che due Seferthorà di quella scrittura mi restarono in mano: vno, di quelli in pergameno, il migliore delli trè puri Ebraici del Chachàm; & vn'altro, che era di vna donna, scritto in carta, ma pur' antichissimo, e molto corretto, come ne' fogli bianchi in fine fanno fede con parole Arabe quattro ò cinque Chachàm, ciascuno de' quali in diuersi tempi dice di hauerlo letto tutto da capo a' piedi, e di non hauerui trouato vn'errore. Presi due di questi libri; perche vno, cioè quello in pergameno, che era di lingua Ebraica con lettere Samaritane, lo voleua per donare al mio Signor di Sansy

Ambasciador di Francia in Costantinopoli, che così lo desideraua, al quale l'hò già mandato ; e l'altro in carta, che non solo è scritto con lettere Samaritane, ma in lingua anche propria de'Samaritani, che è vn misto della Ebraica, e della Caldea, e però al mio parere è forse più curioso e più singolare, voglio, che resti, e lo porto per me ; che se bene infin'adesso non l'intendo, seruirà per orna|mento, trà gli altri libri stranieri, della mia piccola librariuola.   E ne hò gusto grande, perche vna cosa tale, che pur'è di molta stima e per l'antichità, e per la nouità, e per l'utile, che se ne può cauare, come dice il Signor'Ambasciadore ; già che ogni vno, che intende Ebraico, & hà qualche cognition del Caldeo, imparato che haurà l'Alfabeto facilissimo, lo leggerà, & intenderà come l'Ebraico ordinario ; son sicuro che in Italia non vi sarà, forse nè anche in Bibliotheca Vaticana.   Lui, alcuni mi hanno consigliato a donarlo, come cosa rara ; ma io, tanto più che è raro, mi risoluo, e penso, che sia forse meglio di tenerlo appresso di me, mentre viuo : perche nondimeno, nella Libreria Vaticana, doue pochi possono hauere adito, frà tanta moltitudine di libri starebbe in vn certo modo sepolto, e quasi sconosciuto ; doue che in man mia, non solo starà esposto di continuo a publico beneficio di ogni virtuoso, che vorrà seruirsene, e studiarlo, come intendo che debba esser di tutte le altre cose curiose, che hauerò trouate, & acquistate conle mie fatiche ; ma procurerò anche di farlo stampare, se pur mai si trouerà chi sappia farne vna buona traduttione Latina da metterui aggiunta, senza la quale, pare a me, che lo stamparlo poco seruirebbe.   Adesso che io ho il libro, cerco | di hauere ancora la moneta, scritta in Samaritano, per confrontar le lettere : & vna, che ne trouai in Gierusalem, come già dissi, e poteua hauerla, ma non sò per qual negligenza, non hauendo allhora il libro, non la pigliai ; adesso hò mandato là danari per hauerla, e ne hò scritto con diligenza, & aspetto che mi sia mandata sin' in Costantinopoli, doue mi verrà senz' altro ; se però vna Ebrea, che ne era padrona, non fosse pentita di venderla. Basta, per me non mancherà.   Nelle case de' Samaritani, vidi vn'altra cosa curiosa ; cioè, vn materassetto in terra piegato ; & intorno a quello da ogni parte, doue non era il muro, molti sassi piccoli pur'in terra posti in fila per ordine ad vno ad vno, che faceuano quasi siepe al materasso. Domandai che significaua ; e mi dissero, che in quel luogo, frà di loro, staua sempre, senza muouersene mai, la donna, mentre haueua i suoi mestrui, nel qual tempo a loro è vietato di toccarla, e di accostarsi a lei : anzi, che tengono per immonda ogni cosa, che la tocchi ; e però la fanno stare in quel luogo a parte separata, doue niuno si accosta sin'al segno de i sassi in terra : e suole star la donna in questa guisa otto giorni : ma, se in questo tempo non le mancano le purghe ; conuien che ve ne stia otto | altri, e così in che le manchino.   Ceremonia, che gli altri Ebrei ordinarij, non credo, che osseruino con tanto rigore.   Ma torniamo al viaggio.

Translation

(June 1616.) Of all the inconveniences I suffered through this infirmity, I was consoled afterwards in a single morning, when I was taken by Father Michael and a Jewish friend who acted as my interpreter to see a few houses belonging to Samaritan Jews in the gardens outside the city. Here I had such pleasure in visiting the gardens and the houses, which I found (though of mean appearance externally) very fine inside, being all set out with painting in gold with their Samaritan characters cut in and in many places also painted, as is also their Synagogue. Besides this I had the great joy of finding in the house of one of their Chachàms, or sages, four books of the Seferthorà written in their Samaritan script, for which I had been searching for so long. These books were very ancient, all written in Samaritan big characters on parchment. Three of them were in Hebrew only, and one with the addition of certain explanations in Arabic, for these Semrì or Samaritans in Damascus at present speak Arabic. I also saw others of a different sort in the possession of the same person and of others. In conclusion, with the expenditure of a little money and through the diligence of my Jewish interpreter, I succeeded in procuring two of the Seferthorà in that writing. One of them, in parchment, was the best of the three in Hebrew only, belonging to the Chachàm. Another, belonging to a woman, was written on paper, but similarly of great antiquity and extremely correct, as four or five Chachàms who profess to have read it through from beginning to end at different times without having discovered any error, attest in Arabic on the blank pages at the finish. I took two of the books. One, in Hebrew in Samaritan characters, I wanted to give to Signor di Sansy, French Ambassador at Constantinople, who so desired it, and to whom I have already dispatched it. The other on paper, which is not written only in Samaritan characters but also in this language, a mixture of Hebrew and Chaldaic, and therefore in my opinion perhaps stranger and more singular, I have kept back and will take with me; for although I do not thus far understand it, it will serve with other books in foreign tongues to adorn my poor collection. And I take great pleasure in it, because a work of this sort is of great importance both for its antiquity and for its novelty, and for the utility which can be derived from it, as the Ambassador observes. For any one who understands Hebrew and has some knowledge of Chaldaic will read it and understand it like ordinary Hebrew once he has mastered the alphabet, which is very simple. I am, moreover, sure that there is no copy in Italy, except perhaps in the Bibliotheca Vaticana. Some have advised me to present it as a thing of great rarity to that library; but, all the more because it is rare, I am resolved that it will be perhaps better to keep it in my possession as long as I live. For while in the Vatican Library, where few have entrance, it will remain almost unknown and as it were buried amongst such vast numbers of books ; in my possession, on the other hand, it will be continually open to the general benefit to any student who wishes to use it and study it in the same way as I propose with all the other curiosities which I shall have found and acquired through my labours. Moreover, I shall endeavour to have it printed, if only it is possible to find some one to make a good translation of it into Latin to put at its side, without which, in my opinion, printing would be of little use. Now that I have the book, I shall try to acquire also the coin with a Samaritan inscription in order to compare the characters. As I have already said, I found one in Jerusalem and could have had it, but by some negligence I did not take it, not then foreseeing the book. Now I have sent the money to purchase it and have written urgently and expect that it will be sent for me to Constantinople, where it will find me without difficulty, if the Jewess who owned it has not changed her mind about selling it. In any case, I shall leave nothing undone. In the houses of the Samaritans, I saw another curious thing ; to wit, a mattress stretched on the ground, and around it on every side except where the wall was, a number of little stones set in a row one by one on the ground, making a sort of fence around the mattress. I asked what the reason was and they told me that among them a woman stays in that place without moving when she has her periods. In this time it is forbidden them to touch her or to approach her ; what is more they consider unclean anything which she touches. For that reason they make her stay separated in that place, which none approaches beyond the limit of the stones on the ground. The woman remains in this manner for eight days ; but if in this time the stains have not ceased, she must remain another eight, and so on until they are ended—a ceremony which the ordinary Jews do not, I believe, observe with such rigour.

But let us return to my voyage.

APPENDIX III

THE SAMARITAN TENTH COMMANDMENT

In the course of the lectures I have not been able to do more than to point out briefly the difference between the Jewish and Samaritan recension of the Ten Commandments, and to show that great importance is to be attached to this text, and even far more than to the corresponding variants in Deuteronomy. The matter is, however, of such fundamental importance from more than one point of view, that it deserves a much fuller treatment. In order to understand the real character of the Samaritan recension of the Pentateuch no section offers a better example than the one under consideration. The essential feature has been the desire to harmonize the contents of the Bible, to smooth away difficulties, and to fill up the lacunae as much as possible with portions of the text found elsewhere. The book, as it were, was to interpret itself from within. This procedure gave an air of justification for this kind of replenishing the text and completing it, especially as it was designed to be read before the public and to be easily understood by the audience. In this way awkward questions were removed, and the story told in the book made complete as far as possible, first, as already remarked, by words or verses from within, and secondly, by slight additions and interpolations from without. In the Ten Commandments, such as they are found in the books and scrolls, this tendency is made manifest, and quite obviously too.

It is well known that there are two recensions of the Ten Commandments in the Pentateuch, the one in Exodus xx. 1 ff., and the other in Deuteronomy v. 6 ff. There are a good many differences in the Jewish text between the one and the other, which have given rise to many speculations and have led to divergent conclusions. The Samaritans have got over that difficulty by simply harmonizing the two texts; thus every difficulty has been removed, as the two texts now read almost alike ; but this is as nothing compared to the very fundamental change by the addition of a long passage which is counted by them as the Tenth Commandment. It contains the vital dogmatic difference between Jews and Samaritans for the sanctity of Mount Garizim thus proclaimed by God in the grand revelation on Sinai. It stands on the same level with all the other Commandments which form the Covenant between God and Israel, the breaking of which was as heinous an act and as terrible a sin as that of breaking the other Commandments. The selection of Mount Garizim as the chosen spot where the memorial stones were to be placed, upon which the words of these Commandments were to be written, and where an altar was to be built and the sanctuary established, was thus no longer a mere stray Commandment found in various verses in Deuteronomy. This Commandment was, on the contrary, an essential portion of the Divine Revelation. The occurrence of similar verses in Deuteronomy was then, according to this recension, a mere repetition of the Commandment originally given on Mount Sinai, and then repeated by Moses with especial stress when they were approaching the borders of the land of Canaan. It would then be practically the first Commandment in order to be fulfilled as soon as they had taken possession of the land. For the original source was the Divine Revelation. To my mind sufficient attention has not been bestowed upon this cardinal fact, which is the corner-stone of the Samaritan dissidence, and the everlasting bone of contention to this very day. Round it turn all the disputations throughout the ages, and the Samaritans found their strength and justification in the fact that this formed part of the Ten Commandments. It may be that for this reason the reading of the Ten Commandments as part of the liturgy in Jerusalem was dropped after a time ; the reason given was ' because of the Minim '. (See Talmud B. Berakhot f. 11 a.) These were probably the Samaritans, and the leaders in Jerusalem obviously intended to avoid drawing attention to the fundamental difference between the two sects. It is a curious fact, to which attention has already been drawn (p. 128), that this passage had been introduced into the Greek translation, although Origenes does not fail to note that it is absent from the Jewish text, and marks it with an asterisk. Still it is surpassing strange that such an obvious anti-Jewish passage should have been admitted into the Greek text, and above all among the Ten Commandments, thus giving it such a sacred character and such prominent importance. It is no doubt an interpolation from the Samariticon, but still it remains a puzzle.

This, however, does not exhaust the importance of the variants in the Samaritan text. The process of harmonizing has reached here its highest development. A number of verses have been added, and the blending of various texts into one has been here carried out on a far more extensive scale than even in the Ten Commandments. It must not be forgotten that the verses which follow both in Exodus and in Deuteronomy are a direct continuation of the Revelation, and contain a full description of the incidents which happened immediately after the grand act, the discussions between Moses and the people, and the words which God spake to Moses on that occasion, containing also new Commandments. If one compares the two corresponding sections in Exodus and Deuteronomy, the discrepancies are still greater than between the two texts of the Commandments. Surely God could not have spoken differently in one case and differently in another when the same fact is recorded. Either the version in Exodus is the correct record or that in Deuteronomy. The answer to this question is given by the Samaritans, who join the two texts together, and make out of them one complete in Exodus. Thus every difficulty disappears and the text is now fully harmonized. It consists of Deuteronomy v. 21-5 ; Exodus xx. 19 ; Deuteronomy v. 26-9 ; Deuteronomy xviii. 16 ff. ; Exodus xx. 20-6. This composite text has, furthermore, a transcendent value by the interpolation of the passage from Deuteronomy xviii, which becomes clear in the light of the explanation which I have given above (pp. 90-2), when discussing the Samaritan principle of the future Redeemer. He was to be a prophet like unto Moses, and this part of their eschatology agreed in the main with the teachings found in the Apocryphal literature, and above all with the views entertained by the Sadducees, or rather the Ṣadoḳites, of the pre-Maccabean period. By inserting here this promise that a prophet like Moses will arise in the future, who will be sent by God, and to whose voice they are bidden to hearken, a unique importance has been given to it. It has been placed next to the Commandments as being uttered by God on the very same solemn occasion. One cannot over-estimate the value just assigned to it, for it assumes a character of its own and becomes the basis of all the eschatological speculations which are later on crystallized in the belief of a Taheb. No wonder, therefore, that when these Messianic ideas and the outlook for happier times became one of the driving forces in the religious life of the Jews' that the Samaritans should then have rested their belief on this clear pronouncement and Divine promise. They had to seek for a biblical justification for such belief, and nothing lay better to their hands than these words.

The only question which remains which cannot be answered satisfactorily is how old this portion is in the Samaritan Pentateuch. It is older in any case than the Abisha Scroll, and if, as one may assume, it is as old as the Samaritan Tenth Commandment, which, as witnessed by the Septuagint, was already found in their text before the Greek translation, then it belongs indeed to a very high antiquity. To this points also the antiquity of the belief in, or dogma of, the Taheb so fully developed already before the beginnings of the Christian era (John iv. 25). Thus, the Samaritan recension of the Ten Commandments, with the concluding section, contains some of the fundamental dogmas of the Samaritans, and notably those which separate them from the Jews. For this reason I have reproduced here in facsimile two copies of the entire section, including the Tenth Commandment and the succeeding verses. One is taken from a modern scroll, and the other from the ancient parallel Pentateuch preserved in the Kinsha, which contains the Jewish and Samaritan recension side by side. A faithful copy was made for me many years ago by the late High Priest Jacob, and one can see thus at a glance the difference between these two recensions, which I have transliterated and translated here as well.

Besides other slight changes and variations, one more deserves special attention. It shows how careful the Samaritans have been not to allow words to stand in the text, or, according to their statement, not allow words to be introduced, which would change the true meaning and cause even the slightest doubt concerning the Chosen Spot. In the Jewish recension verse 24 reads, 'in *all* places where I will record my Name'; the Samaritan, however, reads, 'in that place where I have caused my Name to be recorded'. Whilst the Jewish recension allows, as it were, many places to be recorded by God, the verb being in the future tense 'I will record', the Samaritan does not allow but one single place, The Chosen Place, which has been recorded by God, here the verb in the past tense, i. e. the place mentioned shortly before in the Tenth Commandment; the change, therefore, is very skilfully done, and shows great tenacity of purpose.

(1) *Modern Scroll Tenth Commandment*

והיה כי יביאך יהוה אלהיך אל ארץ הכנעני אשר אתה בא שמה לרשתה:.
והקמת לך אבנים גדלות: ושדת אתם בשיד: וכתבת על האבנים את כל דברי
התורה הזאת: והיה בעברכם את הירדן תקימו את האבנים האלה אשר אנכי
מצוה אתכם [גיום] בהרגריזים:. ובנית שם מזבח ליהוה אלהיך מזבח אבנים: לא
תניף עליהם ברזל: אבנים שלמות תבנה את מזבח והעלית עליו עלות ליהוה אלהיך
וזבחת שלמים ואכלת: שם ושמחת לפני יהוה אלהיך: ההר ההוא בעבר הירדן
אחרי דרך מבוא השמש: בארץ הכנעני הישב בערבה מול הגלגל אצל אלון מורא
מול שכם:

וכל העם שמע את הקולות ואת קול השופר: וראים את הלפידים ואת ההר
עשן: ויראו כל העם וינעו ויעמדו מרחק:. ויאמרו אל משה הן הראנו יהוה
אלהינו את כבודו ואת גדלו ואת קולו שמענו מתוך האש: היום הזה ראינו כי
ידבר אלהים את האדם וחי:. ועתה למה נמות כי תאכלנו האש הגדלה הזאת
אם יוספים אנחנו לשמע את קול יהוה אלהינו עוד ומתנו: כי מי כל בשר אשר
שמע קול אלהים חיים מדבר מתוך האש כמונו וחי:. ק"ר"ב אתה ושמע את כל
אשר יאמר יהוה אלהינו ואתה תדבר אלינו את כל אשר ידבר יהוה אלהינו אליך
ושמענו ועשינו ואל ידבר עמנו האלהים פן נמות: ויאמר משה אל העם אל תיראו
כי לבעבור נסות אתכם בא האלהים: ובעבור תהיה יראתו על פניכם לבלתי תחטאו:.
ויעמד העם מרחק: ומשה נגש אל הערפל אשר שם האלהים:.

וידבר יהוה אל משה לאמר: שמעתי את קול דברי העם הזה אשר דברו
אליך היטבו כל אשר דברו מי יתן: והיה לבבם זה להם ליראה אתי:
ולשמר את מצותי כל הימים: למען ייטב להם ולבניהם לעולם נביא אקים
להם מקרב אחיהם כמוך ונתתי דברי בפיו: ודבר אליהם את כל אשר אצונו:.
והיה האיש אשר לא ישמע לדבריו אשר ידבר בשמי:. אנכי אדרש מעמו

Deut. 5²¹iii.
– 25

Exod. 20⁹

Deut. 5²⁶

Deut. 18¹⁸

אך הנביא אשר יזיד לדבר דבר בשמי את אשר לא צויתיו לדבר : ואשר ידבר
בשם אלהים אחרים : ומת הנביא ההוא : וכי תאמר בלבבך איך נודע ודבר אשר
לא דברו יהוה אשר ידבר הנביא בשם יהוה : לא יהיה הדבר ולא יבוא : הוא
הדבר אשר לא דברו יהוה בזידון דברו הנביא לא תגור ממנו : לך אמר להם שובו
לכם לאהליכם : ואתה פה עמד עמדי : . ואדברה אליך את כל המצוה החקים

t. 5²⁷

והמשפטים אשר תלמדם ועשו בארץ אשר אנכי נתן להם לרשתה : .

d. 20

וידבר יהוה אל משה לאמר : דבר אל בני ישראל אתם ראיתם כי מן השמים
דברתי עמכם : לא תעשו אתי : אלהי כסף ואלהי זהב לא תעשו לכם מזבח אדמה
תעשה לי : . ובחת עליו את עלותיך ואת שלמיד : מצאנך ומבקרך : . ובמקום אשר
אזכרתי את שמי : שמה אבוא אליך וברכתיך : ואם מזבח אבנים תעשה לי : .
לא תבנה אתהן גזית : . כי חרבך הנפת עליו : . ותחללהו : . ולא תעלה במעלות על
מזבחי אשר לא תגלה ערותך אליו : .

Samaritan Tenth Commandment and Succeeding Verses from my Scroll now in the British Museum

And it shall come to pass when the Lord thy God will bring thee
into the land of the Canaanites whither thou goest to take possession
of it, thou shalt erect unto thee large stones, and thou shalt cover them
with lime, and thou shalt write upon the stones all the words of this
Law, and it shall come to pass when ye cross the Jordan, ye shall
erect these stones which I command thee upon Mount Garizim, and
thou shalt build there an altar unto the Lord thy God, an altar of stones,
and thou shalt not lift up upon them iron, of perfect stones shalt thou
build thine altar, and thou shalt bring up upon it burnt offerings to the
Lord thy God, and thou shalt sacrifice peace offerings, and thou shalt
eat there and rejoice before the Lord thy God. That mountain is on
the other side of the Jordan at the end of the road towards the going
down of the sun in the land of the Canaanites who dwell in the Arabah
facing Gilgal close by Elon Moreh facing Sichem.

And all the people heard the voices and the sound of the trumpets
and they saw the flames and the mountain smoking, and all the people
saw it and they trembled and stood afar off, and they said unto Moses,
'Behold the Lord our God hath showed us his glory and his greatness,
and we have heard his voice out of the midst of the fire; this day have
we seen that God doth talk with man and he liveth. Now therefore
why should we die? for this great fire will consume us; if we should
continue to hear the voice of the Lord our God any more, then we shall
die. For who is there of all flesh that hath heard the voice of the living
God speaking out of the midst of the fire as have we, and yet live?
Go thou near and hear all that the Lord our God shall say, and speak
thou unto us all that the Lord our God shall speak unto thee, and
we will hear and do, but let not God speak with us lest we die.'

And Moses said unto the people, 'Do not fear, for God is come to prove you, and that the fear of him may be before your faces, that ye sin not. And the people stood afar off, and Moses drew near to the thick darkness where was God. And the Lord spake unto Moses, saying, ' I have heard the voice of the words of this people, which they have spoken unto thee ; they have well said all that they have spoken. O that there were such an heart in them that they would fear me, and keep all my commandments always, that it might be well with them and with their children for ever. (Deuteronomy xviii. 18 :) I will raise them up a prophet from among their brethren, like unto thee ; and will put my words in his mouth ; and he shall speak unto them all that I shall command him. And it shall come to pass that whosoever will not hearken unto his words which he shall speak in my Name, I will require it of him. But the prophet which shall presume to speak a word in my Name, which I have not commanded him to speak, or that shall speak in the name of other gods, that same prophet shall die. And if thou sayest in thine heart, How shall it be known that the word is not that which the Lord hath spoken ? When a prophet speaketh in the Name of the Lord, if the thing follow not nor come to pass, that is the thing which the Lord hath not spoken, but the prophet hath spoken it presumptuously : thou shalt not be afraid of him. (Deuteronomy v. 30 :) Go say to them, Get you into your tents again. But as for thee, stand thou here by me, and I will speak unto thee all the commandment, the statutes, and the judgements, which thou shalt teach them, that they may do them in the land which I give them to possess it.' (Exodus xx. 22 :) And the Lord spake unto Moses, saying, 'Speak to the Children of Israel, Ye have seen that I have talked with you from heaven. Ye shall not make with me gods of silver, neither shall ye make unto you gods of gold. An altar of earth thou shalt make unto me, and shalt sacrifice thereon thy burnt offerings, and thy peace offerings, from thy sheep and from thine oxen, and in that place where I have caused my Name to be recorded, thither will I come and bless thee. And if thou wilt make me an altar of stone, thou shalt not build it of hewn stone, for thou hast lifted up thy tool upon it, and thou hast defiled it. Neither shalt thou go up by steps unto mine altar, that thy nakedness be not discovered by it.'

APPENDIX IV

THE STATEMENT OF THE LATE HIGH PRIEST JACOB, SON OF AARON, CONCERNING THE ABISHA SCROLL

כל ימי חייו כתב את ספרה קדישה הממצא בכנשת עיר שכם הקדושה ביד
הכהנים בני לוי עד היום הזה והכתב זה המכתב בהרגריזים בית אל בפתח אהל
מועד ותשקולו ממצא בו בלא מוסף ולא מגרע ועורו מן זבח השלמים : אשר היו
יקריבו אתם את הקהל על המזבח והוא מתשקל באותות בתוך העמודים : מן דברי
התורה באותות מתודעות בתוך העמודים : ותשקולו מן והיה כי יביאך אשר בתר
שמע ישראל וזה מה כתוב בתשקולו : :

אני אבישע בן פינחס בן אלעזר בן אהרן חכהן : להם רצון יהוה וכבודו :
כתבתי זה ספר הקדוש בפתח אהל מועד בהרגריזים ביתאל בשנת שלשה עשר
למושב בני ישראל ארץ כנען אודה את יהוה :. יהוה ישיב עלינו מן ברכאתו
ומברכת אשר כתבו : בידו הקדושה : ומברכת משכן שם יהוה : אשר הכתב
בפתחו : ומברכת המבחר אשר הכתב עליו אמן :.

* * * *

הוה תכלול מן מכתב דן ספרה קדישה ביום הרביעי יט מן חדש אחד עשר
שנת שלשה אלפים וחמש מאות ושבע וארבעים למושב בני ישראל לארץ כנען
על יד המסכין יעקב בן אהרן הכהן יסלח לו יהוה אמן בעמל משה הנבאי" אמן :

Translation

He spent all the days of his life in writing the Holy Scroll which is found in the Kinsha of the holy city Sichem in the hands of the priests the Levites to this very day, and this Writ was written on Mount Garizim Beth El at the gate of the Tent of Assembly and its Colophon (Teshḳul) is found in it without addition or subtraction, and the skin is from the peace offerings, which they did sacrifice with the Congregation on the altar, and this Colophon is made out of the letters which are between the columns, the words of the Law with letters prominently recognizable between the columns, and the beginning of the Colophon is from the words 'and it will come to pass when he shall bring thee' which are after 'Hear, O Israel', and this is what is written in that Colophon :

'I Abisha, son of Pineḥas, son of Eleazar, son of Aaron, the Kohen, to them be the favour of the Lord and his glory. I have written this Holy Scroll at the gate of the Tent of the Assembly on Mount Garizim Beth El, in the thirteenth year of the settlement of the Children of

Israel in the land of Canaan. I thank the Lord.' May the Lord return upon us of his blessing, and of the blessing of him who wrote with his holy hand, and of the blessing of the dwelling-place of the Name of the Lord at the gate of which it was written, and of the blessing of the Chosen Spot upon which it was written. Amen. . . .

And the end of the writing of this Holy Book was on the fourth day (Wednesday), the nineteenth of the eleventh month, in the year 3547 (1909) of the settlement of the Children of Israel in the land of Canaan by the hand of the poor Jacob, son of Aaron the priest. May the Lord forgive him. Amen, for the sake of Moses the prophet. Amen.

A similar Colophon is also given before in Mashalma's letter, both agreeing absolutely with one another. To whatever age this Teshḳul may belong, it is evident that it has been introduced into their most ancient scrolls for the purpose of marking the independence of the Samaritan recension from the Jewish, which, according to their contention, had been falsified by Ezra. They claim thus to have retained the only true recension, tracing it back to the time of the settlement of the Israelites in Palestine. It is a definite repudiation of any possible allegation that their text had anything in common with the 'tainted' copy. It is both more ancient and more accurate in the eyes of the Samaritans.

APPENDIX V

NOTES ON THE ILLUSTRATIONS

I AM giving here some further explanations of the illustrations inserted in the foregoing pages. In the first place, I should like to mention that, with a few exceptions, they are all taken from MSS. formerly in my possession, and now transferred by me to the British Museum, and one of the illustrations is taken from a MS. already before that time in the British Museum, viz. the triglot, *Plate No. 9.*

Plate 1 is taken from the *Atlas Biblicus*, edited by Martin Hagen, Paris, 1907, and gives us the most complete picture of Samaria as it exists in modern times. It would be very difficult to reconstruct it adequately on the basis of Biblical tradition beyond the general outline of the borders.

Plates 2 and *3* are the autographed letter of Abraham ben Jacob, one single folio written on both sides, and, on the whole, sufficiently well preserved. Though greatly reduced, the script is very legible and clear. It is transliterated, translated, and fully explained in Appendix I.

Plate 4 contains the rough drawing in blue chalk of the vessels and various parts of the Tabernacle with a superscription in Samaritan. The subscription reads as follows :

זה תבנית כמו תבנית הנמצא על ארון
אשר הוא בכנשת שכם
לשמרנים :

The translation of it is as follows : ' This is the image of the objects of the Tabernacle as depicted (embossed) on the cover (ark) of the Scroll in the Kinsha of Sichem of the Samaritans.' A photographic copy of that metal case has also happily been taken by me many years ago. It is reproduced here on *Plate 5.* The case consists of three parts, and is used for keeping the special scroll, which is exhibited during the service ; it is covered with various floral and other decorations, all embossed, and with a central diamond-shaped ornament. On the edges Samaritan inscriptions are engraved, and many of the decorations are copies of the vessels of the Tabernacle, from which the designs on *Plate 4* have been drawn. I have been told that this case, which is of copper (or brass), is a copy made in the seventeenth century from an older case which was in silver, and of which the Samaritans had been robbed by the Arabs in Sichem. They insist that the new is an exact replica of the older one. Among other things, we find on it not only the Tables of the Covenant, but the flourishing rod of Moses, with twelve branches. It is not the rod of Aaron which, evidently, according to Samaritan fancy, flourished, but it was the rod of Moses, and to this, as is shown in the text, a special importance has been attached by the Samaritans. The Taheb will bring this rod, and thereby show that he is the proper prophet sent to 'bring back' the Divine Favour.

Plate 6. This is a page from the *Tolidah*, published by Neubauer, Paris, 1873. I am not giving here a transliteration, as the text has already been printed, and is thus accessible. This page has, however, been reproduced here in order to show the somewhat intricate form in which the Samaritans write their genealogies. This may be the cause of much confusion if later copies cannot easily find their way in unravelling these intricacies ; this can thus explain chronological errors, and other mistakes such as have crept in, especially in their chronicles.

Plate 7. A full description of this plate is found in Appendix III. Here we have a complete column, carefully written. Although greatly reduced, it is easily legible. According to the statement of the late High Priest Jacob, from whom I obtained this MS., it is, as far as possible, a faithful copy of their oldest and best scrolls. It is therefore of importance also from a palaeographic point of view, especially as stress has been laid by me on this side of the problem, in connexion with the antiquity of the Samaritan Pentateuch. We have here an exact specimen of the Scroll, with its minor divisions and smaller sections, the proportion of the width of the column to its length, and other details, peculiar to the Scroll, but not to the Pentateuch in book form. The column begins with the word 'Shamor', Exod. xx. 7, the beginning of the Commandment to keep the Sabbath, and it finishes with Exod. xxi. 15.

Plate 8. These are the first lines of the Samaritan phylactery which, from a palaeographic point of view, has been ascribed by me to the second or third century. It is the only Samaritan document thus far known to me in which the words have not been separated by dots, and the characters are very similar to the inscription of Emmaus ascribed to the second century. This text, with the translation and commentary, has been published by me in the *J.R.A.S.*, and is now being reprinted in my forthcoming *Studies and Texts*, p. 480, as well as in the fuller study of the phylacteries in *P.S.P.A.*, also reprinted in the same *Studies and Texts*, pp. 387 ff. The fact that we find in these ancient phylacteries already the characteristic readings of the Samaritan Pentateuch is adduced here as one proof more of the high antiquity of the latter. Only a text considered as sacred down to its minutest details could be used for prophylactic purposes.

Plate 9. This is a portion of the Ten Commandments, Exod. xx. 10–15, with inclusion of Samaritan Tenth Commandment in the most complete triglot—Hebrew, Targum, and Arabic—now, through my intervention, in the possession of the British Museum. It is more complete, and no doubt older, than the Barberini Triglot, hitherto considered as the only one in Europe, and also as the oldest. We find here the text of the two translations already definitely fixed, and here we have the oldest specimens.

Plate 10. A page from a Pentateuch with what I call symmetric writing. It has a peculiarity hitherto not yet observed in some of the oldest and most carefully written copies of the Pentateuch, viz. if in the text the same word or words are often repeated, either in the same verse, or immediately succeeding verses, the copyists try to write these one under the other, as seen in the facsimile. It is a practice also often followed in the Prayer Books when writing the Katef (Florilegium), which consists of a number of similar verses. Whenever possible, the words are so arranged that they form a longer or shorter column. Attention is now drawn here to this peculiarity, for it helps to explain possible mistakes of copyists by the homoioteleuton, which may lead either to verses being omitted or repeated.

Plate 11. At the end of one of the copies of the Pentateuch written by the late High Priest Jacob, he has added, as a kind of colophon, the statement here reproduced in Appendix IV. I had been in communication about it before, and this induced him to enlarge upon the Abisha inscription and this colophon. If compared with the one found in the Meshalma letter, one will find them almost identical. This inscription or cryptogram recurs over and over again in the books written by the Samaritans, but there are greater or smaller discrepancies between them, for very few have really access to the original, and are satisfied to copy it from one another. I believe that the one reproduced also in transliteration and translation, Appendix IV here, is the only authentic one.

Plate 12. This is, as far as I know, the oldest fragment of a scroll, dating 562 Hedge, to equal 1167, in Europe. The text begins Deut. ii. 3, and continues to iv. 32. Once mine, it is now in the British Museum. The cryptogram, consisting of the letters found between the two columns, reads as follows :

בשנת ב וס וה מואן למלכות ישמעאל משם אבה ברבאתיה צדקתה בר אב:

'In the year two and sixty and five hundred, of the kingdom of Ishmael in the name of Abi Barkatiah, Ṣadaḳtah, son of Ab.'

A careful examination will show the system of this cryptogram, inasmuch as each of the letters here given in transliteration, and standing in the middle of columns being read vertically down, are at the same time parts of the words in each of the lines where they stand. No alteration or change would be possible, inasmuch as the word itself would be mutilated. A further comparison of the writing on *Plate 7*, from which this scroll is separated by close upon 800 years, will show how small the change has been from a graphic point of view, and that as far as the internal arrangement is concerned, both follow the same unchanged tradition.

Plate 13. This plate is reproduced from the last page which had been added on to an old MS. of the Pentateuch, written on vellum, the last page of which had disappeared. This was supplemented by the High Priest Tabya (?), who has added various notes at the end, of which the following two lines are at the top of the page :

עתקנו מן אבהתן הטהורים להם הרצאן על מה עתקו על
השבעים היקינים :

'We have received it as ancient tradition from our fathers the pure ones, upon whom be the Favour, who have received it in tradition from the Seventy Elders.'

This statement here put at the end of the Pentateuch is found so expressed also in many other writings of the Samaritans, who believe that the seventy elders lie buried not far from Mount Garizim, and for centuries they have been attending these graves at the place which they call Aburta or Amarta. Many of the Oral Laws are referred by tradition to the seventy elders, but above all do they claim that tradition as vouching for the accuracy of the Pentateuch in their hands. The other notes on that page refer also to the Biblical accents fully described by me in my contribution to the Noeldeke Memorial Volume, now reprinted in my *Studies and Texts*, pp. 614 ff.

Plate 14. The Ten Commandments from the parallel Bible. This is a facsimile of the copy made (so I am told) by the late High Priest Jacob, although I must accept this statement with reserve, since I have learned quite recently that a similar copy is in the hands of a Samaritan, who alleges the work to be of another person. Be it as it may, this is a copy of the very ancient MS. discovered by me in the Kinsha, in which the two recensions are written side by side. As they refused to sell it, I asked for a copy to be made, and the present MS. is the result. In this, the difference between the one and the other, when they are only single letters or words, is that they are written in red ink ; but when the difference consists in longer sections, then a blank space is left in one column or the other to mark the absence of that section. This is seen here by the blank space in the column which contains the Jewish recension.

Plate 15. A page from the copy of the Samaritan Book of Joshua obtained by me from the Samaritans when in London (see *Plate 17*), together with other MSS. they then brought. I have refrained from the transliterating and translating, since that book has been published by me, transliterated and translated, in the *Z.D.M.G.*, vol. 62, 1908, p. 262. I have inserted it here, as special reference has been made to this chapter (p. 139) on the division of the land by Joshua, and the parallel division of the land by the prophet Ezekiel. As a critical edition of this Book of Joshua on the basis of many more MSS. and recensions is being prepared by me, with the assistance of my son, Theodore, further details must therefore be reserved for that publication.

Plate 16. The picture here has been taken from a faint photograph which came into my possession many years ago. It was very faded, and had to be photographed anew and strengthened. I believe it to be the oldest photograph existing of Samaritans, and it is of special importance, inasmuch as it contains the portraits of leading men of the last generation. Not being sure of their identity, I sent the photograph to Nablus, and there Abisha, the son of Pinehas, wrote the names of the persons in Samaritan. This copy has been reproduced here. The persons therein are—first, Pinehas, one of the greatest scholars of the last century, to whom many books have been ascribed. I had occasion to refer to him here only briefly, but I have done so more fully in my article on the Samaritan Arabic literature in the special supplement to the *Encyclopaedia of Islam*. Then there is here in this photo the youthful portrait of the late High Priest Jacob, which must have been taken between 1870 and 1880, if not earlier, for he died, I believe, in 1918, a very old man. To him, Samaritan literature owes a very great debt for the numerous works he copied or compiled. It was his copy of the *Tolidah* that Dr. Neubauer published as far back as 1876, and I possess now a copy of the book with his autograph. The third is the portrait of Isaac, the son of Amram, the man who had been more than once in London, and from whom the British Museum and others have obtained most valuable MSS. He is now the High Priest in Sichem, and his portrait appears also in the next plate, together with that of his companions. The name of the girl has not been communicated, except that she was the daughter of Jacob. The reading, from right to left, is as follows :

יצחק הכהן . נערה ליעקב . יעקב הכהן . פינחס הכהן :

Plate 17. This portrait supplements and completes the preceding one. The central figure is that of Isaac, son of Amram ; the next is Abisha, son of Pinehas ; then there is the figure of Uzzi, the son of the late High Priest Jacob, who has since died and left behind a young lad called Jacob. All these belong to the priestly family. With them came the fourth person, Shalabi, whom I cannot trace any farther, but who proved himself to be an excellent scribe, if the MSS. he brought were indeed written by him. These, with a few more, among them Ab Ḥasda, the son of the late High Priest Jacob, and Abraham ben Pineḥas, represent now the scholarly element of the Samaritans in Nablus.

Plate 18. This is a copy of a photograph taken more than twenty years ago on Mount Garizim, presented to me. I regret I cannot remember the donor. It is included here for its vividness, and for being so far the best copy of a large group of Samaritans with their features clearly distinguished.

Appendix VI. This illustration, giving the ground plan of Mount Garizim with a minute description, is taken from Dean Stanley's *Lectures on the History of the Jewish Church*, vol. i, 2nd ed., 1863, p. 515.

APPENDIX VI

GROUND PLAN OF MOUNT GARIZIM

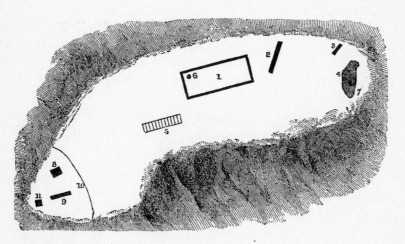

1. Fortress.
2. Seven steps of Adam out of Paradise.
3. Scene of the offering of Isaac—a trough like that used for the Paschal Feast.
4. 'Holy Place.'
5. Joshua's Twelve Stones.
6. 'Tomb of Sheykh Ghranem,' or 'Shechem ben Hamor'.
7. 'Cave where the Tabernacle was built.'
8. Hole where the Paschal sheep are roasted.
9. Trench where they are eaten.
10. Platform for the celebration of the Passover.
11. Hole where the water is boiled.

INDEX

oral law, 46, 48, 49, 51, 63, 65–72, 150.
origin, 6, 7, 11, 16–18.
Pentateuch sole basis of religion, 41–2, 47, 86. 89.
persecutions by Jews and Greeks, 33–6.
Persian settlements, 87.
pronunciation, 134.
rediscovery, 3.
refused permission to worship at Jerusalem, 21.
revival of letters in fourteenth century, 147.
and Sadducees and Pharisees, relationship. 54, 63, 65, 66.
script, 104–17.
Scriptures, *see* Samariticon *and under* Pentateuch.
sects, 86.
Targum, reading by special family, 145.
writers, names, 116, 122, 154, 157.
Samariticon, antiquity, 123.
disappearance, 128.
origin, 117.
See also Pentateuch, Greek translation.
Samuel, joins Eli against Eleazar, 9, 10.
Sanballat (contemporary of Ezra), marriage of daughter, 30.
rebuilding of temple on Garizim, 33.
Sanballat (contemporary of Zerubbabel), dispute with Zerubbabel, 19, 20.
power in Samaria, 18 (foot-note).
Sanchuniathon, history of Phoenicia, 116.
Sansy, de, aid in recovery of Samaritan Pentateuch, 101, 181, 183.
Sargon, colonies established in North Palestine, 16.
Saul, dealings with priestly families, 10.
Scaliger, intercourse with Samaritans, 3, 100, 161, 162, 163, 165.
Schnurrer, copy of letter from Huntington, owned by, 162, 163.
Scribes, *see* Soferim.
'Scroll of Fasting,' *see* Megillat Taanit.
Sebaot, appearance of name in Jewish literature, 9.
'Secrets of Moses,' *see* Asatir Mosheh.
'Seder Olam,' Biblical chronicle, 156.
'Sefer al Tabah,' contents, 151
Seleucids, deportations of Jews and Samaritans, 34.
Septuagint, anti-Samaritan alteration, 8 (foot-note).

based upon more ancient Greek version, 121–2, 129.
Egyptian origin impossible, 115, 117, 122–3.
influence of Samariticon, 128.
origin, legends, 34, 113–15.
truth beneath legends, 35, 120.
and Samaritan Pentateuch, affinity, 50, 102, 112, 126.
'Seventy Elders,' meaning, 119.
Talmudic legends, 120.
Serayah, High Priest—
dispute with Zerubbabel, 19, 20.
invitation to Jews, 19.
Shem Hamitfaresh, mystical amulet, 81, 149.
Shema, meaning, 37 (foot-note), 73, 74.
Shemer, *see* Samaritans, name, derivation.
Shiloh, sanctuary removed to, 9.
Shofet, meaning, 56.
Shomronim, *see* Samaritans, names applied to.
Sibylline Oracles, connexion with Jewish writings, 64, 70, 141.
Sichem, rivalry with Shiloh, 8 (foot-note), 10, 11 (foot-note).
site of true sanctuary, *see* Garizim, Mt.
Simeon, High Priest, persecution of Samaritans, 33, 34.
Simon, King of Jews, persecution of Samaritans, 33.
Slaughter of animals, Jewish and Samaritan practices, 68.
Sofer Mahir, meaning, 27.
Soferim, work of, 110.
Square characters in script of Pentateuch, 104, 106–7.
'Sword of Moses,' Samaritan mystical work, 80.

T

Tabernacle, establishment on Mt. Garizim and Shiloh, 8.
See also Sacred vessels.
Taheb, *see* Messianic idea, Samaritan conception.
Takanah, meaning, 76.
Talmud, evidence as to Septuagint, 120.
Targum, Jewish and Samaritan version, 144–6.
origin, 27, 127.
Samaritan copy obtained by Della Valle, 101, 159, 181.
'Tarikh,' continuation of Abul Fath's chronicle, 157.
Tefillin, Samaritan view, 76.